D1496412

FAITH AND FANATICISM

This book is dedicated to my three children, Dominic, Rebekah and David, who have shown unending patience and support during the preparation of this edition.

FAITH AND FANATICISM

Religious Fervour in Early Modern Spain

edited by

Lesley K. Twomey

assistant editors

Robert Hooworth-Smith
Michael Truman

translator
Michael Truman

Ashgate

Aldershot • Brookfield USA
Singapore • Sydney

Published by   Ashgate Publishing Limited
                      Gower House
                      Croft Road
                      Aldershot
                      Hants GU11 3HR
                      Great Britain

                      Ashgate Publishing Company
                      Old Post Road
                      Brookfield, Vermont 05036–9704
                      USA

ISBN 0 86078 665 X

Front board illustration shows a Spanish fabric design of the fifteenth century, and is taken from the Hart Picture Archives (New York 1978).

British Library Cataloguing-in-Publication Data
Twomey, Lesley K.
Faith and Fanaticism: Religious Fervour in Early Modern Spain.
1.Inquisition—Spain—Congresses. 2. Fanaticism—Religious aspects—Christianity—Congresses. 3. Fanaticism—Spain—History—Congresses. 4. Fanaticism in literature—Congresses. 5. Spain—Church history—Congresses. I. Twomey, Lesley K. II. Hooworth-Smith, Robert. III. Truman, Michael.
282.4'6'09031

U.S. Library of Congress Cataloging-in-Publication Data
Faith and Fanaticism: Religious Fervour in Early Modern Spain / edited by Lesley K. Twomey; assistant editors, Robert Hooworth-Smith, Michael Truman; translator, Michael Truman.
       p. cm.
Primarily papers presented at a meeting, University of Humberside, May 1996.
Includes bibliographical references and index. 1. Fanaticism—Spain—History. 2. Spain—Religion. I. Twomey, Lesley K. II. Hooworth-Smith, Robert. III. Truman, Michael.
BL53.5.F35   1997   97-30474
274.6'06—dc21   CIP

This volume is printed on acid-free paper.

Printed in Great Britain by Galliard (Printers) Ltd, Great Yarmouth

Contents

List of Contributors

John Edwards, formerly Reader in Spanish History, *University of Birmingham*

Ronald Cueto, Reader in Spanish History, *University of Leeds*

Lesley K. Twomey, Senior Lecturer in Spanish, *University of Lincolnshire and Humberside*

Terence O'Reilly, Associate Professor in Spanish, *University College, Cork*

A. Gordon Kinder, Honorary Research Fellow in Spanish and Portuguese Studies, *University of Manchester*

Michael Alpert, Reader in Spanish, *University of Westminster*

Nicholas Griffiths, Lecturer in Hispanic Studies, *University of Birmingham*

Hilary Pomeroy, Postgraduate student in Hispanic Studies, *Queen Mary and Westfield College, University of London*

Encarnación Sánchez García, Riccerciatore, Dipartimento di Studi Letterari e Linguistici dell' Occidente, *Istituto Universitario Orientale, Naples*

John A. Jones, Senior Lecturer in Hispanic Studies, *University of Hull*

Editor's Preface

Lesley K. Twomey

The present volume contains a series of papers presented at the first Hispanic Conference held at the University of Humberside in May 1996. The one-day conference was entitled *Fervor y Fanatismo* and brought together Hispanists regionally, nationally and internationally, united by their interest in the fanaticism and religious fervour which has marked literature and history in early modern Spain. Whilst the call for papers was open to specialists in any century, the final selection of papers centred naturally on the sixteenth and seventeenth centuries, and that has given the focus to this edition. The conference and this volume were the vision of the editor, and in the venture I was ably supported by my two colleagues in the Spanish section, Mr Michael Truman and Mr Robert Hooworth-Smith.

From this first conference came six of the articles included in this volume and to those original articles were added contributions from Nicholas Griffiths, Terence O'Reilly and John Jones, complementary to the original conference papers and developing aspects of some of the main themes. In this way, the current edition can make a contribution to deepening understanding of Spain at her zenith and beyond.

The holding of this conference and the publication of this volume have been made financially possible by support from the Department of Modern Languages, Hull Business School, the University of Lincolnshire and Humberside. The editor and assistant editors wish to thank colleagues in the Department of Modern Languages, especially Mr Ian Scott, Head of Languages, for their unremitting support for this project.

I am grateful to Dr John A. Jones for his invaluable comments on the text of this volume.

Introduction

John Edwards

In the western world of today, at least as it is portrayed by the mass media, activity and attitudes undertaken in the name of 'religion' (especially, one might observe, if the participants are Muslims) are commonly described as 'fanatical' or, using a twentieth-century American Christian coinage, 'fundamentalist'. The original title of the University of Humberside conference at Hull on 11 May 1996, *Fervor y Fanatismo*, focuses sharply and aptly a dilemma of religious belief. If faith in a set of religious beliefs is expressed in action, in accordance, for example, with a person or group's understanding of the Jewish, Christian and Muslim scriptures, and, therefore, that action inevitably has consequences, does it remain mere 'faith' or does it become 'fervour' or even 'fanaticism'? In the eighth edition of the *Concise Oxford Dictionary of Current English*, published in 1990, 'faith' is first defined as 'complete trust or confidence', then as 'firm belief, esp. without logical proof', thirdly, as 'a system of religious belief' (with the Christian faith given as an example) and, fourthly, as a 'duty or commitment to fulfil a trust'. This blend of the 'religious' and the 'secular' (terms still used in a manner so faithful to late medieval western European ecclesiastical thought) is not continued into the 1990 *Concise Oxford* definition of 'fervour', which refers to 'vehemence, passion, zeal' and, in accordance with the more literal medieval French and Middle English usage, a 'glowing condition, intense heat'. The religious category is also absent from the 'current' definition of a fanatic (hence 'fanaticism') : 'a person filled with excessive and often misguided belief'. However, the current usage of the word 'fundamentalism' to apply to Islam, regardless of its origin in American Protestant Christianity, is also reflected in this source. Yet many questions remain, especially for those who, as do the contributors to this volume, attempt to apply these concepts to late medieval and early modern Spain.

The nine studies included in this volume come at the vexed question of faith, fervour and fanaticism from angles as diverse as their authors, who have in common a commitment to our understanding of the complex religious experience of fifteenth-, sixteenth- and seventeenth-century Spaniards, whatever their individual understanding of that experience may have been.

Lesley Twomey's study, based on evidence from the Valencian poetry competitions of the fifteenth century, makes a valuable contribution to the theme by emphasizing the Christian majority context in which Jewish and Muslim life, as well as that of converts from those religions, was lived in the period. For Twomey, fervour did turn into fanaticism when the opponents of the doctrine that the Virgin Mary was sinless (immaculate) from the very moment of her conception, which was a novelty, as a proposed dogma, of the late Middle Ages, came to be held as political traitors by its supporters among the Valencian poets. The parallel between this situation and that of supposedly judaizing *conversos*, in the same period, who were regarded by their enemies as politically disloyal, is both obvious and neglected.

A further element in the religious equation of sixteenth-century Spain, the influence of Erasmian Christian humanism, is to be found in Encarnación Sánchez García's careful study of the anonymous *Viaje de Turquía*, which again illustrates preoccupations among Spanish Christians beyond those of Jews, Muslims and *conversos*, as Renaissance turned into Golden Age. The concern here was not just a revival of Classicism, but the reform and reunification of the Church, an agenda which went back to the humanism of the fifteenth century, in Spain as elsewhere. Terence O'Reilly's study of Spanish contemplative spirituality, and its attempted transmission to the laity, for example by Juan de Valdés, illustrates the strength of such ideas, which pre-dated the influence of Erasmus in Spain, and also shows the anxiety among conservatives, such as Melchor Cano, which was induced by this type of activity.

From a very different perspective, Gordon Kinder's careful study, which is 'fervent' in the best sense, takes the story of the Spanish Reform forward into the later sixteenth century, when a number of Spaniards, at great personal cost, explicitly attached themselves to the ideas and institutions of Calvin, Bucer and others. Neither Reformed nor Catholic thinkers in Golden Age Spain were as isolated from outside influence as has often been supposed.

Ronald Cueto's wide-ranging study turns from the Mother of God to more earthly Spanish women, who, like her, regarded themselves as responding to spiritual or angelic messages. The evidence shows that, by the beginning of the seventeenth century, inquisitors had transferred some of their attention from supposed practitioners of Judaism or Islam, as well as Protestant Christians, to the female visionaries whose efforts had caused such disturbance to ecclesiastical and secular hierarchies since long before the time of Joan of Arc. Nicholas Griffiths provides a specific context for such repression, or at least suspicion, of unorthodox belief, in an explicitly Christian context, in his detailed study of the treatment of such matters by the inquisitorial tribunal of Cuenca, in the late sixteenth and seventeenth centuries.

Judaism and Islam continued, however, to be the preoccupation (fervour?), or obsession (fanaticism?) of all too many in early modern Spain, as Hilary Pomeroy illustrates in her study of the development of the rich Castilian ballad tradition in its treatment of Jews, Moors and their religion. What is striking in these ballads is how their original Christian content seems to have been kept alive by Jewish and Muslim exiles, but with a kind of 'literary revenge' on those who had persecuted their communities in the Iberian Peninsula.

Yet there were still reasonable people in the Iberian Peninsula, even after the introduction of the Inquisition, the conquest of the Muslim kingdom of Granada, and the expulsion of Jews who refused to convert to Christianity. As John Jones demonstrates, the tradition of 'gentle' Christian evangelism which Hernando de Talavera had initiated, as first archbishop of Granada after Ferdinand and Isabella's conquest, was ably and sympathetically continued in literary form, in the tortured political climate of the years around 1600, by Pedro de Valencia. In his treatise on the *Moriscos*, who were supposedly Christian converts from Islam, like *judeoconversos* a century or so earlier, Pedro de Valencia indeed managed to avoid crossing the line between fervour and fanaticism. He was, of course, attempting to prevent the repetition for 'converted' Muslims, in his own day, of the action taken against Jews (not against *judeoconversos*, who were too integral and valuable a part of the Spanish status quo, circa 1500), at the end of the previous century.

Perhaps one of the reasons for the failure of Pedro de Valencia's advocacy of keeping the Muslim converts in Spain is to be found in Michael Alpert's study of an *auto de fe* in Madrid in 1632, in which various supposed Jews were 'processed' as supposed desecrators of an image of the *Cristo de la Paciencia*. As Alpert shows, the story was transferred into later literature, thus perhaps illustrating the truth of the often-made observation that anti-Jewish feeling does not depend on the presence of Jews. It seems more than probable that the expulsion of the *moriscos*, in 1609-1610, owed as much to memories of supposed earlier atrocities by Jews and converts from Judaism, such as the 'ritual murder' of the 'holy child' of La Guardia which immediately preceded Ferdinand and Isabella's expulsion edict of 1492, as to any actions on the part of converts from Islam.

Probably in any country, society and period, and certainly in late medieval and early modern Spain, the expressions of religious experience and commitment were, and are, so diverse that all analysts have an insurmountable problem in attempting to order them into any pattern. Yet large movements did take place. Between the mid-fifteenth century and 1620, open and lively Jewish and Muslim communities did disappear from the Iberian Peninsula. Notions of Christian reform, so lovingly nurtured by the Spanish followers of Erasmus in the earlier decades of the sixteenth century, were crushed, at least on the surface, by the repression of Lutheranism, and the crushing of religious dissidence which was still, even in and after 1700, frequently described in the by then outmoded categories of the late medieval war against the Muslim, and his supposed Jewish ally, which had in reality finished with Ferdinand and Isabella's entry into Granada in 1492. The essays in this volume should serve to remind all students of Spain, and other readers, of the multifaceted nature of religious experience in any time and place. If they raise more questions than they answer, they have succeeded. The concepts of 'faith', 'fervour' and 'fanaticism' remain as elusive and subjective as ever.

Oxford

Part I

The Quest for Orthodoxy

1

Fervor / Fanatismo or *Entorno / Enfoque*: The Problem of the Female Visionary in the Catholic Monarchy

Ronald Cueto

An American specialist on early modern French social history has pinpointed the abundance of contemporaneous Spanish material dealing with women.[1] It is not necessary for the student to explore the holdings of the Biblioteca Nacional in Madrid to confirm the validity of the observation. If the *Biblioteca de Autores Españoles* is accessible then a perusal of Manuel Serrano y Sanz's *Apuntes para una biblioteca de escritoras españolas* soon proves to be both revealing and rewarding.[2] The sheer quantity of material is in itself rather overpowering, if not off-putting. And it is not just a question of those holy women writers who became national figures during the sixteenth and seventeenth centuries: the justly celebrated Teresa de Jesús, María de Jesús de Agreda or Luisa de la Ascensión de Carrión. This Catholic Monarchy phenomenon includes characters such as Doña María de Robles y Belluga whose spiritual writings 'ocupan nada menos que once gruesos tomos en folio', the Dominican Sor Hipólita de Jesús who produced 24 volumes, and so on (vol. 270, 149-150). And, one insists on it being treated as a Catholic Monarchy phenomenon, for it is to be seen not only in the Peninsula but also in the Indies, as may be confirmed in the case of Angela Carranza:

> embaucadora nacida en Córdoba de Tucumán, [quien] por los años 1665 y siguientes fingió tener éxtasis y raptos. Hacía un tráfico importante con medallas, rosarios y otros objetos, que aseguraba tenía milagrosas virtudes. Procesada por el Santo Oficio en 1688, fue recluida en un beaterio.

Apparently, 'en quince años escribió quince libros, compuestos de 543 cuadernos, con más de 7.500 hojas' (vol. 268, 216).

---

[1] Natalie Z. Davis, *Society and Culture in Early Modern France* (London: Duckworth, 1975), 85.
[2] Manuel Serrano y Sanz, *Apuntes para una biblioteca de escritoras españolas* in *Biblioteca de Autores Españoles* (Madrid: Atlas, 1975), vols 268-271.

From the very waning of the Middle Ages the loquacity of female visionaries has caused serious problems for the authorities of Catholic Christendom. To cut a rather complicated story very short, the student soon becomes aware that two assessments of the writings of St Bridget were seen to be crucial *a posteriori*. The Sorbonne theologian Gerson recommended prudence in his *De probatione spiritum* in 1415. Possibly more telling was the very influential Dominican cardinal Juan de Torquemada who came out in defence of the Swedish visionary and prophetess in his *Defensorium super revelationes S. Birgittae* of 1433. Ironically, his fellow Dominican, the future saint, Vincent Ferrer, regarded female visionaries and their revelations with profound distrust, in spite of being the personification of the trump of doom himself. Sixteenth-century scandals involving Cordovan Poor Clares, Lisbonian Dominicans and Madrilenian *beatas* had grave repercussions far beyond the confines of the Iberian Peninsula. In the seventeenth century, the Cistercian Cardinal Bona with his *De discretione Spiritum* of 1671 attempted to provide an overall view on the basis of the experience of the great mystics and spiritual directors. In the eighteenth century, the Jesuit Giovanni Battista Scaramelli with his *Discernimento degli spiritii* of 1753 was to produce what was to prove to be the most popular guide ever to the thorny problem of discernment of spirits.

It is not too difficult to find examples of seventeenth-century *calificadores* showing an almost innate dislike of having to judge manuscripts dealing with visions and revelations. The Dominican Francisco de Araujo, one of the most distinguished Thomists of his age, had to admit that:

> aunque es verdad, lo que dizen los Doctores arriba citados, que semejantes revelaciones y visiones se hazen sospechosas, o por frequentes, por no ser Dios loquaz, y menos en la Ley Evangélica, y serlo mucho el Demonio: o por ser el sugeto que las recibe del sexo femenino, por que las mugeres son flacas de cabeza, y abundar en ellas el humor viscoso, apto para recibir, y conservar los varios, y diferentes fantasmas: Y por estar de ordinario sugetas al vicio de la vanidad, y por la vehemencia de sus passiones, reyna en ellas más que en los hombres; por lo qual fácilmente juzgan que es Dios, o Angel de luz, el que las habla, que es más juzgar por el antojo de la passion, que por la verdad del objeto .[3]

Likewise, the Discalced Franciscan, Fray Gerónimo Planes, was convinced that: 'De los engaños de las mugeres en esta materia, podríamos escriuir un tratado'. The trouble was that: 'Y oy passa esto; que viendo los simples que

---

[3] Miguel Batista de Lanuza, *Vida de la Sierva de Dios, Francisca del Santmo. Sacramento, Carmelita Descalza, del Conuento de S. Ioseph de Pamplona* (Zaragoza: Joseph de Linaja y Lamarca, 1659), 537.

vna persona tiene arrobamientos, sin más consideración se van empos della: y la predican por santa'.[4]

Clearly the problem was compounded by the low status accorded to women in general at this time. However, there were other factors involved, factors concerned with the very nature of religious life during this period. As was pointed out by a Discalced Franciscan authority publishing in 1615, singularity was to be avoided like the plague by the true religious. For Fray Juan de Santa María:

> La que siempre se ha temido, y tenido por muy dañosa en esta vida común, ha sido el vicio de la singularidad. Y assí los muy santos han tenido en esto más punto, y huydo con mayor cuydado esta tentación, por no dar que dezir a otros, y huyr la vanagloria del mundo, anteponiendo el orden, y común modo de viuir, que todos los demás religiosos guardan conuentualmente a qualquiera otro exercicio, y particular deuoción suya: porque el que haze alguna cosa con publicidad que los demás no hazen, da con ella ocasión de que vnos se admiren, y otros murmuren: hasta el silicio, la cadena, y qualquiera otra cosa particular que alguno trae, que no es como los que vsan los demás, se sabe que otros lo saben, se lo quita, o de tal manera lo dissimula que no puede ser oydo, ni visto, por no parecer singular. No tiene mucho deseo de viuir desconocido al mundo, y escondido a la opinión, y fama vulgar, el que no sigue la comunidad, que los más zelosos, más reformados, y mejores religiosos, siguen y guardan conforme a los precetos y documentos de su regla y profession, y si alguna singularidad ha de ser en la más rigurosa y perfecta obseruancia de su misma regla, y en essos mismos actos conuentuales con singular pureza de intención y deuoción.[5]

Furthermore, one did not need to be a qualified theologian to realize that good pickings could be found amongst the credulous. The upward link between the path of virtue and what we now call social mobility was plain for all to see, particularly the inquisitors. By the same token, even in the seventeenth century certain would-be manifestations of holiness were seen as too crude for comfort. The saying of prayers in Discalced Carmelite toilets whilst exercising necessary bodily functions did not strike all *calificadores* as worthy of praise or emulation. Thus it was that the Dominican Fray José Buenaventura Ponz, *catedrático de Escoto* in the University of Zaragoza, in the case of the Discalced Carmelite Francisca del Santísimo Sacramento felt bound to agree with Our Lady, who had suggested to her: 'no rezasse en la cama su Corona, ni en el lugar deputado a los oficios menos decentes del cuerpo; ni prosiguiesse allí sus devociones, aunque las tuviesse començadas' (Lanuza, 522). Moreover, the strengthening

---

[4] Gerónimo Planes, O.F.M.D., *Tratado del Examen de las Revelaciones verdaderas y falsas, Y de los raptos* (Valencia: Viuda de Juan Chrysóstomo Garriz, 1634), 271ᵛ, and 387ʳ.

[5] Juan de Santa María, O.F.M.D., *Chronica de la Provincia de San Joseph*, 2 vols (Madrid: Imprenta Real, 1615-1618), I, 271.

of this sense of impropriety in influential places can easily be traced in the eighteenth century. Thus it was that a Jesuit missioner could approve the prohibition of a biography of a reformed prostitute, even though it had been penned and published by a General of the Praemonstratensians. The justification for such a drastic and humiliating course of action could not have been simpler: in La Quintana's reported visions Our Lady appeared in 'alpargatillas', whilst Our Lord was 'un hombre baxo ayrado con el brazo remangado'.[6] A couple of decades later Cardinal Lorenzana, an enlightened Archbishop of Toledo, preached caution to his own preachers:

> En referir exemplos de milagros, de almas condenadas o salvadas, y de apariciones, han de ser muy *cautos* los Predicadores, porque entre gente entendida se pierde mucho fruto.[7]

It is well known that in the nineteenth century a leading Spanish historian quoted a papal librarian to the effect that Spanish history was but an Augean stable in desperate need of a good cleansing.[8] There can be little doubt that Serrano y Sanz set about his part of this mammoth task with relish, criticizing right, left and centre. In the case of the previously mentioned Angela Carranza, he quoted with approval Toribio de Medina, specialist on the Lima Tribunal of the Holy Office, who claimed that:

> quitada la máscara a esta esfinge diabólica, se halló todo el prodigio de sus maravillas, portento de embustes, ficciones y vanidades ridículas, irrisorias, contradictorias y disparatadas por la mayor parte en las revelaciones. Sus escritos un seminario de herejías, errores, malsonancias, temeridades, escándalo de proposiciones cismáticas, impías, blasfemias peligrosas.

And Serrano y Sanz agreed with all this because he was of the opinion that with reference to the 'más de 500 cuadernos refiriendo sus imaginarias visiones, quemólos la Inquisición y con esto libró a los eruditos de perder el tiempo en leerlos para dar cuenta de las necedades que contendrían' (vol. 268, 216). However, it is with the aristocratic Dominican Sor Hipólita de Jesús Rocaberti that he really goes to town:

> Pocos libros se han publicado, no ya en España, mas en toda Europa, tan indigestos y farragosos como los de la Madre Hipólita. (...) Son montones de hojarasca, en mala hora editados por el celo indiscreto del Arzobispo

---

[6] Pedro de Calatayud, S.J., *Opusculos, y doctrinas practicas* (Logroño: Francisco Delgado, 1754), 338.

[7] Francisco Antonio Lorenzana, *Coleccion de las Pastorales, y Cartas* (Madrid: Joachín Ibarra, 1779), 'Avisos (...) a los Predicadores de su Arzobispado', 6.

[8] Modesto Lafuente, *Historia General de España*, 6 vols (Barcelona: Montaner y Simón, 1877-1885), V (1879), 411.

Rocaberti, quien se imaginaba tener en su familia una nueva Santa Teresa (vol. 270, 151).

It goes without saying that this was the approach that was to flourish amongst twentieth-century historians, whether lay or religious. Even loyalty to the Order, normally sacrosanct amongst religious, was to be tested to breaking point by leading scholars. The Augustinian, Fr Santiago Vela, had no hesitation in dismissing much of this type of Augustinian literature as so much rubbish.[9] The dismissive severity of the Dominican Fr Beltrán de Heredia is worthy of quotation:

> Su estudio, que sólo puede interesar a la psicología de anormales, es con todo un antecedente obligado para explicar el origen de esa suspicacia (...) de la doctrina de la Santa Reformadora.[10]

For the highly respected Ramón Ezquerra Abadía, the use of visionaries for political purposes was an 'indicio triste de decadencia'.[11] His better-known contemporary Gregorio Marañón was even more critical, and was convinced that it was all 'absolutamente típica de la profunda y degradante corrupción del alma popular en aquellos siglos'.[12] Obviously, such readings pose serious problems for the academic student of the Court of Madrid under the Hapsburgs, whether it be in the case of Philip II, Philip III, Philip IV, or Charles II. What is one to make of Philip II in the Escorial spending time and money on one of the world's great collections of relics? Is one to ignore the findings of Patrick Williams and see Philip III purely and simply as a bigot, who preferred visiting monasteries and convents to defending his inheritance? And the problem becomes even more acute in the case of that born courtier, Philip IV. Has the Nun of Agreda to be brushed aside as a coarse purveyor of superstition, working in league with venal Confessors Royal and bogus prophets? Then there is the justly celebrated painting of Charles II adoring the Blessed Sacrament in the Escorial. Is the commitment of the House of Hapsburg to the Catholic sacrament *par excellence* mere fervour or mere fanaticism? Surely it makes much more sense to explore this link between religion, art and politics in a more detached manner, for there must be some significance in the fact that

---

[9] Gregorio de Santiago Vela, O.S.A., *Ensayo de una Biblioteca Iberoamericana de la Orden de San Agustín*, 8 vols (Madrid-El Escorial: Imprenta Asilo de Huérfanos, 1913-1931).

[10] Vicente Beltrán de Heredia, O.P., *Miscelánea*, 4 vols (Salamanca: Dominicos de las Provincias de España, 1972-1973), III, 335.

[11] Ramón Ezquerra Abadía, *La conspiración del Duque de Híjar (1648)* (Madrid: Borondo, 1934), 122.

[12] Gregorio Marañón, *El Conde-Duque de Olivares (La pasión de mandar)*, 2nd edn (Madrid: Espasa Calpe, 1945), 205.

Philip IV slept in the presence of a depiction of the Emperor Rudolph I venerating the Blessed Sacrament.

No doubt the development of this highly critical response, which pays such small regard to the historical *entorno*, suggests the need for caution on the part of the revisionist. Of course, the modern student may smile on learning that the Conceptionist Sor Inés de Jesús de Franco struggled womanfully in her convent in Miedes against 'inauditas lascivas sugestiones y con obscenas horribles apariencias' (Serrano y Sanz: vol. 269, 417), as did the future beatified Sor María de Jesús of the Discalced Mercedarians against visions of 'hombres luxuriosos y deshonestos con desnudez maliciosa'.[13] However that may be, here an attempt will be made to examine the validity of the 'common-sense approach' with reference to particular cases in the major Orders.

There is no need to stress the importance of the Trinitarians in the Court of Madrid in the first half of the seventeenth century. Lerma was a major patron of both the Calced and Discalced branches. Fray Hortensio Félix de Paravicini was arguably the finest Court preacher of his day. Fray Simón de Rojas was Queen Margarita de Austria's confessor. The bed-bound Fray Tomás de la Virgen was on familiar terms with Philip IV, Isabel de Borbón, Olivares, and all the major courtiers. Fray Juan de San Francisco was Haro's confessor. For all these reasons the chronicles of the Discalced Trinitarian Fray Alejandro de la Madre de Dios prove to be most illuminating.[14] On the one hand this Trinitarian world is clearly a world of demons, angels, mortifications, and what seem to us to be all sorts of excesses. Thus, before the novices started eating in the refectory:

> Precedían, y preceden a esta tal comida, varias y frequentes mortificaciones: se ponen a la puerta del Refectorio postrados para que los que entran los pissen como vasura. Otros entran en el mesmo Refectorio con una Cruz muy grande a cuestas, o se ponen a los pies de él, los brazos levantados en Cruz, o postrados en el suelo con la mesma figura de Cruz, o entran con una calabera en la mano izquierda, dándose grandes bofetadas con la derecha, o golpes en los pechos con una piedra, o en las espaldas con una disciplina, que suele ser de cadenas. Estas mortificaciones duran hasta que el Presidente haze señal para que cessen (II, 5)

As the General of the Order, Fray Martín de la Asunción, acutely observed:

---

[13] Serrano y Sanz, vol. 269, 565. For a detailed case-study of the sexual entanglements of *beatas* in sixteenth-century Toro, see Francisco Javier Lorenzo Pinar, *Beatas y mancebas* (Zamora: Editorial Semuret, 1995).

[14] Alejandro de la Madre de Dios, O.SS.T.D., *Chronica de los Descalzos de la Santissima Trinidad (...)*, *Segvnda Parte* (Alcalá de Henares: J. García Briones, 1706), and *Tercera Parte* (Madrid: Imprenta Real, 1707).

> Mas una cosa es pintarlo aora, y otra muy distincta verlo entonces. Nadie
> dexaría de juzgar, que nos sustentaba Dios milagrosamente, y yo lo creo assí
> sin duda alguna (II, 6).

Yet this Order is seen at the same time as: 'Tálamo de la Perfección, Jardín
Ameno, y Palacio hermoso, que edificó la Divina Sabiduría' (II, 3). Trinitarian
beatas are treated with respect. And the list of holy women flourishing in the
Catholic Monarchy is no less impressive for all its predictability. For this
chronicler there cannot be any doubt that:

> Aunque siempre es admirable Dios en sus santos, parece que en estos últimos
> siglos ha estendido los braços de su misericordia, para manifestar su poder en
> las Santas, y en muchas mugeres, que florecieron en virtud, especialmente en
> nuestra España, lo qual causa digna admiración a los que piadosamente lo
> consideran, y son movidos a rendir las gracias al Padre de las cumbres, de
> quien desciende toda la perfección de las almas. En tiempos que casi pisaron
> los umbrales de nuestros años, escogió Dios a la seráfica Madre Santa Teresa
> de Jesús, y a muchas hijas, y compañeras suyas, y también a la inestimable flor
> la Infanta Sor Margarita de la Cruz, y a la muger fuerte Doña María de Vela,
> que como luminar segundo después de Santa Teresa, ilustró a Avila, su dichosa
> cuna y feliz sepulcro. A la ilustrada Doña Marina de Escobar, glorioso timbre
> de Valladolid. A la Sabia de Coria, verdaderamente sabia, pues supo tan
> perfectamente las prácticas de el divino Amor. A la Extática Virgen María de
> Jesús de Villarrobledo. A la nueva maravilla de la Gracia Sor Juana de Jesús,
> corona gloriosa para la Cabeça de Castilla, más que quantas ciñeron sus
> ínclitos Reyes: Y a la Madre María de Jesús, Abadesa de Agreda, y escritora
> de los libros que divinamente pintan al vivo los esmaltes de la Santa Ciudad de
> Dios, que es María Santíssima (III, 209).

Yet the critical faculty as we understand it is not lost. One *beata's* visions are
easily explained by her Trinitarian confessor: 'Essa es la visión, el no aver
cenado' (III, 335). This chronicler does not quote Dr Pérez de Valdivia, but he
is clearly aware of the influence of diet on the contemplative life. Certainly, the
leading Golden Age authority on *beatas* had no doubt that:

> Los manjares que, a mi parecer, no son buenos para la castidad son todos los
> muy calientes o ventosos, como son, de las cosas de la carne, el macho
> principalmente; hay otros que, aunque no tanto, por ser muy ordinarios
> manjares no se cuentan en particular. No nombro aves, aunque algunos no son
> manjares castos, porque la gente recogida o no los come, o muy poco; y lo
> poco no hace mal, aunque no sea muy bueno.
> El pescado casi todo es amigo de la castidad, como no sea muy salado, ni de
> mala digestión(...).
> Los huevos no son muy contrarios a la castidad, a lo menos las yemas, que la
> clara no es muy casta por su naturaleza.

> De las frutas, las secas, que no son muy calientes, son las más sanas y más
> castas, especialmente pasas y granadas sin cibera, o granillos, y peros cuando
> están maduros.
> De los licuores, el aceite es malo contra la castidad (...).
> El vino es malvadísimo para la gente casta, y se ha de beber como medicina
> (...). De las legumbres, garbanzos y habas son ventosos y desayudan a la
> castidad.[15]

Needless to say, the more thoughtful also reflected on the bodily effects of
contemplation, and within their own terms were capable of producing a
perfectly rational explanation. Thus Huarte was convinced:

> El rezar y meditar se hace subiendo el calor natural a la cabeza, por cuya
> ausencia quedan las demás partes del cuerpo frías; y si es con mucha atención,
> se viene a perder el sentido del tacto, del cual dijo Aristóteles que era necesario
> para la vida de los animales, y los demás sentidos servían de ornamento y
> perfección, aunque sin gusto, olfato, vista y oído vemos que se puede vivir.
> Mas estando el ánima elevada en alguna profunda contemplación, no envía la
> facultad animal a las partes del cuerpo, sin la cual ni los oídos pueden oír, ni
> los ojos ver, ni las narices oler, ni el gusto gustar, ni el tacto tocar. Por donde
> ni sienten frío los que están meditando, ni calor, ni hambre, ni sed, ni
> cansancio. Y siendo el tacto la centinela que descubre al hombre quién es que
> le hace bien o mal, no se puede aprovechar de él; y así, estando helado de frío o
> abrasándose de calor o muerto de hambre, pasa por ello sin sentirlo, porque no
> hay quien le avise.[16]

Likewise Fray Alejandro shows awareness of the psychological ravages to
which contemplatives are exposed, and quotes cases where 'su entendimiento
estaba como farol apagado'. This thought-provoking Discalced Trinitarian
chronicler is both touching and telling when describing the despair of his brother
in Christ, Fray Luis de la Santísima Trinidad, for he continues:

> Su memoria, como si jamás se hubiera acordado de Dios, ni hubiera de
> acordarse, y los objetos santos se le representaban como especies estrañas, y
> de lexos, y como bienes agenos. Las obras buenas, que avía hecho las miraba
> sin estimación, y como el que después de aver empleado su caudal en Indias,
> lo perdió todo en la Mar, y él quedó cautibo, pobre, y miserable. La voluntad
> estaba tambien trémula, y cobarde, sin que se le descubriese una centella de
> devoción sensible, y sin poder atravesar una gota de agua dulce, porque las

[15] Diego Pérez de Valdivia, *Aviso de gente recogida* (Madrid: Fundación Universitaria
Española-Universidad Pontificia de Salamanca, 1977), 610-611.
[16] Juan Huarte de San Juan, *Examen de ingenios. Para las sciencias,* Rodrigo Sanz (ed.), 2
vols (Madrid: Espasa Calpe, 1930), I, 70, quoted by Alvaro Huerga, O.P., *Historia de los
Alumbrados*, 5 vols (Madrid: Fundación Universitaria Española, 1978-1994), II (1978), 361.

> olas de aquella tempestad le avían hecho tragar muchas aguas amargas, que
> llenaban todas sus potencias, y avían entrado hasta su alma. Quando bolvía
> los ojos a mirarse, y se hallaba en su interior tan desdichado, crecía en su
> entendimiento el exceso de su temor, [como David se juzgaba] desechado de
> los ojos de Dios (Alejandro de la Madre de Dios: II, 273-274).

And no attempt is made to cover up the scandalous aspects of the case:

> En algunas ocasiones fue acometido con tentaciones de blasfemia, y de ira,
> contra Dios, contra sí mesmo, y contra todas las criaturas. Sentía unas
> violencias, o rápidos movimientos, que se llaman primeros, a los quales resistía
> la razón, pero luego bolvía el combate, sin cesar. Acompañaba a este desusado
> exercicio la falta que tenía de satisfacción, con lo qual al principio, por la
> novedad comenzó notablemente a afligirse. Experimentaba, que ni las vigilias,
> ni la oración, ni las penitencias era remedio eficaz, para sosegar la imaginación,
> y lleno de pena suplicó a su Magestad, por medio de la Reyna de los Angeles,
> que le librase de aquellas violencias fantásticas que le atormentaban el corazón
> (II, 267).

The conversion of the 'jardín ameno' into a lunatic asylum was not
exceptional. When the Recollect Augustinians took over the Concepción in
Salamanca, for instance, 'hallaron en ella dos locas'.[17] But where there was the
possibility of the loss of wits, there was also the possibility of sanctity. By
1695, 53 Discalced Franciscan nuns had died since their ´foundation in
Salamanca. Of these, 'de Veinte y siete se escrivieron las vidas', and well could
an admirer exclaim: 'Rara maravilla, por cierto, cargar de tanto fruto en tan
breve tiempo este Paraíso'. [18] And, as will be seen, the horticultural image is
important.

Again, the sublunary world of the Recollect Augustinian Sor Mauricia del
Santísimo Sacramento is, naturally enough, a world of devils and angels, visions
of heaven and hell, of saints and patriarchs, and things marvellous and
miraculous. But it is at the same time a lower-class world of frightening
brutality, of abused children and battered wives, of blackmail and violence, of
abortion and murder. This girl bride, who leaves her only child and brute of a
husband, chose the path of virtue instead of prostitution in order to survive.
Through her down-to-earth autobiography, the modern student of Golden Age
Spain is brought into close and disconcerting contact with the fact that Sor
Mauricia's world is now foreign and remote even for her Spanish

---

[17] Alonso de Villerino, O.S.A., *Esclarecido Solar de las Religiosas Recoletas de Nvestro
Padre San Agvstin*, 3 vols (Madrid: Bernardo de Villadiego-Juan Garciá Infanzón, 1690-
1691-1694), II, 9.

[18] Manuela de la Santísima Trinidad, O.F.M.D., *Fvndacion del Convento de la Pvrissima
Concepcion de Franciscas Descalzas de la Civdad de Salamanca* (Salamanca: María Estévez,
1696), in 'Aprobacion de la Orden', no pagination.

correligionists.[19]   The same may be said of the world of the Discalced
Franciscan Sor Beatriz de la Concepción, an illegimate daughter of the Duke of
Terranova, who died in 1646 at the age of 54. Nobody wanted to be with her in
the kitchen because 'se quedava en Cruz toda la mañana' (Manuela de la
Santísima Trinidad, 316). To make sure that it was not just an act: 'Hiziéronla
mil martirios, para ver si volvía de los arrobos (...): por brazos y pies la metían
alfileres grandes, y la traspasavan de parte à parte (...)'(Manuela de la Santísima
Trinidad, 277).

And this handmaid of the Lord was not singular in her bearing of pain. Her
sister in Christ, Sor Micaela de Jesús, had to have her left hand amputated. The
operation - with many *botones de fuego* and the fumes of burning flesh
suffocating the weeping onlookers - was carried out with her singing: 'En el
Molino de Amor / se deshaze mi alma con este favor' (Manuela de la Santísima
Trinidad, 259).

The sheer foreignness of this world is further underlined in the case of Sor
Bernardina del Sacramento, a niece of the Condes de Fuentes:

> Era enfermíssima, porque tenía en la cabeza vn cerco de lobanillos, que parecía
> corona de espinas; estos estavan de ordinario tan enconados, que padecía
> intolerables dolores: en medio de este cerco tenía vn lobanillo tan grande como
> vn meloncillo, que era el que más le fatigava. Trataron, después de muchos
> años que le tenía, de cortárselo, y se executó teniendo apercibido el Confessor,
> que entró con el Médico, y Cirujano, porque tuvieron por cierto moriría en el
> sacrificio: determináronse a él, por estar antes tan en peligro su vida, como en
> la cura que la hazían: ciñéronle el lobanillo con vna sábana gruessa, y
> aparejados todos los instrumentos, se le cortó el Cirujano, y estando todos los
> que lo miravan atemorizados, ella no se quexó más que si estuviera muerta,
> sólo dixo muy passo: Sea por amor de Dios: diéronle muchos botones de fuego,
> y de mil maneras la atormentaron, quedando edificadíssimos los Doctores de su
> sufrimiento: quitáronla la sábana, que estava bañada en sangre, y otros muchos
> paños, que parecía avérsele ido quanta avía en su cuerpo, y la descubrieron el
> rostro, (que aunque era ya vieja, no tenía nada acabada la hermosura) que
> estava mucho más linda con los hilos de sangre que se le bañavan, no bastando
> tantos dolores para que la tuviesse desapacible, porque tenía grandíssimo
> consuelo en padecer por su Amado (Manuela de la Santísima Trinidad, 160-
> 161).

If the link between religion and politics may only be ignored at the risk of
serious distortion, the same applies to the connection between religion and
medicine.

---

[19] Ronald Cueto, 'La mentalidad barroca segoviana a través de los recuerdos de una abuela
visionaria y monja', in *Segovia 1088-1988. Congreso de la historia de la ciudad. Actas.*
(Segovia: Academia de San Quirce, 1992), 519-536.

By the same token, it is at one and the same time a world that is both *coherente y consecuente*. Precisely because Sor Mauricia was such an intelligent operator of the system, this visionary grandmother was eventually to join one of the Catholic Monarchy's most exclusive female Orders. In the process, she was to become co-foundress of the Recollect Augustinian convent in Gijón, with all the prestige that such status involved. Whether in Segovia, Valladolid, Madrid or Asturias, Sor Mauricia always had an expert eye for the main chance, whether it were Discalced Franciscan, Dominican, Brigettine or Augustinian.[20] It is worth recalling that, in the space of the 99 years from 1589 to 1688, no fewer than 45 convents of Recollect Augustinians were founded in the Peninsula.[21] In the case of their Madrid convent of the Encarnación, there was a passage which led directly to the Alcázar Real. A close reading of this autobiography confirms the suspicion that rather than talk in general terms of credulity or superstition, it is more profitable to explore the case of each individual writer.

Again Sor Hipólita de Jesús proves to be yet another case in point. Born in Barcelona in 1549, this aristocrat took the Dominican habit at the age of 11 and professed five years later. She went to her Maker in 1624. She came from a family with pretensions to sanctity. It is all very well for Serrano y Sanz to score easy points against her nephew. But Fray Juan Tomás de Rocaberti has to be placed in context.

One can but suspect that Serrano y Sanz accepted Modesto Lafuente's assertion: 'Era Rocaberti más fanático y crédulo, que avisado y docto', for it is clear from his entry on the Rocabertis that he was blissfully unaware of the work of a Catalan scholar who was to become Bishop of Vic. Dr Torras maintains that Lafuente could only have known of Rocaberti by name. In point of fact, Fray Juan Tomás de Rocaberti was one of the most learned Dominicans of his age. Born around 1620, after a promising academic career, he became prior of Tarragona in 1663, provincial of Aragon in 1664, and Master General of the Order in 1670. He was presented to the see of Valencia by Charles II in 1676. Fray Rocaberti's first major work, *Alimento Espiritual*, had appeared in 1668, and had been quickly followed by *Teología mística* in 1669. International celebrity was to come with his *De Romani Pontificis auctoritate*, which was to be attacked by Bossuet and other supporters of Gallicanism. It was after the *Parlement* of Paris had condemned his *magnum opus* that Fray Rocaberti had published in Rome, in 20 volumes, his *Bibliotheca maxima Pontificia*.

---

[20] Ronald Cueto, 'Connexions and Interests on the Path of Virtue: Mauricia Pérez de Velasco and the Expansion of the Augustinian Recollection', in Colin Richmond and Isobel Harvey (eds), *Recognitions: Essays Presented to Edmund Fryde* (Aberystwyth: The National Library of Wales, 1996), 351-374.

[21] Villerino, op. cit., II, 'Indice', no pagination.

Fray Juan Tomás was finally appointed Inquisitor General in 1695, a post he held until his death in 1699. He had already acted twice as Viceroy of Valencia.[22] To treat a Dominican scholar and politician of this eminence as the persistent victim of misguided zeal and ignorance begs far too many questions. And, of course, the point is a sharp one for, when he was appointed Inquisitor General, Archbishop Rocaberti was assured by the King's secretary:

> me manda S. M. asegurar a V. E. solamente ha intervenido la gran justificación de S. M., y su Real propensión a la persona de V. E., fundada en el justo respeto que se merece V. E. por sus muchas prendas, igual amor y zelo a su servicio (Torras i Bages, 17).

In the event a close examination of Serrano y Sanz's own predilections helps to explain much. The clue is provided in the entry on Madre María Magdalena de San Jerónimo, where he notes:

> Muchas veces nos hemos dolido en esta obra de que abunden las noticias biográficas de monjas ilusas, y en cambio apenas se encuentren de algunas cuyos nombres merecen veneración (vol. 270, 304).

This nun dedicated her life to trying to tackle the problem of prostitution. In the on-going debate between Martha and Mary it is not too difficult to see where Serrano y Sanz's sympathies lie. It is the subtle, and often unrecognized, presence of the influence of a very unsubtle positivism that so often militates against a tenable reading of Spanish Golden Age religiosity. The problem may be encapsulated in a short quotation: 'El P. Pedro de San Cecilio, en su Crónica, tomo II, dice que [Sor María de la Antigua] "dejó escritos más de 1.300 cuadernos de alta y sustancial doctrina, dictados por Dios'"(vol. 268, 42). And, of course, the sting is in the tail.

Recently students of post-Tridentine religion have tended to stress the insurance policy aspect of the subject.[23] Religion provided the reassurance and protection that the civil authorities could not provide. But the question is more complex than insurance policies, for it also involves post-Tridentine understanding of knowledge and of the sources of knowledge. Before the growth of modern science, several sources of knowledge were seen as legitimate. It is neither helpful nor historical to dismiss everything other than modern science as so much superstition and ignorance. The sixteenth- and seventeenth-century subjects of His Catholic Majesty were neither uninformed nor silly. Their criteria were different in that they were overwhelmingly

---

[22] Josep Torras i Bages, *En Rocaberti y en Bossuet* (Barcelona: Jaume Jepús y Roviralta, 1898), *passim*.

[23] Jean Dulumeau, *Rassurer et protéger le sentiment de securité dans l'Occident d'autrefois* (Paris: Fayard, 1988).

Christocentric. Hence, with reference to spirituality, the on-going problem was one of discernment of spirits. For this reason it would be difficult to exaggerate the importance of the horticultural imagery previously noted. In this context, it was not so much a question of the Good Shepherd leading his flock, but rather of the *Divino Agricultor* producing fine trees with good crops. Hence the importance attached to the combination of rapidity and quantity, whether it were the number of new foundations or the numbers of saints. And it was not just a question of the phenomenal spread of the Discalced Carmelites. The Capuchins, for instance, between 1592 and 1594 opened seven noviciates in the Spanish Netherlands to cope with the flood of vocations.[24] Neither was it a question of some sort of other-worldliness. As even the most cursory inspection of almost any ecclesiastical archive in the Hispanic world will confirm, Golden Age clerics knew how to keep ledgers.

Rather than sum up in the usual fashion, it may be more helpful to quote Serrano y Sanz yet again. Sor Jerónima de la Asunción sent back to Spain from Manila an account of the revelations of her sister Poor Clare, Sor Juana de San Antonio (vol. 270, 225). For anyone who has seen Velázquez's magnificent portrait of Sor Jerónima, it becomes impossible to think in terms of *monjas ilusas* or fanaticism and superstition, when dealing with Spanish Golden Age spirituality. Needless to say, visions, revelations and prophecy have never found much favour in Academe. Even a retired *catedrático de prima* and *regente de estudios de San Esteban* in the seventeenth century in Salamanca saw the need to be even-handed. According to Fray Gerónimo de Matamá:

> De las visiones, y revelaciones, es doctrina común, que aprobarlas todas, es levedad; reprobarlas todas dureza. Lo cierto es, que no hazen Santos, sino suponen la Santidad, si son seguras. Por muchas se hazen sospechosas todas, como enseña S. Francisco de Sales, a quien sigue el Cardenal Bona, y más en sugetos melancólicos, de vehemente aprehensión, afligidos con dolores y enfermedades, que debilitan el celebro, y enflaquecen la cabeza.[25]

Even so, in the case of the post-Tridentine Catholic Monarchy one might be inclined to go along with a specialist in Reformation popular piety, when he suggests:

> [the future] seems likely to lie with those who, in pursuing the detailed local investigations we still need, are self-conscious about the dangers of anachronism, hesitant about distinguishing too confidently between "religion"

---

[24] Francis Xavier Martin, O.S.A., *Friar Nugent. A Study of Francis Lavalin Nugent (1569-1635) Agent of the Counter-Reformation* (Rome-London: Capuchin Historical Institute-Methuen, 1962), 28.

[25] Manuela de la Santísima Trinidad, op. cit., 'Dictamen', no pagination.

and "superstition", and open in their interpretation to the insights of the sociologists, cultural anthropologists, and students of comparative religion.[26]

Bibliography

Beltrán de Heredia, Vicente, O.P., *Miscelánea*, 4 vols (Salamanca: Dominicos de las Provincias de España, 1972-1973)

Calatayud, Pedro de, S.J., *Opusculos, y doctrinas practicas* (Logroño: Francisco Delgado, 1754)

Cueto, Ronald, 'La mentalidad barroca segoviana a través de los recuerdos de una abuela visionaria y monja', in *Segovia 1088-1988. Congreso de la historia de la ciudad. Actas.* (Segovia: Academia de San Quirce, 1992), 519-536

----------, 'Connexions and Interests on the Path of Virtue: Mauricia Pérez de Velasco and the Expansion of the Augustinian Recollection' in Colin Richmond and Isobel Harvey (eds), *Recognitions: Essays Presented to Edmund Fryde* (Aberystwyth: The National Library of Wales, 1996), 351-374

Davis, Natalie Z., *Society and Culture in Early Modern France* (London: Duckworth, 1975)

Dulumeau, Jean, *Rassurer et protéger le sentiment de securité dans l'Occident d'autrefois* (Paris: Fayard, 1988)

Ezquerra Abadía, Ramón, *La conspiración del Duque de Híjar (1648)* (Madrid: Borondo, 1934)

Huarte de San Juan, Juan, *Examen de ingenios. Para las sciencias,* Rodrigo Sanz (ed.), 2 vols (Madrid: Espasa Calpe, 1930)

Huerga, Alvaro, O.P., *Historia de los alumbrados*, 5 vols (Madrid: Fundación Universitaria Española, 1978-1994), II (1978)

Lafuente, Modesto, *Historia General de España*, 6 vols (Barcelona: Montaner y Simón, 1877-1885), V (1879)

Lanuza, Miguel Batista de, *Vida de la Sierva de Dios, Francisca del Santmo. Sacramento, Carmelita Descalza, del Conuento de S. Ioseph de Pamplona* (Zaragoza: Joseph de Linaja y Lamarca, 1659)

Lorenzana, Francisco Antonio, *Coleccion de las Pastorales, y Cartas* (Madrid: Joachín Ibarra, 1779), 'Avisos (...) a los Predicadores de su Arzobispado'

---

[26] Francis Oakley, 'Religious and Ecclesiastical Life on the Eve of the Reformation' in Steven E. Ozment (ed.), *Reformation Europe: A Guide to Research* (St. Louis: Centre for Reformation Research, 1982), 21.

Lorenzo Pinar, Francisco Javier, *Beatas y mancebas* (Zamora: Editorial Semuret, 1995)

Madre de Dios, Alejandro de la, O.SS.T.D., *Chronica de los Descalzos de la Santissima Trinidad* (...), *Segvnda Parte* (Alcalá de Henares: J. García Briones, 1706), and *Tercera Parte* (Madrid: Imprenta Real, 1707)

Marañón, Gregorio, *El Conde-Duque de Olivares (La pasión de mandar)*, 2nd edn (Madrid: Espasa Calpe, 1945)

Martin, Francis Xavier, O.S.A., *Friar Nugent. A Study of Francis Lavalin Nugent (1569-1635) Agent of the Counter-Reformation* (Rome-London: Capuchin Historical Institute-Methuen, 1962)

Oakley, Francis, 'Religious and Ecclesiastical Life on the Eve of the Reformation' in Steven E. Ozment (ed.), *Reformation Europe: A Guide to Research* (St Louis: Centre for Reformation Research, 1982)

Pérez de Valdivia, Diego, *Aviso de gente recogida* (Madrid: Fundación Universitaria Española-Universidad Pontificia de Salamanca, 1977)

Planes, Gerónimo, O.F.M.D., *Tratado del Examen de las Revelaciones verdaderas y falsas, Y de los raptos* (Valencia: Viuda de Juan Chrysóstomo Garriz, 1634)

Santa María, Juan de, O.F.M.D., *Chronica de la Provincia de San Joseph*, 2 vols (Madrid: Imprenta Real, 1615-1618)

Santiago Vela, Gregorio de, O.S.A., *Ensayo de una Biblioteca Iberoamericana de la Orden de San Agustín*, 8 vols (Madrid-El Escorial: Imprenta Asilo de Huérfanos, 1913-1931)

Santísima Trinidad, Manuela de la, O.F.M.D., *Fvndacion del Convento de la Pvrissima Concepcion de Franciscas Descalzas de la Civdad de Salamanca* (Salamanca: María Estévez, 1696), in 'Aprobacion de la Orden', no pagination

Serrano y Sanz, Manuel, *Apuntes para una biblioteca de escritoras españolas* in *Biblioteca de Autores Españoles* (Madrid: Atlas, 1975), vols 268-271

Torras i Bages, Josep, *En Rocaberti y en Bossuet* (Barcelona: Jaume Jepús y Roviralta, 1898)

Villerino, Alonso de, O.S.A., *Esclarecido Solar de las Religiosas Recoletas de Nvestro Padre San Agvstin*, 3 vols (Madrid: Bernardo de Villadiego-Juan Garciá Infanzón, 1690-1691-1694)

2

'Cechs són aquells que tenen lo contrari': Fanatical Condemnation of Opponents of the Immaculate Conception in Fifteenth-Century Valencia

Lesley K. Twomey

The association between the doctrine of the Immaculate Conception, supporters of which considered that the Virgin Mary was untainted by original sin from the very moment of her conception, and religious fervour makes an article on it indispensable in any book dedicated to fervour and fanaticism. If we take as our starting point René Laurentin's image of the 'marée montante', which he uses to explain the development of mariology, it is apparent that both fervour and fanaticism are integral to the development of Marian doctrines:

> Comme les vagues se soulèvent, culminent, puis s'étalent et refluent jusqu'à ce que la suivante porte plus loin son élan, ainsi chaque période pressent quelque aspect caché du visage de la Vierge, le découvre avec ferveur non sans excès parfois, et souvent non sans lutte.[1]

The development of the Conception doctrine from the celebration of the feast-day in the eastern Church, whence it spread to Britain and then to France where it became established, to its acceptance across Christendom has been charted by theologians and religious historians.[2] Many in the Church could not accept the celebration of

---

[1] René Laurentin, *Court traité sur la Vierge Marie*, 5th edn (Paris: Lethielleux, 1967), 15.

[2] For the development of the doctrine in the eastern Church, cf. P Martin Jugie, A.A., *L'Immaculée Conception dans l'Écriture Sainte et dans la tradition orientale*, Bibliotheca Immaculatae Conceptionis, III, Textus et Disquisitiones (Rome: Academia Mariana Internationalis, 1952); for a general overview of mariology and its development, including the Immaculate Conception, cf. Hilda Mary Graef, *Mary: A History of Doctrine and Devotion*, 2 vols (London: Sheed and Ward, 1963-1965); Marina Warner also devotes a chapter to the Immaculate Conception, *Alone of All her Sex: The Myth and Cult of the Virgin Mary* (London: Weidenfeld and Nicolson, 1976), chapter 16. For a detailed overview of all aspects contributing to the development of the doctrine, see E. D. O'Connor, C.S.C. (ed.), *The Dogma of the Immaculate Conception: Its History and Significance* (Notre Dame: University of Notre Dame Press, 1958); for details of the spread of the feast-day to western Europe, see Dom Alberic Stacpoole, O.S.B., 'The English Tradition of the Doctrine of the Immaculate Conception' in Alberic Stacpoole, O.S.B. (ed.), *Mary's Place in Christian Dialogue* (Middlegreen: St Paul's Publications, 1982), 217-231.

the feast; indeed, St Bernard's opposition to its celebration is well known and is encapsulated in his Letter to the Canons of Lyons.[3] Lesmes Frías documents the celebration of the Conception feast in Spain considering that its first recorded mention was in a statute dating from 1309.[4]

St Thomas Aquinas was one of many thirteenth-century theologians who opposed the doctrine.[5] The first tentative steps towards wider acceptance of the doctrine were taken early in the fourteenth century by scholastic teachers, particularly at the University of Oxford, where John Duns Scotus taught.[6]

In the fifteenth century itself, the doctrine was by no means universally accepted: impassioned debate and violent reprisals against opponents were the norm. Debate about the doctrine was divided into two main camps. The Dominican Order of Preachers, following the school of thought of St Thomas Aquinas, was maculist, or sanctificationist, since Dominican scholars believed that the Virgin Mary was sanctified immediately after her conception and were opposed to the idea that Mary might have been set apart from the rest of humanity by the privilege of an Immaculate Conception, whilst the Franciscans, disciples of Scotus, were immaculist and promoted the doctrine. The difference between the two camps centred on whether the Virgin Mary was pure from the very moment of her conception or whether she was sanctified, or made holy, immediately after her conception.[7]

---

[3] St Bernard of Clairvaux, *Epistola* 174, Ad canonicos Lugdunenses: De conceptione S. Mariae, *Patrologia Latina*, vol. 182, 332-336; for details of the controversy, see Graef, I, chapter 5.

[4] See Lesmes Frías, S.J., 'Antigüedad de la fiesta de la Inmaculada en España, *Miscelánea Comillas*, 23 (1955), 31-85, especially 37-39.

[5] St Thomas Aquinas, *Summa Theologiae*, Thomas Gilby (ed.), 61 vols (New York: McGraw Hill; London: Blackfriars with Eyre and Spottiswoode, 1964-1976), vol. 51, Thomas R. Heath (ed.) (London: Blackfriars, 1969), especially Liber III.27 art.2; for an analysis of Aquinas's views, see Marie-Joseph Nicolas, O.P., 'The Meaning of the Immaculate Conception in the Perspectives of St Thomas' in E.D. O'Connor, C.S.C. (ed.), *The Dogma of the Immaculate Conception: Its History and Significance* (Notre Dame: University of Notre Dame Press, 1958), 327-345; also, Graef, I, 279-281. For a summary of key theologians' views on the Immaculate Conception, see Francisco de Guimaraens, O.F.M. Cap., 'La Doctrine des théologiens sur l'Immaculée Conception de 1250 à 1350', *Etudes franciscains*, 9 (1952), 181-205; 10 (1953), 23-53 and 167-187.

[6] Carlo Balic, O.F.M., 'The Medieval Controversy over the Immaculate Conception up to the Death of Scotus' in E.D. O'Connor, C.S.C. (ed.), *The Dogma of the Immaculate Conception: Its History and Significance* (Notre Dame: University of Notre Dame Press, 1958), 161-212, 202.

[7] Wenceslaus Sebastian, O.F.M., 'The Controversy over the Immaculate Conception from after Scotus to the End of the Eighteenth Century' in E.D. O'Connor, C.S.C. (ed.), *The Dogma of the Immaculate Conception: Its History and Significance* (Notre Dame: University of Notre Dame Press, 1958), 213-270.

By the fifteenth century, the leading role played by Spanish theologians in the Conception debate is attested by the fact that, at the Council of Basle, the session on the Immaculate Conception was due to be led for the maculists by the Dominican, Cardinal Juan de Torquemada, and for the immaculists by Juan de Segovia. In the event, only Juan de Segovia's side of the argument was heard at the Council. The pronouncement of the dogma of the Immaculate Conception, published on 17 September 1439, was never recognized, since the Council's decrees had been invalidated by the withdrawal of the papal legates in September 1437.[8] Sebastian, nevertheless, considered that the decree contributed to the spread of the doctrine in those countries which recognized the Council, amongst which, he includes Aragon (272).

An example of the virulence of debate about the Immaculate Conception at a local level in Spain can be found in the *Papeles relativos a las riñas y disputas que hubieron en Valladolid los frailes franciscanos con los dominicos acerca de la Inmaculada Concepcion y en especial el guardian de San Francisco, fray Martin de Alva, con el prior de San Pablo a principios del siglo XVI*.[9] Following a sermon about the Immaculate Conception preached by the Franciscan, Fray Martin de Alva, the Dominicans preached sermons in return raising various points of disparity with Fray Martin. The dispute was eventually settled by the ruling of the *Cancilleria de Valladolid*, commanding the two sides to put their past differences behind them:

> Primeramente rogamos e encargamos a los dichos padres... que vivan e esten en paz y sosiego segund pertenesce a varones de tanta religion, e que ni los unos ni los otros ... murmuren de las cosas pasadas [...].[10]

More interestingly, the Franciscan was commanded not to preach on the subject in the Valladolid area: 'so pena de obediencia e descomunion' (*Sentencia*, 283).

The existence of opposition to the Immaculate Conception in the kingdom of Aragon itself is revealed by edicts, supporting the Immaculate Conception, which were promulgated by Juan I, Martín I and Doña María de Aragón.[11] From the late

---

[8] The text of the decree is reproduced in Sebastian, 232, n.113.

[9] Archivo Histórico Nacional, Universidades y Colegios, Libro 1196. Epígrafe general: *Papeles relativos a la Purísima Concepción*. Reproduced in full by Julio Rodríguez Puértolas, *Fray Íñigo de Mendoza y sus 'Coplas de Vita Christi'* (Madrid: Gredos, 1968), Apéndice VIII, 281-282.

[10] *Sentencia de la Cancilleria de Valladolid sobre la disputa anterior*, Archivo Histórico Nacional, Universidades y Colegios, Libro 1196. Epígrafe general: *Papeles relativos a la Purísima Concepción*, reproduced by Rodríguez Puértolas, Apéndice, IX, 283-284.

[11] X. Le Bachelet, 'L'Immaculée Conception' in Jean Michel Alfred Vacant, Eugene Margenot, Emile Amann, Bernard Lott, Marc Albert Michel (eds), *Dictionnaire de théologie catholique contenant l'exposé des doctrines de la théologie catholique, leurs preuves et leur*

fourteenth century onwards, the Catalan monarchy had been particularly active in the promulgation of such decrees, which demanded loyalty to the doctrine as a prerequisite of loyalty to the state. What is more, confessors and preachers to the Kings of Aragon were now exclusively drawn from the Franciscan Order which gave them an important political advantage.[12] It was difficult for the maculist viewpoint to be heard in Aragon, since its adherents were powerfully prevented from putting their case before the Church as a whole by threat of exile and charges of high treason.[13]

Interest in the Conception doctrine, fanned by Franciscan preachers, was reflected in the literature of the period. The support of Juan I for the doctrine is recorded in Bernat Metge's *Lo Somni*, where the king appears after death to the author and attests that upholding the doctrine of the Immaculate Conception has brought certain advantages:

> No et pens, però, que per tenir aquesta opinió sien damnats los doctors dessús dits que a bona intenció la tengueren, e no és contra article de fe ne cuidaven errar. Bé emperò és ver que aquells qui la vera opinió han tenguda e creeguda fermament, a honor e reverència de la Mare del Fill de Déu són estats diversament privilegiats en paradís, e han obtenguts remissió de llurs delictes e s'alegren contínuament entre los sancts de prerrogatives singulars.[14]

Not only does the immaculist monarch continue to support the doctrine after death, when he might be expected to finally know the truth about the doctrine, but he underlines the remission for sins and the privileges which belief in the doctrine can bring. It is clear that royal support from beyond the grave for the doctrine is used to add weight to the case for the Immaculate Conception. Although he does not consider the maculist view heretical and, indeed, rather seems to pity the maculists for their views, it is noteworthy that Metge is quick to accord status to the doctrine of the Immaculate Conception, terming it 'la vera opinió'. In this way, Metge quite

---

histoire, 16 vols (Paris: Letouzey, 1899-1950), VII, 846-1218, 1088; Suzanne L. Stratton, *The Immaculate Conception in Spanish Art* (Cambridge: Cambridge University Press, 1994), 6-7.

[12] P. Alejandro Recio, O.F.M., 'La Inmaculada en la predicación franciscano-española', *Archivo Ibero-Americano*, núm extraord. 57-58 (1955), 105-200, 112; David J. Viera refers to the many gifts and foundations conferred on the Franciscan Order by the royal house of Aragon in 'Francesc Eiximenis and the Royal House of Aragon: A Mutual Dependence', *Catalan Review*, 3:2 (1989), 183-189.

[13] Recio includes the text of the main decrees promulgated in the period. For example, Juan I's decree of 2 February 1394 commands all maculist preachers 'cierren su boca y callen perpetuamente' and the penalty for failing to observe the royal command is exile: 'sean totalmente expellidos y echados, así de sus conventos e iglesias como de sus casas'.

[14] Bernat Metge, *Lo Somni*, Marta Jordà (ed.), 4th edn, Les millors obres de la literatura catalana, 41 (Barcelona: Edicions 62 i La Caixa, 1991), 73.

evidently shows which of the two approaches to the doctrine he considers to be the true opinion, as well as indicating that there is a false opinion about the Immaculate Conception in existence at the time of writing, 1398-1399.

The Conception doctrine is no less promoted in poetry amid such a climate of immaculist devotion in the kingdom of Aragon. In fifteenth-century Valencia, in particular, certàmens, or poetry competitions, modelled on the Toulouse troubadour *puys*, were held in honour of the Virgin Mary and even, on two occasions, specifically in honour of her Immaculate Conception.[15] The 1440 certamen, entitled 'Certamen en llaors de la 'Concepció de Nostra Dona', followed the pronouncement of the thirty-sixth session of the Council of Basle, in September 1439, considered a magnificent victory by the immaculists. The 1486 certamen, 'Certamen poètic en honor de la Sacratíssima Concepció', followed on the heels of the Papal Bulls, *Grave Nimis*, in 1482-1483, which were also considered a fillip for the immaculist cause. The poems submitted to these poetry competitions, published by Ferrando Francés, provide an interesting insight into the approach to defence of the doctrine of the Immaculate Conception in poetry.

It is first to be noted that the proclamation of the second immaculist certamen by Ferrando Díeç in 1486 is pugnacious; Ferrando Francés himself refers to the tone of the *Llibell* and *Introit*, written by Díeç, as 'militància immaculista' (*CP*, 379). Entrants are expressly forbidden to defend the maculist view: 'No admetent dients en lo contrari' (*Llibell* I, *CP*, 433). The Franciscans and other immaculists, just after the publication of *Grave Nimis* (1484), felt that support for the Conception doctrine had been vindicated by the Franciscan Pope, Sixtus IV, firstly by his recognition of the Conception feast, and secondly by his intimation that the doctrine might become dogma at some later stage.[16] The *Introit* to the 1486 certamen contains an allusion to the recognition of the Conception feast by the Pope:

> Ja lo Sixt papa declarar
> vol en l'offici
> tan gran misteri .n benefici
> dels crestians (*Introit, CP*, 436).

---

[15] Antoni Ferrando Francés, *Els certàmens poètics valencians del segle XIV al XIX*, Institut de literatura i estudis filològics, Institució Alfons el Magnànim (Valencia: Diputació de Valencia, 1983), 30 ff. Hereinafter referred to as *CP*.

[16] Cf. Ch. Sericoli, 'De praecipuis Sedis Apostolicae documentis de B.M.V. Immaculata Conceptione', *Antonianum*, 29 (1954), 373-408: 'constat doctrinam de Immaculata Conceptionis per xystinas constitutiones maiorem saltem probabilitatem ac securitatem obtinuisse' (380), particularly in the word 'nondum': 'cum nondum sit a romana ecclesia et apostolica sede decisum' (380).

Díeç refers not only to the benefits the celebration of the Conception office will bring, in pardons obtained for its celebration,[17] but also takes the opportunity to condemn roundly those priests who are refusing to celebrate the new office:

> Mas huy los nostres capellans
> seguir no .l volen,
> puix tals laors cantar no solen
> del ver parer (*Introit, CP*, 436).

Ferrando Francés referring to this passage, notes that it alludes to the wave of opposition to the Conception 'dogma' after the Council of Basle, when the 'fort moviment antiimmaculista que s'oposava que el papa Sixt IV confirmàs la declaració dogmàtica sobre la Immaculada aprovada al Concili de Basilea' (*CP*, 384). However, it should be remembered that the priests who refused to adopt the new office were perfectly within their rights, since the institution of the feast in *Grave Nimis* declared the Immaculate Conception to be an optional observance explicitly stating those who chose not to subscribe to the doctrine of the Immaculate Conception could not be called heretics.[18]

The aggressive exclusion, from the competition, of poets opposing the 'ver parer' explains why the 1486 certamen, dedicated expressly to the defence of the Immaculate Conception and to proselytism on its behalf, produces poetry which seeks to denigrate the maculists. Despite the wording of *Grave Nimis*, which expressly forbids those who oppose the doctrine to be called heretical, Ferrando Díeç tars opponents of the Immaculate Conception with implied heresy from the outset:

> Al descubert, giramantells,
> Qui la regiren,
> molt prop d'eretges, si bé miren
> lo que .ns ha dit
> sent Agostí, del qu.és escrit
> dient: 'Qui u glosa
> al seny que vol, ab mala glosa
> sia maleyt' (*Introit, CP*, 436).

---

[17] Sericoli cites the text of the papal decree, *Libenter* (1480) which accords indulgences for the celebration of the new Conception office: 'qua indulgebat ac concedebat ut omnes "pro devotione sua, dicere et recitare libere et licite" possent officium Conceptionis B. V. Mariae a Bernardino de Bustis, O.F.M.' (377).

[18] Sericoli notes that, whilst the Bull appeared to be even-handed, it, in fact, favours the immaculist position (379-380).

By referring to St Augustine, Díeç seems to be the recalling the stance the saint took against the Pelagian heresy and to tar the 'turncoat' maculists with the brush of heresy. He also takes the opportunity to cast aspersions on the thought processes of the maculists; the implication is that the maculists in following their human reasoning are falling short of the leap of faith required by belief in the Conception doctrine, since, after all, who can know the mind of the Almighty: '¡Qui pot saber la prescièntia \ de l'Infinit!' (*Introit, CP*, 435).

The main purpose of the immaculist poets when they refer to opposition to the Conception doctrine in the certamen poems is to establish the folly of the opinions of those who dispute the doctrine. Díeç roundly asserts that the maculists show their own ignorance in their opposition to the doctrine, since they condemn the Virgin to being stained with original sin: 'Qual ignorant és tan malvat \ que us posa .n culpa' (*Introit, CP*, 435).

Similarly, Vinyoles, in his poem submitted for the Rod of Jesse prize, affirms the Immaculate Conception, asserting that opponents of the doctrine are blind to the truth; that their reasoning is flawed and that they are unable to reason: 'Cechs són aquells que tenen lo contrari' (*CP,* 449).[19]

For the most part, certamen poets are content to hint at a group of people holding the maculist viewpoint, referring to opposition to the Immaculate Conception in generic terms, rather than indicating any specific person or persons by name. Vilaspinosa affirms that the Virgin was exempt from original sin and does not brook any opposition to the statement: 'Callen doctors lo general edicte' (*CP*, 445). The opponents are unspecified, although they are doctors of theology. The command 'callen' seems to echo the words of the edict of 1394. The important point is, however, that debate is not permitted. Vilaspinosa also uses a rhetorical question to doubt the reasoning powers of those who hold the maculist viewpoint:

> Donchs ¿qui pot dir que no fósseu vós sana
> del crim d'Adam tenint vós tals estrenes? (*CP*, 445)[20]

However, on two occasions, in the poems, it is precisely the Dominicans who, as firm opponents of the immaculist position, are singled out by name for opprobrium. The first of the poems describes the Virgin throughout in terms of a marzipan sweet,

---

[19] For the 1486 certamen, for example, the prizes include a Rod of Jesse, a navigators' map and a marzipan sweet. For details of the use of the Rod of Jesse as an immaculist symbol, see Stratton, 13 ff ; see also my unpublished doctoral thesis, 'The Immaculate Conception in Castilian and Catalan Poetry of the Fifteenth Century: A Comparative Thematic Study' (University of Hull, 1995), 144-145.

[20] For further details of the use of scholastic rhetoric in fifteenth-century poetry, see Twomey, 44-100.

'letovari', since Centelles, the poet, is seeking to win the marzipan prize (*CP*, 502). The maculists are begged by the poet to taste the new doctrine 'gustau un poquet':

> Hoiu, pricadors,   les santes doctrines,
> gustau un poquet   d'aquest letovari.
> A fe que són dolces,   sabors tenen fines,
> hoiu lo concert   de cobles divines
> de crim preservant   lo digne sacrari.
> Lexau per mercé   la fe tan errada,
> bateu-vos los pits,   digau vostra culpa (*CP*, 501-502).

The doctrine both tastes 'sabors tenes fines' and sounds sweet 'lo concert   de cobles divines'.   The association of the host and the doctine of the Immaculate Conception is hinted at, since the Virgin is the ombrey which holds the consecrated wafers.

According to the poet, the Dominicans, referred to as 'pricadors', since they are the Order of Preachers, should leave behind their misguided opinions on the Immaculate Conception: 'fe tan errada'. These opinions are treated as sinful and the Dominicans are urged to respond in a penitential manner. Like penitents, they are told: 'bateu-vos los pits,   digau vostra culpa'. In Centelles' poem, the Dominicans are not merely described as misguided but they are depicted with all the actions typical of sinners.

The Dominicans are singled out once again by name in one of the 'sentèntias' which gives a judgement on a series of poems submitted for a particular 'joya' (or prize). On presentation of the poetic prize to Roïç, Ferrando Díeç, the judge, states that the reason for the selection of Roïç's poem is that 'contra .ls malignes \ de pricadors frares   rahons diu insignes' (Sentèntia, *CP*, 507). It is noteworthy that the winning poem is selected not purely on literary merit but because of its powers of reasoning and the fact that it serves as a weapon against the Dominican school of thought.   The Dominican train of thought, once considered the orthodox response to the burgeoning doctrine of the Immaculate Conception, is termed 'maligne' by Díeç.

The debate between followers of Scotus and Aquinas is mentioned in Pere d'Anyó's poem, which was entered for the 1474 certamen in the hope of winning the prize of a navigators' map :

> Les grans escotilles   ab proves fundades
> les han sobre .ls núvols   axí sublimades,
> que resta per terra   l'inich tomatista (*CP*, 514).

By 'les escotilles', Pere d'Anyó is referring to the disciples of Scotus, associating them with the celestial opinion on the doctrine 'sobre .ls núvols' and also with the opinion which is gaining ground 'ab proves fundades'.   The term 'follower of Aquinas' exemplifies the Dominican Order, since Aquinas had long provided the theological position on the Immaculate Conception to Dominican theologians; Aquinas's opposition to the doctrine established the Dominican response for many centuries. In the poem, the term 'tomatista' is used scornfully as a term of abuse.

In addition, it should be noted that the Dominican position is associated with the earthly point of view 'resta per terra', and also with the devil's viewpoint, the devil being termed the enemy on occasion in the poems.[21]   The Dominicans, by being earth-bound, are also placed clearly on the losing side in the debate.

Johan Sent Climent, writing for the 1474 certamen, goes one step further than other poets of his generation. This poem is particularly relevant to the theme of *fervor* and *fanatismo*, since it combines references to opposition to the doctrine and anti-Moorish sentiments which form a backdrop to the poem. In the first stanza, the poet asks for protection from 'that wicked sect': 'Que .m guardeu   d'aquella mala secta \ dels peccadors,   qui són ferits de verga' (*CP*, 302). In a note on the third line of the poem, Ferrando Francés indicates that Sent Climent is referring to the Moors as 'mala secta'. In fact, 'mala secta' is made more explicit in the second stanza: 'Vós confoneu   de Mahomet la secta' (*CP*, 303). The fourth stanza combines these references with a reference to original sin:

> No us ha pogut   fer nafrar la vostr. arma
> lo vil Satan   ab la seu cruel vergua,
> d'aquell peccat   original, que .ls òrphens
> fels cristians   són guardats del sepulcre
> de l'infern brau (*CP*, 303).

The effect of juxtaposing 'Satan' and 'nafrar' is to create a resonance of the protoevangelical conflict between the woman, her seed and the serpent, in the reader's mind. This resonance is from Genesis 3,15.[22] The 'cruel vergua' of Satan echoes the 'ferits de verga' of the first stanza except that Satan's rod has now become explicitly identified with original sin. The wording of 'no us ha pogut fer nafrar la vostr. arma' echoes Genesis 3,15: 'he shall bruise her heel'. In this case, instead of bruising the heel of the Virgin, the serpent or Satan, is unable to bruise her

---

[21] Cf. Vallmanya's entry to the 1486 certamen, where he terms the devil, 'l'adversari' (*CP*, 465). The devil is most regularly termed 'Satan' (*CP*, 460; 456; 446; 526; 527), 'lo diable' (CP, 440), 'Lucifer' \ 'Lucibell' (*CP*, 455, 472; 477; 486), 'la serp' (CP, 518).

[22] Warner notes that: 'In the "woman", Christians had seen a prophecy of the Virgin Mary ever since the fourth century, and the promised victory over the serpent had been used to develop the image of the second Eve who triumphs where the first Eve failed, [...]. When the controversy over the question of the Virgin's original sin became inflamed, this victory over the devil was used to prove that Mary was from the time of the creation predestined to escape altogether the devil's power' (245).

soul. In turn, 'nafrar vostr. arma' echoes 'Simeon dix   vos travessarà l'arma' from the end of the previous stanza. In this way, the poet links the Genesis text to the sword which Simeon prophesied would pierce the Virgin's soul in Luke 2.35. The link is indirect, depending on the *encadenación* practised by the poet, but is, nevertheless, striking. The bruising is made explicit and refers directly to original sin 'ab sa cruel vergua \ d'aquel peccat   original' (*CP*, 304).

As has been the case in several of the certamen poems, the poet condemns those who doubt the victory of the Virgin. The poets care little whether the doubters are opponents of the new doctrine or the infidel Moors: 'E qui dirà "yo hu dubte" \ de paradís   no veurà may la cambra' (*CP*, 303). It would seem that the nature of the doubt, which is not explicit in the poem, is intended to be interpreted as doubt of the Christian faith. Moreover, orthodox Christian belief is intimately bound up with the doctrine of the Immaculate Conception. The poem's preoccupation with the Moors causes the poet to give an additional twist. Those who do not believe the doctrine will be equivalent to those won over by the Moors: 'Aquests seran   semblants dels qui la secta \ de Mahomet   han tengut en lo segle' (*CP*, 303). Whilst the poet's technique is less than perfect, the strength of his opinion and the poem's contribution to the defence of the Immaculate Conception make it an interesting comment on anti-maculist and anti-Moorish sentiment. It is noteworthy that in the debate in Valladolid mentioned above (24-25) the Dominicans referred to the Franciscan preacher, Martin de Alva, as a heretic and also as an infidel preacher:

> Ytem los dominicos dijeron en Valladolid como los fraires de Sant Francisco predicaban la Ley de Mahoma, por dos testigos (Rodríguez Puértolas, Apéndice VIII, 282).

The combined evidence of the two sources suggest that such insults were common. Other insults directed at Fray Martin were that he was 'majadero porro, badaxo e discipulo del Ante Christo e necio que mentia'.

Sant Climent's poem with its anti-Moorish opinions may assist in explaining an oblique reference in a later certamen poem. Miralles's entry to the Rod of Jesse prize in the 1486 certamen refers to the doctrine of the Immaculate Conception and explains how the Virgin Mary could be conceived from a sinful mother and remain sinless, using the image of how gold is mined 'en aspres lochs' (*CP*, 454). The image develops with Miralles associating the opponents of the doctrine with the search for gold:

> Hi .ls qui diran   contra ço rahons tristes,
> pobres prelats   iran com alquimistes (*CP*, 456).

Once again, the reasoning power of maculist prelates is found wanting. What is more, the image of alchemists in this context is striking. Perhaps Miralles may mean that the impecunious prelates are in search of the pure metal of the truth, but only end up with a base product, in other words with dishonouring the Virgin. However, it is possible that Miralles refers to opponents of the doctrine as alchemists in order to associate them with the Moors, who were noted alchemists and, thus, once again obliquely link maculism with the infidel.

Finally, the certamen in honour of the 'Vingt triunphes', written before the capture of Granada, shows how high feelings against the Moors were running in Valencia in the late fifteenth century. Ferrando Francés notes that the economic and military investment made in Granada by the Valencians was costly (*CP*, 362). It therefore comes as no surprise that the poem which celebrates twenty events in the life of the Virgin, including her Immaculate Conception, should end on a note of anti-Moorish sentiment:

> Máre de Déu,   qui .ls superbos deposa,
> Nostre rey sanct   haja son cor complit,
> que .l moro rey   qui .n Granada reposa
> sie expel.lit
> y Jesucrist   hi sia beneït (*CP*, 377).

Religion and political loyalty are thus linked, giving an insight into why the Dominicans are so vehemently condemned for failing to support the Immaculate Conception. Even prior to the Reformation, support for the Conception doctrine shows links with politics and national correctness.

Study of the Conception poems from the early immaculist certàmens reveals that the lively debate about the Immaculate Conception in the fifteenth century used the terms of reference of its day to condemn opponents of the doctrine. In Valencia, given the official support for the immaculist viewpoint, poets were in the vanguard of support for the doctrine. Certainly, maculist poems were not welcome at the certàmens and would not have been favourably regarded by the ruling elite. Condemnation of opponents, as has been seen, ignored the papal ruling on heresy and associated opponents with heretical splinter groups from previous controversies as well as with the centuries' old opponents of the state, the Moors. Fanatical support for the Immaculate Conception in this series of poems was unbounded. *Fervor* for the Immaculate Virgin slipped into *fanatismo* as anti-maculist sentiment fused with opposition to the enemies of the state, the Moors. The immaculist certamen poets' association of the Dominicans, who failed to support the Immaculate Conception, with the Moors and other heretics, is a way of discrediting opponents of the doctrine and underpinned the poets' advocacy of the adoption of the 'ver títol', Immaculate, for the Virgin Mary.

Bibliography

Aquinas, St Thomas, *Summa Theologiae*, Thomas Gilby (ed.), 61 vols (New York: McGraw Hill; London: Blackfriars with Eyre and Spottiswoode, 1964-1976), vol. 51, Thomas R. Heath (ed.) (London: Blackfriars, 1969)

Balic, Carlo, O.F.M., 'The Medieval Controversy over the Immaculate Conception up to the Death of Scotus' in E.D. O'Connor, C.S.C. (ed.), *The Dogma of the Immaculate Conception: Its History and Significance* (Notre Dame: University of Notre Dame Press, 1958)

Ferrando Francés, Antoni, *Els certàmens poètics valencians del segle XIV al XIX*, Institut de literatura i estudis filològics, Institució Alfons el Magnànim (Valencia: Diputació de Valencia, 1983)

Frías, Lesmes, S.J., 'Antigüedad de la fiesta de la Inmaculada Concepción en España, *Miscelánea Comillas*, 23 (1955), 31-85

Graef, Hilda Mary, *Mary: A History of Doctrine and Devotion*, 2 vols (London: Sheed and Ward, 1963-1965)

Guimaraens, Francisco de, O.F.M. Cap., 'La Doctrine des théologiens sur l'Immaculée Conception de 1250 à 1350', *Etudes franciscains*, 9 (1952, 181-205; 10 (1953) 23-53; 167-187

Jugie, P. Martin, A.A., *L'Immaculée Conception dans l'Écriture Sainte et dans la tradition orientale*, Bibliotheca Immaculatae Conceptionis, III, Textus et Disquisitiones (Rome: Academia Mariana Internationalis, 1952)

Laurentin, René, *Court traité sur la Vierge Marie* (Paris: Lethielleux, 1967)

Le Bachelet, X., 'L'Immaculée Conception' in Jean Michel Alfred Vacant, Eugene Margenot, Emile Amann, Bernard Lott, Marc Albert Michel (eds), *Dictionnaire de théologie catholique contenant l'exposé des doctrines de la théologie catholique, leurs preuves et leur histoire*, 16 vols (Paris: Letouzey, 1899-1950), VII, 846-1218

Metge, Bernat, *Lo Somni*, Marta Jordà (ed.), 4th edn, Les millors obres de la literatura catalana, 41 (Barcelona: Edicions 62 i La Caixa, 1991)

Nicolas, Marie-Joseph, O.P., 'The Meaning of the Immaculate Conception in the Perspectives of St Thomas' in E.D. O'Connor, C.S.C. (ed.), *The Dogma of the Immaculate Conception: Its History and Significance* (Notre Dame: University of Notre Dame Press, 1958), 327-345

O'Connor, E.D., C.S.C. (ed.), *The Dogma of the Immaculate Conception: Its History and Significance* (Notre Dame: University of Notre Dame Press, 1958)

Recio, P. Alejandro, O.F.M., 'La Inmaculada en la predicación franciscano-española', *Archivo Ibero-Americano*, núm extraord. 57-58 (1955), 105-200

Rodríguez Puértolas, Julio, *Fray Íñigo de Mendoza y sus 'Coplas de Vita Christi'* (Madrid: Gredos, 1968), Apéndice VIII, 281-282; Apéndice IX, 283-284

Sebastian, Wenceslaus, O.F.M., 'The Controversy over the Immaculate Conception from after Scotus to the End of the Eighteenth Century' in E.D. O'Connor, C.S.C. (ed.), *The Dogma of the Immaculate Conception: Its History and Significance* (Notre Dame: University of Notre Dame Press, 1958), 213-270

Stacpoole, Dom Alberic, O.S.B., 'The English Tradition of the Doctrine of Immaculate Conception' in Alberic Stacpoole, O.S.B. (ed.), *Mary's Place in Christian Dialogue* (Middlegreen: St Paul's Publications, 1982), 217-231

Stratton, Suzanne L., *The Immaculate Conception in Spanish Art* (Cambridge: Cambridge University Press, 1994)

Twomey, Lesley K.,'The Immaculate Conception in Castilian and Catalan Poetry of the Fifteenth Century: A Comparative Thematic Study' (unpublished doctoral thesis, University of Hull, 1995)

Viera, David J., 'Francesc Eiximenis and the Royal House of Aragon: A Mutual Dependence', *Catalan Review*, 3:2 (1989), 183-189

Warner, Marina, *Alone of All her Sex: The Myth and Cult of the Virgin Mary* (London: Weidenfeld and Nicolson, 1976)

3

Meditation and Contemplation:
Monastic Spirituality in Early Sixteenth-Century Spain

Terence O'Reilly

The history of monastic spirituality in sixteenth-century Spain has not been fully explored or described. It, therefore, raises many questions to which no firm answer can be made.[1] Some of these have to do with its role in the renewal of religious life that bore fruit in the reign of *los reyes católicos*.[2] Did this renewal involve a return to the ancient sources of monastic spirituality? And, if it did, by what means were they recovered? Others concern its influence on new forms of spirituality that developed outside the cloister after 1520: illuminism,[3] Erasmianism,[4] the teachings of Juan de Avila[5] and of Juan de Valdés,[6] and the *Exercises* of Ignatius Loyola.[7] Did these involve, in some sense, a break with monastic tradition? Or did they adapt

---

[1] By 'monastic spirituality' in this context is meant traditions of spiritual teaching and practice developed within and for religious orders living the *vita contemplativa* and committed to celibacy and enclosure. The term distinguishes such traditions from the relatively 'decloistered' spiritualities of other, more active orders, and of the laity itself. In sixteenth-century Spain, 'monastic' and 'decloistered' spiritualities flourished side by side. I am grateful to Joseph Veale, S.J., for his helpful comments on this and other points made in an earlier draft of the argument presented here.

[2] José García Oro, *La reforma de los religiosos en tiempo de los Reyes Católicos* (Valladolid: Instituto Isabel la Católica, 1969), and 'Conventualismo y observancia: La reforma de las órdenes religiosas en los siglos XV y XVI' in José Luis González Novalín (ed.), *La Iglesia en la España de los siglos XV y XVI* (Madrid: Editorial Católica, 1979), 211-349.

[3] Alistair Hamilton, *Heresy and Mysticism in Sixteenth-Century Spain: The 'Alumbrados'* (Cambridge: James Clarke, 1992).

[4] Marcel Bataillon, *Erasme et l'Espagne*, Daniel Devoto and Charles Amiel (eds), 2nd edn, 3 vols (Geneva: Droz, 1991).

[5] Baldomero Jiménez Duque, *El maestro Juan de Avila* (Madrid: Editorial Católica, 1988).

[6] A. Gordon Kinder, 'Juan de Valdés', *Bibliotheca Dissidentium*, 9 (1988), 111-195.

[7] Ignacio Iparraguirre, S.J., *Práctica de los Ejercicios de san Ignacio de Loyola en vida de su autor (1522-1556)* (Bilbao: El Mensajero del Corazón de Jesús; and Rome: Institutum Historicum Societatis Iesu, 1946).

it to new ends? Other questions again concern the place of monastic spirituality in the debate about orthodoxy that culminated during the 1550s in the arrest of Bartolomé Carranza and in the *Index of Prohibited Books*.[8] Was it central to the debate or marginal? And, once the crisis had passed, how was the monastic tradition affected by its outcome? The present paper can do no more than touch on some of these questions by focusing on one aspect of monastic spirituality, the practice of meditation as a prelude to contemplation, a practice which developed out of the ruminative reading of Scripture involved in *lectio divina*, and which was disseminated widely in the later Middle Ages, both within the cloister and outside it.[9] This will be considered in three representative texts: the manual of spiritual exercises published in 1500 by the Abbot of Montserrat, García Jiménez de Cisneros;[10] the *Alfabeto cristiano* written by Juan de Valdés,[11] probably in 1536; and the *Libro de la oración y meditación* that Luis de Granada published, incomplete, in 1554, and that he later revised and reissued at the Inquisition's behest.[12]

I

Modern studies of the reforms in Montserrat that García Jiménez de Cisneros pioneered have shown the importance he attached to meditation, and how, to this end, he introduced into the monastery methods of mental prayer that had been developed outside the Peninsula by writers associated with the *devotio moderna*.[13] His reasons may be inferred from a passage in his writings inspired by Ubertino de Casale that pinpoints a feature of contemporary religious life which caused him deep concern:

---

[8] José Ignacio Tellechea Idígoras, *El arzobispo Carranza y su tiempo*, 2 vols (Madrid: Guadarrama, 1968).

[9] Jean Leclercq, O.S.B., *Études sur le vocabulaire monastique du moyen âge* (Rome: Pontificium Institutum S. Anselmi, 1961); Simon Tugwell, O.P., *Ways of Imperfection: An Exploration of Christian Spirituality* (London: Darton, Longman and Todd, 1984), 93-124.

[10] García Jiménez de Cisneros, *Obras completas*, Cipriano Baraut (ed.), 2 vols (Montserrat: Abadía, 1965). The *Exercitatorio de la vida spiritual* is edited in both Latin and Spanish in volume II.

[11] Juan de Valdés, *Alfabeto cristiano*, Benjamin B. Wiffen (ed.), (London: Reformistas Antiguos Españoles, 1861; Facsimile reprint, Barcelona: Diego Gómez Flores, 1983).

[12] Fray Luis de Granada, *Libro de la oración y meditación*, Álvaro Huerga (ed.) (Madrid: Fundación Universitaria Española, 1994). To trace the complex history of the *Libro* it is suntil necessary to consult the edition of the text provided in *Obras de Fray Luis de Granada*, Justo Cuervo (ed.), 14 vols (Madrid: Gómez Fuentenebro, 1906), II.

[13] G.M. Colombás, *Un reformador benedictino en tiempo de los Reyes Católicos, García Jiménez de Císneros, abad de Montserrat* (Montserrat: Abadía, 1955), and his more recent article, 'García Jiménez de Cisneros' in *Dizionario degli Istituti di Perfezione*, V, 311-312; see too the lengthy introduction by Baraut in volume I of his edition of the *Obras completas*.

gran parte de los religiosos deste tiempo son no solamente sin experientia de los interiores y mentales excessos, mas aun los vocablos ignoran... de aquí es que... no curando de los lacrimosos y mentales excessos, en sola la oración vocal confían (II, 507-508).

To tackle this problem he composed two manuals, the *Exercitatorio de la vida spiritual* and the *Directorio de las horas canónicas*. The first is a *florilegium*, or collection of monastic texts, drawn from throughout the western tradition and translated into Spanish. It is not, however, just an anthology, for its contents are edited and combined with a clear purpose in view, to prepare the monk for contemplation:

En este libro, hermanos muy amados, tractaremos cómo el exercitador y varón devoto... por çiertos y determinados exerçicios, según los días de la semana, meditando, orando, contemplando, ordenadamente podrá subir a alcançar el fin desseado, que es ayuntar el ánima con Dios, lo qual es dicho de los sanctos verdadera y no conoscida sabiduría (II, 90).

The Constitutions of the house indicate how meditation was used to renew the elements of the monastic round. In the novitiate, the young monks were introduced to the *Exercitatorio* and were shown how to practise the spiritual exercises set out in its opening chapters (II, 529). Later, as professed members of the community, they were expected to become familiar with the whole work before passing on to other studies (II, 519). In choir devout recitation of the office was valued as a sign of fidelity to the rule (II, 6), but it does not seem that great importance was attached to the vocal prayer of which it was composed. Instead the monks were encouraged to meditate while they sang on the events of Christ's life, death and resurrection, following, as they did so, the instructions set out in the *Directorio* (II, 20-33). At other times of the day the monk was expected to practise private prayer and fixed periods for this were set aside, the longest being after Matins when the community stayed in or near the cloister for 30-45 minutes and practised the exercises that the *Exercitatorio* contained (II, 513-514).

In Chapter 10 of the *Exercitatorio*, Cisneros explains how its exercises are structured. The spiritual life of the monk is seen as a progression from one kind of fear to another. It begins with servile fear when one turns towards God terrified by the punishments that follow on sin, including hell. And it ends with filial fear when one adheres to God anxious never to be parted, a fear that springs not from terror but from love. In between there is initial fear, a half-way state in which terror and love are combined. Cisneros sums it up:

el temor servil... es aquel por el qual el honbre dexa de pecar por temor de la pena. El temor filial es aquel por el qual se contiene y aparta de pecar por temor de la

offensa de Dios; ca de los fijos es temer la offensa del padre. El temor inicial es dicho
aquel por el qual el honbre por lo uno y por lo otro, conviene a saber, por la offensa
de Dios y por la pena del infierno, se abstiene y aparta de pecar (II, 136).

He concludes by indicating to the monk the journey before him:

Estos temores havemos aquí declarado porque puedas conoscer en quál espeçie dellos
estás, y dexes el amor de siervo y te allegues al filial (II, 138).

The meditations that follow in three cycles are designed to encourage the monk on
his way.[14] The first cycle begins with meditations on sin, death, judgment and hell,
which inspire *temor servil*. While he makes them, the monk sees himself as a jester
petitioning his Lord and as a criminal facing his judge. But it ends on a positive
note, with meditations on the Passion and on Paradise that encourage grateful love,
the beginnings of *temor inicial*. In the second cycle, initial fear is deepened by
meditations on God's *beneficios* or gifts in which gratitude is allowed to grow. But
the monk is urged on further towards *temor filial*:

no devemos principalmente amar a Dios por sus beneficios, mas por su bondad sin
medida y por sí mismo (II, 200).

The third cycle focuses attention on the infinite perfection of God, and, as the monk
meditates, his love is expected to become less preoccupied with self. He is
encouraged to pray, like the psalmist:

Señor, puramente os amo, no por los dones de los çielos, ni tanpoco por los dones de
sobre la tierra, mas por vuestra soberana bondad y por vos mismo.

He sees himself, as he does so, as a lover and as a son (II, 238). When the third
cycle ends, the monk is reminded of the ideal towards which his prayer should tend,
a love that is not mercenary but pure:

El fin de la meditaçión, oraçión y contemplaçión, no sea por tu provecho, no por
evadir las penas o por esperança de ganançia o del premio celestial... porque este tal
sería amor merçenario. Mas medita, ora y contempla por puro y filial amor (II, 446).

---

[14] The analysis presented here is based on my more detailed study, 'The Structural Unity of
the *Exercitatorio de la vida spiritual*', *Studia Monastica*, 15 (1973), 287-324, reprinted in
*From Ignatius Loyola to John of the Cross: Spirituality and Literature in Sixteenth-Century
Spain* (London: Variorum, 1995).

He is given prayers that express a longing for union with God, and, in the fourth part of the work that follows, he goes on to consider what such union involves, and to meditate on the humanity of Christ that by it he might attain to His divinity.

The teaching on fear and love on which the *Exercitatorio* is based shows that Cisneros was concerned to renew monastic spirituality by returning to the sources from which it sprang. St Basil the Great had affirmed:

> We obey God and avoid vices from the fear of punishment and in that case we take on the resemblance of slaves. Or we keep the precepts because of the utility that we derive from the recompense, thus resembling mercenaries. Or finally, for love of Him who has given us the law we obey with joy at having been judged worthy of serving so great and good a God, and thus we imitate the affection of children towards their parents.[15]

Later the same points were made in the writings of John Cassian and in the Rule of the Master, from where they passed into the Benedictine Rule that the monks of Montserrat observed.[16] In chapter seven, St Benedict compares the monk's life to a ladder of humility that begins in fear of hell and ends in love. He writes:

> When he has climbed all these rungs of humility, a monk will immediately come to that love of God which when perfect casts out fear... By this love, without any trouble, as it were naturally, by habit, he will begin to keep everything... no longer now by fear of hell but by the love of Christ (Chapter 7, 67-69).

Later in the Middle Ages, St Benedict's teaching was developed further, most notably by Bernard of Clairvaux.[17] Cisneros may be said in short to have enabled his monks to recover the original charism of their founder, and to have done so by teaching them methods of meditation that in the Spain of his time were relatively new.

II

The reform of Montserrat coincided with the beginnings of printing in Spain, and the writings of Cisneros were part of a stream of religious literature that was deeply

---

[15] *Patrologia Graeca*, vol. 31, 895-896. See Friedrich von Hügel, *The Mystical Element of Religion as studied in Saint Catherine of Genoa and her Friends*, 2 vols, fourth impression (London: Dent and Clarke, 1961), II, 165-166.

[16] Cassian, *Institutes* 4, 39, 3; *Conferences* 11, 7, 13; 11, 6; 11, 8, 1. *Rule of the Master* 10, 92-122. See George Holzherr (ed.), *The Rule of Benedict: A Guide to Christian Living*, (Dublin: Four Courts, 1994), 111.

[17] Etienne Gilson, *The Mystical Theology of St Bernard*, trans. A.H.C. Downes (London: Sheed and Ward, 1940), 95-96.

monastic in character.[18] When, however, new forms of popular spirituality emerged during the 1520s, the leading figures in reform came to include not only members of the orders but humanists like Juan and Alfonso de Valdés, secular clerics such as Juan de Avila and Constantino Ponce de la Fuente, and even unlettered laymen such as Ignatius Loyola and Pedro Ruiz de Alcaraz. Their various spiritual teachings differed in content and in style and were sometimes mutually incompatible. They had certain features in common, however, including a desire to help people in all walks of life, especially laymen, and usually their apostolates developed, not in monasteries and convents, but in the towns, courts and universities of the Peninsula.

Their relationship with the religious orders was complex. On the one hand, there was discontinuity and sometimes tension. Alcaraz and his fellow illuminists, the *dexados*, were at loggerheads with the Franciscan *recogidos*. Avila, as a young man, entered one of the mendicant orders, but for reasons that are unknown he did not persevere, and he left before being professed.[19] The humanists, following Erasmus, were openly critical of the orders. And Loyola, though personally more sympathetic to monastic tradition than Erasmus, appears to have held similar views on the need for a renewal of religious life, and on the form it might take.[20] In this respect they may be said to have shared a sentiment expressed in the famous phrase: 'monachatus non est pietas' (Bataillon [1991], 206). On the other hand, it is clear that they were familiar with monastic spirituality and drew sustenance from it. Alcaraz was well read in monastic writings in Spanish, including, it seems, the manuals of Cisneros.[21] Loyola was converted on reading the *Vita Christi* of Ludolph the Carthusian and the *Flos sanctorum* of Jacopo di Voragine; later, at Montserrat, he appears to have encountered the methods of prayer that Cisneros had introduced.[22] At a more scholarly level, the Erasmian concern to renew and

---

[18] Melquíades Andrés, *Historia de la mística de la Edad de Oro en España y América* (Madrid: Editorial Católica, 1994), 151-157.

[19] Luis Sala Balust (ed.), *Obras completas del santo maestro Juan de Avila*, revised by Francisco Martín Hernández, 6 vols (Madrid: Editorial Católica, 1970), I, 27.

[20] Marcel Bataillon, 'D'Erasme à la Compagnie de Jésus: Protestation et intégration dans la Réforme Catholique au xvie siècle', *Archives de Sociologie des Religions*, 24 (1967), 57-81; reprinted in *Erasme et l'Espagne*, III, 279-304. On the 'decloistered' spirituality of Loyola see Joseph Veale, S.J., 'Saint Ignatius speaks about "Ignatian Prayer"', *Studies in the Spirituality of Jesuits*, 28:2 (St Louis: The Seminar on Jesuit Spirituality, 1996). `

[21] A. Gordon Kinder, '"Ydiota y sin letras": Evidence of Literacy among the *Alumbrados* of Toledo', *Journal of the Institute of Romance Studies*, 4 (1996), 37-49. During his trial Alcaraz referred to 'un libro que se llama *Directorio de la vida espiritual...* que se decía ser hecho del bienaventurado sant Benito'. The *Directorio* and the *Exercitatorio* were published in 1500 in Latin, as well as Spanish, and the Latin editions were bound together in one volume (Jiménez de Císneros, I, 45). It is possible, therefore, that Alcaraz conflated the two titles in his testimony (see Kinder's article, 48, n.44).

[22] José Ignacio Tellechea Idígoras, *Ignacio de Loyola, solo y a pie*, 2nd edn (Madrid: Ediciones Cristiandad, 1987), 93-95, 139-140; Aimé Solignac, S.J., 'Le "Compendio breve"

popularize *lectio divina* by restoring the ruminative reading of Scripture left its mark not only on the Valdés brothers but on Juan de Avila too.[23]   This familiarity, moreover, is evident in their writings where one finds many themes of monastic spirituality, but reformulated and transposed to new contexts and ends. An example is the *Alfabeto cristiano*, which was written a few years after its author arrived in Naples, there to enjoy, like Garcilaso, the favour of Don Pedro de Toledo, the Spanish viceroy.[24]

The *Alfabeto* records in dialogue form a conversation that took place one evening between Valdés and a young widow, Giulia Gonzaga.[25] They met as she was returning from a sermon by Bernardino de Ochino whose words had disturbed her deeply for reasons she could not understand. Valdés, after listening, was able to tell her why:

> teméis el infierno por interés vuestro, amáis el paraíso por interés vuestro: teméis la confusión del mundo por vuestro interés, amáis la gloria y el honor del mundo por vuestro interés. De suerte que en todas las cosas que teméis o amáis, mirado bien, os encontraréis a vos misma (24-25).

He goes on, at her request, to offer a solution: she must move away from preoccupation with herself and turn instead towards God. And to help her do so, he prescribes certain exercises similar in theme to the ones set out in the manual of Cisneros. Each day she must meditate on two subjects; first, her own weakness and limitations, which will teach her knowledge of self; and second, the goodness of God. His hope is that she will pass from the stage of fear towards love:

> quiero que caminéis por este camino como señora y no como sierva, como libre y no como esclava, con amor y no con temor (109).

Giulia is willing to comply, but confesses to a further doubt that holds her back: the teaching of Ochino that works performed without pure love have no merit in the eyes of God:

---

de l'"Exercitatorio" de Cisneros et les "Exercices spirituels"', *Archivum historicum Societatis Iesu,* 63 (1994), 141-159.

[23] Marcel Bataillon, 'Jean d'Avila retrouvé (À propos des publications récentes de D. Luis Sala Balust)', *Bulletin Hispanique,* 57 (1955), 5-44.

[24] A. Gordon Kinder, 'Juan de Valdés' in Hans J. Hillerbrand (ed.), *The Oxford Encyclopedia of the Reformation,* 4 vols (Oxford and New York; Oxford University Press, 1996), IV, 212-214.

[25] The *Alfabeto cristiano* was published in Venice in 1545 and 1546. The first modern edition of the Italian text was published in 1861 by Benjamin B. Wiffen (n.11 above). The quotations in the present article are from the Spanish version included in Wiffen's edition. In reproducing them, I have modernized the orthography.

> El predicador dice que solamente acepta Dios aquellas buenas obras que nosotros hacemos puramente movidos por el amor de Dios, sin que a ello nos mueva ni temor de infierno, ni deseo o amor de gloria.

This makes her wonder how she can be saved:

> hallo que no me movería a obrar cosa ninguna si no fuese por temor del infierno y, a veces, por amor de la gloria, mas ninguna por puro amor de Dios: porque yo sé de mí que si no hubiese infierno ni paraíso me lo pasaría bien en este mundo (165-166).

Valdés's response is to explain that God draws us to Him in stages, beginning with fear of hell and moving on to the attractions of Paradise. Eventually, we come to know that He is truly good and to love him with a passion that is disinterested:

> Con este conocimiento comenzamos a enamorarnos de Dios, y a obedecerlo y servirlo, no ya por miedo del infierno, ni por amor de la gloria, sino solamente porque hemos conocido que Él es digno de ser amado y que infinitamente nos ama.

When this stage is reached one is free:

> Entonces Dios nos da carta de libertad, y nosotros no salimos de su servicio por haber tenido la libertad, antes le estamos más sujetos y más obedientes, pero no como esclavos sino como libres, no como mercenarios sino como hijos: y en esto consiste la libertad cristiana (169).

His words reveal how familiar he was with the traditions of monastic spirituality, a familiarity confirmed by his reply when Giulia asks him what she should read. The works he recommends are all monastic in provenance: the writings of Cassian; Jerome's lives of the early hermits; and the *De imitatione Christi* of à Kempis (145). He adds that he himself had found them helpful.[26]

However, although its author's teaching on fear and love draws on the same sources as Cisneros, the *Alfabeto* differs from the Abbot's manual in two ways. First, the context is distinct. Giulia is a noblewoman involved in the activities appropriate to her class, and Valdés is not a cleric but a layman. The setting of their

---

[26] It has been argued that in Italy Valdés came to know the writings of the Benedictine Congregation of Santa Giustina of Padua, and that they left their mark on his theological works: Barry Collett, *Italian Benedictine Scholars and the Reformation: The Congregation of Santa Giustina of Padua* (Oxford: Clarendon Press, 1985), 168, n.36. His first contacts with monastic spirituality may have occurred earlier, in Spain, perhaps during his time in the household of the Marqués de Villena, where he would have known Pedro Ruiz de Alcaraz (Kinder ([1988], 111).

dialogue is urban, feminine, domestic. The contrast becomes apparent when Valdés explains the times and places for meditation. Cisneros pictures his monks meditating round the cloister in the middle of the night and strictly observing the times prescribed for private prayer (vol. II, 512-514). Valdés pictures Giulia in her home and in her bedroom meditating at whatever times suit her best:

> no quiero que toméis supersticiosamente estos ratos de tiempo que yo digo... quiero que los toméis con libertad de ánimo, en la hora que más os agradare, y en la parte de vuestra casa que más os acomodare, y cuando no os venga bien otro tiempo me contentaré con que toméis aquél cuando estáis despierta en la cama, o me contentaré con aquél cuando andáis paseando por casa, diciendo Padrenuestros [...] (109-110).

Like Cisneros, Valdés recommends the highest Christian ideals, but, unlike him, he emphasizes that these may be lived in the heart of society. When Giulia begs him to teach her how to lead a committed religious life that is private, and hidden from the gaze of others (70-71), he does so by showing her that to be perfect one does not have to abandon the world and take religious vows. His words astonish her, for she had always supposed that the state of perfection was reserved for friars and nuns, but he insists that she is mistaken. All Christians, whether clerical or lay, will be judged by the same standard:

> *Valdés*: Y digo que tengáis este mandamiento por vuestra regla principal, porque la perfección cristiana consiste en amar a Dios sobre todas las cosas, y al prójimo como a vos misma.

> *Julia*: Maravíllome de esto que dezís, porque toda mi vida he oído decir que los frailes y las monjas tienen el estado de perfección por los votos que hacen, si los guardan.

> *Valdés*: Dejadlos decir, Señora, y creedme; que tanto tendrán de perfección cristiana los frailes, y los no frailes, cuanto tuvieren de fe y amor de Dios, y ni un adarme de más (37-38).

Second, the two works have different ends. Cisneros urges his monks towards union with God in contemplation. Valdés, similarly, sets before Giulia the goal of union with Christ (xiv). The focus of his attention, however, is not this but the spiritual problems that afflict her, problems that appear to have been widespread at the time. She is anxious because she feels unable to perform properly what she sees as her part in the drama of personal salvation. Similar anxieties may be observed in the spiritual crises of her more famous contemporaries, Gasparo Contarini, Martin

Luther and Ignatius Loyola,[27] all of whom were assailed, in different ways, by what has been termed, 'the sense of the nothingness of man's efforts at sanctity that seems to have pervaded the later Middle Ages'.[28] The causes appear to lie in the popular theology of the period, and they may be connected, as Anthony Levi has shown, with the impact on religious practice of the tenets of Nominalism.[29] In Giulia's case, the anxiety she felt was, in a sense, well-founded, for it was orthodox to suppose that good works lacked merit unless informed by love. The teaching was formulated by Augustine,[30] and became part of monastic tradition. It is mentioned in the manual of Cisneros, though only in passing (II, 134). The advice, moreover, that she receives from Valdés, to journey from fear to love, is also the solution he proposes to the more general crisis of the day, with which he was familiar, not only through his own experience, but through his reading of Protestant theology.[31]

---

[27] Edward Yarnold, '*Duplex iustitia:* The Sixteenth Century and the Twentieth', in *Christian Authority: Essays in Honour of Henry Chadwick* (Oxford: Clarendon, 1988), 204-223 (especially 210-213); Terence O'Reilly, '*The Spiritual Exercises* and the Crisis of Medieval Piety', in *The Way*, Supplement 70 (Spring 1991), 101-113, reprinted in O'Reilly (1995).

[28] Charles Trinkaus, 'The Religious Thought of the Italian Humanists and the Reformers: Anticipation or Autonomy?' in Charles Trinkaus and Heiko Oberman (eds), *The Pursuit of Holiness in Late Medieval and Renaissance Religion* (Leiden: Brill, 1974), 339-366, 350.

[29] Erasmus of Rotterdam, *Praise of Folly and Letter to Martin Dorp, 1515*, trans. Betty Radice with an introduction and notes by A.H.T. Levi (Harmondsworth: Penguin, 1971), 16-21.

[30] *Patrologia Latina*, vol. 38, 857: 'Qui enim adhuc ideo bene agit, quia poenam timet, Deum non amat, nondum est inter filios'. For further references see Jiménez de Cisneros, II, 134-135, n.2.

[31] It is possible that Valdés began to read Reform writings before he left Spain. However, the precise nature and extent of his debt to Protestant theology is not yet clear. On the one hand, it has been argued that there are parallels beween his teaching in the *Alfabeto* and certain writings of Calvin (Collett, 167-168) and Luther: Massimo Firpo, *Tra alumbrados e "spirituali": Studi su Juan de Valdés e il valdesianismo nella crisi religiosa del '500 italiano* (Florence: Olschki, 1990), 63-64; and verbal parallels have been found between passages in his earlier *Diálogo de doctrina christiana* (Alcalá de Henares, 1529) and texts of Luther: Carlos Gilly, 'Juan de Valdés, traductor y adaptador de escritos de Lutero en su *Diálogo de doctrina christiana*' in Luis López Molina (ed.), *Miscelánea de estudios hispánicos: Homenaje de los hispanistas de Suiza a Ramón Sugranyes de Franch* (Montserrat: Abadía, 1982), 85-106. On the other hand, a cautionary note has been struck by Margherita Morreale, who has pointed to the difficulty of interpreting such evidence: 'Juan y Alfonso de Valdés: de la letra al espíritu' in Manuel Revuelta Sañudo and Ciriaco Morón Arroyo (eds), *El erasmismo en España* (Santander: Sociedad Menéndez Pelayo, 1986), 417-427, 426 n.18; and the differences between Valdés's teaching on justification and that of the Wittenburg Reformers have been underlined by Alister E. McGrath in his *Iustitia Dei: A History of the Christian Doctrine of Justification*, 2 vols (Cambridge: Cambridge University Press, 1986), II, 55-56.

People who seek to be justified by the good works they carry out are moved by a love that is self-interested:

> Es que cuando sirven como esclavos, y cuando sirven como mercenarios, se tienen y juzgan ser perfectos, y no buscando otra perfección se quedan siempre en aquella servidumbre, como dice san Pablo, que no teniendo noticia de la justicia con la qual Dios justifica a los que en Él creen, y queriendo justificarse por sus obras, no llegan jamás a parte de la justicia de Dios (170).

They need to grow further into a love that is pure. How can they do so? By considering the Passion of Christ:

> Amad, Señora, si queréis desterrar de vuestra alma todo el temor, porque no puede morar temor ninguno en aquella persona que con un vivo y eficaz pensamiento pone los ojos de su alma en Cristo crucificado, considerando con entera fe que Cristo satisface y paga por ella (59).

This combination of two traditions, the teaching on fear and love and devotion to Christ's Passion, may be found in monastic spirituality before Valdés, most notably in the meditations of the pseudo-Anselm.[32] In his writings, however, it was accorded a central place, and, partly through his influence, it became a distinctive feature of devotion to the *beneficio de Cristo*, a devotion celebrated even more intensely in the works of his contemporary Juan de Avila.[33]

III

Many works on the interior life influenced by the *beneficio de Cristo* were included in the *Index of Prohibited Books* issued in 1559 by the Inquisitor General, Fernando de Valdés. One of them was Luis de Granada's *Libro de la oración y meditación*. Later Granada was permitted to revise it, and when the book was reissued in 1566 it was greeted with renewed acclaim and soon became a classic of devotional writing. The reasons for its prohibition in the first place, and the alterations that Granada subsequently made, merit close examination, for they throw light on the controversy about meditation and contemplation that arose in Spain at the time.

---

[32] *Patrologia Latina*, vol. 158, 761-762, in meditation X, on the Passion of Christ: 'Nihil quaero nisi teipsum, quamvis nulla merces repromitteretur: licet infernus et paradisus non essent, tamen propter dulcem bonitatem tuam, propter teipsum adhaerere vellem tibi'. See Marcel Bataillon, 'El anónimo del soneto "No me mueve, mi Dios"...' in his *Varia lección de clásicos españoles*, trans. José Pérez Riesco (Madrid: Gredos, 1964), 419-440, 423 n.14.

[33] Massimo Firpo, 'Da Erasmo al "Beneficio di Christo"' in his *Riforma protestante ed eresie nell' Italia del Cinquecento: Un profilo storico* (Rome and Bari: Laterza, 1993), 89-100; 190-191; Melquíades Andrés, 'En torno a la "Theologia crucis" en la espiritualidad española', *Diálogo Ecuménico*, 6 (1971), 359-390.

The first edition of the *Libro* makes plain the original intention of the work. It opens with two chapters on prayer, lyrical in tone and drawn in part from St Bonaventure. In the first, mental prayer is described as the goal of all other spiritual exercises:

> A ésta se ordenan todos los buenos ejercicios, el ayuno, la lición, el coro, las vigilias y las otras penitencias y asperezas (597).

Its ultimate end is said to be the union with God which is wisdom:

> Oración es subir el ánima sobre sí y sobre todo lo criado, y juntarse con Dios... Éste es el camino de la verdadera sabiduría (593; 597).

In these two respects, Granada's view of prayer coincides with the one set out earlier by Cisneros. To them, he adds a third point not emphasized by Cisneros, but one of which Juan de Valdés would have approved: such prayer is available and desirable for all Christians, clerical, religious and lay:

> Venid a esta fuente a beber de todos los estados: los casados, los religiosos, los sacerdotes, los del mundo y fuera del mundo (596-597).

In the preface, he gives some idea of how his book is designed to prepare its readers for the goal of union. The first of its three parts, he explains, will provide material for meditation, the second, material to stir devotion, while the third, he indicates, will consist of various kinds of prayer:

> en ella se ponen diversas oraciones y meditaciones, unas para antes de confesión, otras para antes y después de la comunión, otras para calentar y ejercitar el corazón en el amor de Dios, y así otras semejantes (648).

The structure Granada intended becomes clear when one examines the meditations in Part One. Two cycles of meditation are proposed: the first, on sin and virtue, runs in the evenings of the week, the second, on the Passion of Christ, is scheduled for the mornings. He describes this arrangement as designed to inspire fear and love:

> Y porque la común materia de esta oración [mental] es la consideración de la pasión de Cristo y de otros artículos y misterios de nuestra fe, que inducen al hombre al amor y temor de Dios, por esto pareció que sería cosa conveniente poner aquí las meditaciones de estos misterios, y repartirlos por los días de la semana, para que tenga el hombre cada día nuevo manjar en que rumiar (599-600).

A detailed analysis of the meditations would be needed in order to show exactly how, as they unfold, fear and love are aroused, but it is clear, even from a general examination, that in both cycles the monastic teaching on the grades of fear left its mark.[34] The evening exercises begin by focusing on the nature of sin and its consequences, notably death, judgment and the fires of hell. In doing so, they appeal to *temor servil*. They end, however, with the rewards due to virtue and the gifts bestowed by God, particularly the life of the blessed in paradise, and in this way they encourage the growth of *temor inicial*. In the morning exercises, meanwhile, the love of God that springs from self-interest, and that corresponds to *temor inicial*, is encouraged throughout. It is expressed in thanksgiving for the redemption of humanity that Christ achieved in his Passion. From the start, however, it is combined with appeals to a more selfless, compassionate love which corresponds to *temor filial*, and which is clearly distinguished as the more excellent kind. As the cycle develops, this latter form of love gradually takes precedence over the former in the prayers proposed. In a note, Granada indicates that, in principle, the evening meditations should be practised first, for they are more suited to beginners (117). Seen in this light, the meditations of Part One may be said to take the reader away from *temor servil* and towards *temor filial*. Granada, it would seem, planned to confirm this process in Part Three. His original description of its contents reminds one of the short treatises that he published in Evora in 1554, and it may be, as Fr Huerga has suggested, that he intended to re-edit them in the *Libro*.[35] Their tone is lyrical, and they are suffused with an ardent longing for transforming union, like the prayers prescribed by Cisneros in the third part of his manual.[36]

The original design of the *Libro*, in other words, would have made it a handbook for contemplatives, like the *Exercitatorio* of Cisneros but directed to Christians in general. This plan, however, was never realized. In 1554 only the first two parts appeared in print. Granada apologized and explained that Part Three had been left out because of lack of space:

> Aquí falta, cristiano lector, la tercera parte deste libro que en el prólogo prometimos: la cual dejó de imprimirse porque el volumen con las dos primeras partes creció tanto que no parecía dar lugar para la tercera. Pero placerá a nuestro Señor que ésta con algunas otras cosas añadidas a ella salga a luz en otro pequeño volumen (Granada [1906], 433).

---

[34] The discussion that follows is based on the more detailed analysis presented in my unpublished doctoral thesis, 'The Literature of Spiritual Exercises in Spain, 1500-1559' (University of Nottingham, 1972), 347-410.

[35] Alvaro Huerga, *Fray Luis de Granada: Una vida al servicio de la Iglesia* (Madrid: Editorial Católica, 1988), 120-121.

[36] Marcel Bataillon, 'La Genèse et métamorphoses des oeuvres de Louis de Grenade' in *Annuaire du Collège de France, 48ᵉ année* (Paris: Imprimerie Nationale, 1948), 194-201, 195.

His reasons, however, were probably more complex than he implied. In 1555 he reissued the work with a third part included, but instead of the prayers he had promised he provided three sermons on mental prayer not lyrical but didactic in tone. Then, to compound confusion, he published in 1556 the *Libro llamado Guía de pecadores* with the claim that it was the third part he had promised in 1554:

> Resta... avisar al cristiano lector que aquí va la tercera parte que prometimos en la primera impresión del libro de la Oración, aunque acompañada con otras cosas.[37]

Again, however, the tone and contents differed from the prayers he had originally announced.

The unspoken reasons for Granada's hesitancy came to the surface eventually when he heard in 1559 that the *Libro* and his other works were to be included in the *Index of Prohibited Books*. He travelled to Valladolid to see and speak with Fernando de Valdés, only to find him under the spell of the conservative Melchor Cano. Officials assured him that he would be allowed to recast the *Libro* as the Inquisition wished, but their words did not relieve him of concern. As he explained in a letter to Carranza written on 25 July, the Inquisitor was critical of the *Libro* because he did not believe it was right to set before ordinary lay people the riches of contemplation:

> Y con todo esto habrá un pedazo de trabajo, por estar el arzobispo tan contrario a cosas (como él llama) de contemplación para mujeres de carpinteros, etc.[38]

When, seven years later, a reformulated *Libro* appeared in print the difference between it and the first edition was striking. In Part One, the opening chapters (one and two) were suppressed. In Part Two, a series of *avisos* were inserted, warning against the dangers of illuminism, and extolling the value of vocal prayer, self-denial, and the rites of the Church. In Part Three, the sermons added in 1556 were replaced by three *tratados*, only one of which was on prayer: the other two were on fasting and the giving of alms, described as prayer's 'companions' (648).[39] In the *tratado* on prayer itself some of the original chapter one was included, but parts of it were omitted, including the appeal to all Christians to make mental prayer their own,

---

[37] Fray Luis de Granada, *Guía de pecadores*, M. Martínez Burgos (ed.) (Madrid: Espasa-Calpe, 1929), 13.

[38] Fray Luis de Granada, *Epistolario*, Alvaro Huerga (ed.), 2nd edn (Córdoba: Monte de Piedad and Caja de Ahorros, 1991), 41-43.

[39] Alvaro Huerga, 'Fray Luis de Granada entre mística, alumbrados e inquisición' in his *Historia de los alumbrados*, 5 vols (Madrid: Fundación Universitaria Española, 1978-1994), V, 261-279 (especially 269-272).

and the statements that such prayer is the end of every spiritual exercise and that it leads one, eventually, to union with God. Instead, prayer is praised as a means to acquire virtue and strengthen it:

> el siervo de Dios tenga por fin de su vida alcanzar la perfección de las virtudes; y porque éstas no se pueden bien alcanzar sin el socorro de la oración, aprovéchese fielmente de este socorro, para que así pueda perseverar en aquel trabajo (513).

In this way, a book that had been planned originally as a manual for contemplatives became in the end a work whose tone and aim were ascetical. It went on, nonetheless, to become one of the best-sellers of the age, perhaps because it retained, amid all the changes to the text, a central concern with the themes of the *beneficio de Cristo* (Bataillon [1948], 200).

The drama surrounding the *Libro* reveals that, by the middle of the century, the traditions of monastic spirituality had become controversial, especially the monastic view that meditation should prepare the soul for contemplation. Why this should have been so is suggested by certain comments of Melchor Cano in his *censura* of the catechism of Carranza in which he mentions the *Libro* specifically and raises two objections.[40] First, Granada encouraged the laity to aspire to the perfection that contemplatives pursue:

> a frai Luis le podía la Iglesia reprehender gravemente... La una, en que pretendió hazer contemplativos e perfectos a todos, e enseñar al pueblo en castellano lo que a pocos dél conviene... (351)

To his mind the contemplative life was not compatible with the vocation of lay Christians. It required solitude, time and attention that the laity could ill afford, and if they aspired to it they would abandon the works proper to their calling. As evidence, he refers to the *dexados* who, he claims, were led by a desire for contemplation to neglect their jobs and their families, and he concludes that to encourage contemplation among the laity is dangerous to individual souls and to the Republic at large (305-306). It was his conviction, also, that one should not discourage indiscriminately the fear of hell and the desire for heaven. These were imperfect motives, he held, but they were not reprehensible: 'el temor de la pena eterna, aunque no es perfecta fructa [de la fe informe] es buena fructa, e ni mas ni menos la esperança de la gloria' (257). He was particularly opposed to any suggestion that the saving Passion of Christ had made it unnecessary for sinners to fear God's judgment. On the contrary, he affirmed, most people needed to fear hell with greater intensity, not less (265).

---

[40] Fray Bartolomé Carranza, *Documentos históricos*, J. Ignacio Tellechea Idígoras (ed.), 6 vols (Madrid: Real Academia de la Historia, 1962-1981), VI, 225-384.

Cano's second objection to the *Libro* was that Granada had misled the laity by suggesting that Christian perfection could be attained without taking the three vows of the religious life:

> Lo otro en que frai Luis justamente será reprehendido es en aver prometido camino de perfectión común e general a todos los estados sin voctos de castidad, pobreza e obediençia (351-352).

He reproached Carranza for the same fault (323-324). In his opinion, it was insufficient to recommend the interior practice of the vows in place of their solemn profession. This had been the error of Erasmus and Luther who had argued that not only religious renounce the world, and that the Apostles, for instance, had done so as ordinary lay Christians, thus implying that the religious life had not been counselled by Christ but invented by men. To him, the notion that perfection is possible for all who renounce the world in their hearts posed a threat to the religious orders, and to the spiritual health of the laity:

> E así el que sin vocto de castidad, antes con estado de matrimonio; sin vocto de obediençia, antes con libertad; sin vocto de pobreza, antes con riquezas, solamente con preparaçión de el ánimo halla camino hordinario para la perfectión christiana, es destruidor de las religiones, es engañador de el pueblo, e aun blasphema de la sabiduría de Christo (309).

His comments reveal among other things a concern to underscore the distinctive character of monastic and religious life and to do so by drawing a firm line between monastic and lay spirituality.

IV

The consequences of the events of the 1550s for monastic spirituality in Spain lie beyond the confines of this paper, but some comments may perhaps be made. The victory of Melchor Cano and of the theological opinions he voiced was in a sense a limited one, for it did not stem the flow of writings in Spanish about the experience in prayer of loving union with God. In the works of authors such as Luis de León, Diego de Estrella, Alonso de Orozco, and above all Santa Teresa, the devout layman of the late sixteenth century continued to have access to the riches of monastic spirituality. In another sense, however, Cano's victory was decisive, for the issues he had raised became central, even for his foes, and may be said to have conditioned the ways in which such writings were written and read. Was contemplation a normal fruit of the interior life of all Christians, one to which everyone could rightfully aspire? Or was it a special grace accorded only to a few, and only after many trials and tribulations? Was it compatible with the state of married people and of single but unconsecrated men and women, who owned property and who were living busy lives? Or was it linked indissolubly to the monastic conditions of virginity, asceticism, and enclosure? Was it an inevitable concomitant of union with God, an intrinsic part of the call to perfection? Or were such union and such perfection possible without it?[41]

In the period that followed the *Index* of 1559, the official line in such matters was cautious. The kind of meditation favoured for the laity was one that normally issued not in longings for union but in firm resolutions to shun evil and do good. And in monastic spirituality the distinguishing feature of the religious life tended to be found not in contemplation but in the solemn vows. In both kinds of spirituality, in fact, one notes the stress on activity that H.O. Evennet saw as characteristic of the Counter-Reformation Church.[42] But despite deep suspicion of its credentials the contemplative tradition that left its mark on Cisneros, Valdés and Granada was not suppressed, and the unresolved problems that the sixteenth century left behind continued to surface in the Church, most notably during the period that followed, in the debates about fear and love that divided Fénélon and Bérulle,[43] and in the controversies incited in Rome by the writings of Miguel de Molinos.[44]

---

[41] These issues were treated at length by the Dominican contemporary of Cano and Granada, Fray Juan de la Cruz, O.P., in his *Diálogo sobre la necesidad de la oración vocal* (Salamanca: Juan de Canova, 1555). There is a modern edition in Melchor Cano, Domingo de Soto, Juan de la Cruz, *Tratados espirituales*, Vicente Beltrán de Heredia, O.P. (ed.) (Madrid: Editorial Católica, 1962). See Ramón Hernández, O.P., 'El dominico fray Juan de la Cruz, compañero del padre Granada: Historia y espiritualidad' in Antonio García de Moral, O.P., and Urbano Alonso del Campo, O.P. (eds), *Fray Luis de Granada: Su obra y su tiempo*, 2 vols (Granada: Universidad de Granada, 1993), II, 333-353; Simon Tugwell, O.P., 'Jean de la Croix, le dominicain', *Courants dominicains de spiritualité*, 2 (1993), 57-65.

[42] H. Outram Evennett, *The Spirit of the Counter-Reformation*, John Bossy (ed.) (Cambridge: Cambridge University Press, 1968), 36-37, 41-42.

[43] Elfrieda Dubois, 'Fénélon and Quietism' in Cheslyn Jones, Geoffrey Wainwright and Edward Yarnold, S.J. (eds), *The Study of Spirituality* (London: SPCK, 1986), 408-415; Louis Dupré, 'Jansenism and Quietism' in *Christian Spirituality: Post-Reformation and Modern* (London: SCM, 1989), 138-141.

[44] J. Ignacio Tellechea, 'Molinos y el quietismo español' in Antonio Mestre Sanchis (ed.), *La Iglesia en la España de los siglos XVII y XVIII* (Madrid: Editorial Católica, 1979), 475-521; Miguel de Molinos, *Defensa de la contemplación*, Eulogio Pacho, O.C.D., (ed.) (Madrid: Fundación Universitaria Española, 1988).

Bibliography

Andrés Martín, Melquíades, 'En torno a la "Theologia crucis" en la espiritualidad española', *Diálogo Ecuménico*, 6 (1971), 359-390

----------, *Historia de la mística de la Edad de Oro en España y América* (Madrid: Editorial Católica, 1994)

Avila, Juan de, *Obras completas*, Luis Sala Balust (ed.), revised by Francisco Martín Hernández, 6 vols (Madrid: Editorial Católica, 1970)

Bataillon, Marcel, 'El anónimo del soneto "No me mueve, mi Dios"...' in his *Varia lección de clásicos españoles*, trans. José Pérez Riesco (Madrid: Gredos, 1964), 419-440

----------, *Érasme et l'Espagne*, Daniel Devoto and Charles Amiel (eds), 2nd edn, 3 vols (Geneva: Droz, 1991)

----------, 'La Genèse et métamorphoses des oeuvres de Louis de Grenade' in *Annuaire du Collège de France, 48ᵉ année* (Paris: Imprimerie Nationale, 1948), 194-201

----------, 'Jean d'Avila retrouvé (À propos des publications récentes de D. Luis Sala Balust)', *Bulletin Hispanique*, 57 (1955), 5-44

Carranza, Bartolomé, O.P., *Documentos históricos*, J. Ignacio Tellechea Idígoras (ed.), 6 vols (Madrid: Real Academia de la Historia, 1962-1981)

Collett, Barry, *Italian Benedictine Scholars and the Reformation: The Congregation of Santa Giustina of Padua* (Oxford: Clarendon Press, 1985)

Colombás, G.M., O.S.B., *Un reformador benedictino en tiempo de los Reyes Católicos, García Jiménez de Cisneros, abad de Montserrat* (Montserrat: Abadía, 1955)

----------, 'García Jiménez de Cisneros', *Dizionario degli Istituti di Perfezione*, V, 311-312

Dubois, Elfrieda, 'Fénélon and Quietism' in Cheslyn Jones, Geoffrey Wainwright and Edward Yarnold, S.J. (eds), *The Study of Spirituality* (London: SPCK, 1986), 408-415

Dupré, Louis, 'Jansenism and Quietism' in *Christian Spirituality: Post-Reformation and Modern* (London: SCM, 1989), 138-141

Erasmus of Rotterdam, *Praise of Folly and Letter to Martin Dorp, 1515*, trans. Betty Radice with an introduction and notes by A.H.T. Levi (Harmondsworth: Penguin, 1971)

Firpo, Massimo, 'Da Erasmo al "Beneficio di Christo"' in his *Riforma protestante ed eresie nell' Italia del Cinquecento: Un profilo storico* (Rome and Bari: Laterza, 1993)

----------, *Tra alumbrados e "spirituali": Studi su Juan de Valdés e il valdesianismo nella crisi religiosa del '500 italiano* (Florence: Olschki, 1990)

García Oro, José, *La reforma de los religiosos en tiempo de los Reyes Católicos* (Valladolid: Instituto Isabel la Católica, 1969)

----------, 'Conventualismo y observancia: La reforma de las órdenes religiosas en los siglos XV y XVI' in José Luis González Novalín (ed.), *La Iglesia en la España de los siglos xv y xvi* (Madrid: Editorial Católica, 1979), 211-349

Gilly, Carlos, 'Juan de Valdés, traductor y adaptador de escritos de Lutero en su *Diálogo de doctrina christiana*' in Luis López Molina (ed.), *Miscelánea de estudios hispánicos: Homenaje de los hispanistas de Suiza a Ramón Sugranyes de Franch* (Montserrat: Abadía, 1982), 85-106

Granada, Luis de, O.P., *Obras*, Justo Cuervo (ed.), 14 vols (Madrid: Gómez Fuentenebro, 1906), II

----------, *Epistolario*, Alvaro Huerga (ed.), 2nd edn (Córdoba: Monte de Piedad and Caja de Ahorros, 1991)

----------, *Libro de la oración y meditación*, Alvaro Huerga (ed.) (Madrid: Fundación Universitaria Española, 1994)

Hamilton, Alistair, *Heresy and Mysticism in Sixteenth-Century Spain: The 'Alumbrados'* (Cambridge: Clarke, 1992)

Hernández, Ramón, O.P., 'El dominico fray Juan de la Cruz, compañero del padre Granada: Historia y espiritualidad' in Antonio García de Moral, O.P., and Urbano Alonso del Campo, O.P. (eds), *Fray Luis de Granada: su obra y su tiempo*, 2 vols (Granada: Universidad de Granada, 1993), II, 333-353

Huerga, Álvaro, O.P., *Fray Luis de Granada: Una vida al servicio de la Iglesia* (Madrid: Editorial Católica, 1988)

----------, 'Fray Luis de Granada entre mística, alumbrados e inquisición' in his *Historia de los alumbrados*, 5 vols (Madrid: Fundación Universitaria Española, 1978-1994), V, 261-279

Iparraguirre, Ignacio, S.J., *Práctica de los Ejercicios de san Ignacio de Loyola en vida de su autor (1522-1556)* (Bilbao: El Mensajero del Corazón de Jesús; and Rome: Institutum Historicum Societatis Iesu, 1946)

Jiménez de Cisneros, García, O.S.B., *Obras completas*, Cipriano Baraut (ed.), 2 vols (Montserrat: Abadía, 1965)

Jiménez Duque, Baldomero, *El maestro Juan de Avila* (Madrid: Editorial Católica, 1988)

Juan de la Cruz, O.P., *Diálogo sobre la necesidad de la oración vocal* in Melchor Cano, Domingo de Soto, Juan de la Cruz, *Tratados espirituales*, Vicente Beltrán de la Heredia, O.P. (ed.) (Madrid: Editorial Católica, 1962)

Kinder, A. Gordon, 'Juan de Valdés', *Bibliotheca Dissidentium,* 9 (1988), 111-195

----------, 'Juan de Valdés' in Hans J. Hillerbrand (ed.), *The Oxford Encyclopedia of the Reformation*, 4 vols (Oxford and New York; Oxford University Press, 1996), IV, 212-214

----------, "'Ydiota y sin letras": Evidence of Literacy among the _alumbrados_ of Toledo', _Journal of the Institute of Romance Studies_, 4 (1996), 37-49

Leclercq, Jean, O.S.B., _Études sur le vocabulaire monastique du moyen âge_ (Rome: Pontificium Institutum S. Anselmi, 1961)

McGrath, Alister E., _Iustitia Dei: A History of the Christian Doctrine of Justification_, 2 vols (Cambridge: Cambridge University Press, 1986), II

Molinos, Miguel de, _Defensa de la contemplación_, Eulogio Pacho, O.C.D. (ed.) (Madrid: Fundación Universitaria Española, 1988)

Morreale, Margherita, 'Juan y Alfonso de Valdés: de la letra al espíritu' in Manuel Revuelta Sañudo and Ciriaco Morón Arroyo (eds), _El erasmismo en España_ (Santander: Sociedad Menéndez Pelayo, 1986)

O'Reilly, Terence, _From Ignatius Loyola to John of the Cross: Spirituality and Literature in Sixteenth-Century Spain_ (London: Variorum, 1995)

Outram, Evennett, H., _The Spirit of the Counter-Reformation_, John Bossy (ed.) (Cambridge: Cambridge University Press, 1968)

Solignac, Aimé, S.J., 'Le "Compendio breve" de l'"Exercitatorio" de Cisneros et les "Exercices spirituels"', _Archivum Historicum Societatis Iesu_, 63 (1994), 141-159

Tellechea Idígoras, José Ignacio, _El arzobispo Carranza y su tiempo_, 2 vols (Madrid: Guadarama, 1968)

----------, _Ignacio de Loyola, solo y a pie_, 2nd edn (Madrid: Ediciones Cristiandad, 1987)

----------, 'Molinos y el quietismo español' in Antonio Mestre Sanchis (ed.), _La Iglesia en la España de los siglos XVII y XVIII_ (Madrid: Editorial Católica, 1979), 475-521

Trinkaus, Charles, 'The Religious Thought of the Italian Humanists and the Reformers: Anticipation or Autonomy?' in Charles Trinkaus and Heiko Oberman (eds), _The Pursuit of Holiness in Late Medieval and Renaissance Religion_ (Leiden: Brill, 1974), 339-366

Tugwell, Simon, O.P., _Ways of Imperfection: An Exploration of Christian Spirituality_ (London; Darton, Longman and Todd, 1984)

----------, 'Jean de la Croix, le dominicain', _Courants dominicains de spiritualité_, 2 (1993), 57-65

Valdés, Juan de, _Alfabeto cristiano_, Benjamin B. Wiffen (ed.) (London: Reformistas Antiguos Españoles, 1861; Facsimile reprint, Barcelona: Diego Gómez Flores, 1983)

Veale, Joseph, S.J., 'Saint Ignatius speaks about "Ignatian Prayer"', _Studies in the Spirituality of Jesuits,_ 28:2 (St Louis: The Seminar on Jesuit Spirituality, 1996)

von Hügel, Friedrich, _The Mystical Element of Religion as studied in Saint Catherine of Genoa and her Friends_, 2 vols (London: Dent and Clarke, 1961)

Yarnold, Edward, '*Duplex iustitia:* The Sixteenth Century and the Twentieth' in *Christian Authority: Essays in Honour of Henry Chadwick* (Oxford: Clarendon, 1988), 204-223

Part II

The Imposition of Orthodoxy

4

Spain's Little-Known 'Noble Army of Martyrs' and the Black Legend

A. Gordon Kinder

The majority of my research effort during the last thirty years or so has been dedicated to studying the Protestants of sixteenth-century Spain. Over the period it has become quite clear to me that the Reformation did not pass Spain over - *qualitatively,* that is, although *quantitatively* no one would wish to claim that the movement achieved great numbers. The mere fact that there were definite repercussions in Spain to the Reformation movement set in motion in northern Europe may come as a revelation to certain people. Whenever it is mentioned, there is usually some expression of surprise at the very idea of Protestants in sixteenth-century Spain.

Spain, however, was the only country touched by the Reformation that had in place the machinery to seek its adherents out systematically and by various means eliminate them. It is true that the Spanish Inquisition was not set up with the Protestants in mind; indeed, its foundation went back to a time before Luther's birth. In the late 1470s, as the conquest of the last vestige of Moorish domination hove in sight, the crusader spirit reasserted itself, putting an end to the *convivencia* of the three religions that had characterized most of Spain's mediaeval period (give or take several serious anti-Jewish riots and the perpetual Christian-versus-Muslim frontier fighting). Although the Inquisition's brief was never actually to convert non-Christians to the faith, one of Spain's main problems was felt to be Jews (principally) and Muslims, who, having been baptized, often by coercion, were continuing in non-Christian practices, defined, therefore, as heresy.

The spiritual ferment that was affecting Europe in the late fifteenth and early sixteenth centuries, prompting people to desire a form of Christianity purified from abuses, corruption, and the accretions of the past, was evident in Spain as much as anywhere. In that country, as elsewhere, numbers of works were written criticizing the papacy, the clergy, and the greed and venality in the practices of the Church.[1]   When a monk called Martin Luther in distant Germany began to bring together these criticisms and to articulate them, gathering support, it was unlikely that there would be no repercussions in Spain. International trade brought the news; books know no frontiers, all the more so, when Charles I came to the throne (soon also becoming the Emperor Charles V), with dominions in Naples, Sicily, Sardinia, Flanders, Franche Comté, Austria, Bohemia, and the Tyrol, not to mention America and the Far East. Ideas moved around rapidly, as courtiers and officials moved amongst the centres of government in his various territories, and soldiers passed from one war-zone to another.

The approach of this paper is twofold: firstly, to survey some of the better known victims of anti-Protestant activity in and by Spain, who, although often ignored, are part of the noble army of martyrs and confessors of the Christian faith, since for some the suffering was that of long exile from their homeland. To these people, about whom a certain amount is known, can be added others who have come down as little more than names on lists. Flowing from this, the second intention is to show how their sufferings, often related by those who escaped, were used in their day for their own ends by Protestant nations to construct the so-called Black Legend.

Exactly when and where in Spain the Erasmianism of the early part of the century and the illuminism of the 1510s and 1520s began to turn into a definite Protestantism is difficult to determine. The illuminist movement, often known by its Spanish name of the *Alumbrados* of Toledo, has an importance well beyond its numbers and limited geographical extent.[2]   It affected an indeterminate number of people in a part of Spain that can roughly be contained in the area bounded by Toledo, Salamanca, Valladolid, Alcalá de Henares, and Madrid. Its significance is that it seems to have been the product of a wholly (or at least, largely) native Spanish inspiration. Discussion rages as to whether there was any direct influence from the Protestant Reformers, and protagonists in this debate can be allocated to various camps: those who claim a totally indigenous origin, those who point to Erasmus as the main inspiration, and those who would see the Reformers in the equation (that is, if we discount fantastic theories involving early Christian Gnosticism or Muslim Shadilíes, and so on).   The movement apparently started amongst Franciscan friars and thence

---

[1] See A. G. Kinder, 'Le Livre et les idées réformées en Espagne' in J-F. Gilmont (ed.), *La Réforme et le livre: L'Europe de l'imprimé (1517-v. 1570)* (Paris: Cerf, 1990), 301-326.

[2] For the *Alumbrados* of Toledo, see Alastair Hamilton, *Heresy and Mysticism in Sixteenth-Century Spain: The Alumbrados* (Cambridge: Clarke, 1992).   Later outbreaks of a similar kind must not be confused with this movement, although Spaniards called them also '*Alumbrados*' in their day, and continue to do so, despite there being no link between them, nor more than a superficial resemblance.

passed to lay tertiaries and others. The branch that eventually came under condemnation was one that was designated as *dexado* (meaning 'abandoned to the love of God'), the leadership of which moved on from the friars to lay people amongst the literate servants of noblemen's houses, employed as bookkeepers, dressmakers, and so on. There are already some indications of a drift towards Protestantism in the fact that, although, in general, the *Alumbrados* did not receive heavy penalties - by the standards of the day - for their deviation from perceived orthodoxy, no more than five perished at the stake in the early 1530s: Juan López de Celaín, Alonso Garzón, Diego Barreda, Juan Ramírez, and Juan del Castillo, against all of whom there were accusations of Lutheranism mingled with that of illuminism. These were arguably the first Protestant martyrs of Spain; although their principal accusation was that they were *Alumbrados*, they perished because they, alone of all the *Alumbrados*, had the taint of so-called Lutheranism in their cases. The majority of their companions, after the due processes of the Inquisition, and the consequent punishments, returned, sadder and wiser, to their former occupations, often still under the protection of their noble patrons.

Juan de Valdés seems to have come under *Alumbrado* influence in the household of the Marqués de Villena. As early as 1530 the inquisitorial examination of his *Dialogo de doctrina christiana* in Alcalá made Valdés himself and several others feel the need to flee abroad. Recent discovery of the use of works by Protestant Reformers in the work's compilation indicate that there were some grounds for their anxiety.[3] The Inquisition archives show that both Juan de Valdés and his brother Alfonso, if not actually tried *in absentia,* were at least under investigation, doubtless because of their *Alumbrado* connections, if not because of their writings. Alfonso had written two works, *Diálogo de las cosas acaescidas en Roma* and *Diálogo de Mercurio y Carón,* to justify the Emperor's part in the Sack of Rome in 1527, in which he had some hard things to say about the failures and abuses of the papacy and the Church in general. He remained outside Spain with the Emperor's court, and his death from plague in Vienna seems to have rescued him from facing the Inquisition.[4] Apart from the above-mentioned *Dialogo,* Juan de Valdés published nothing before his death in 1542, although when he died he left a

---

[3] See Carlos Gilly, 'Juan de Valdés, traductor y adaptador de escritos de Lutero en su *Diálogo de doctrina christiana'* in Luis López Molina (ed.), *Miscelánea de estudios hispánicos: Homenaje de los hispanistas de Suiza a Ramón Sugranyes de Franch* (Montserrat: Abadía, 1982), 85-106; id., 'Juan de Valdés: Übersetzer und Bearbeiter von Luthers Schriften in seinem *Diálogo de doctrina',* *Archiv für Reformationsgeschichte,* 74 (1983), 257-306.

[4] For Alfonso de Valdés, see Dorothy Donald & Elena Lázaro Corral, *Alfonso de Valdés y su época* (Cuenca: Diputación Provincial, 1983).

considerable corpus of works in manuscript. After living in Rome for a few years, he took up residence in Naples, living in a secluded manner, but with considerable spiritual influence on a large number of Italian patricians. By avoiding controversial topics, he escaped the attentions of the Inquisition. The evidence of action against the Valdés brothers comes in the form of extracts from Inquisition documents concerning them, which were supplied for use in the trials of others. If they were indeed tried in their absence from Spain, no documents of the actual cases have so far come to light, although these extracts suggest a strong likelihood of their having taken place.[5]

One of those who fled originally to Paris was the already mentioned Juan del Castillo, who was eventually picked up in 1533 in Bologna, where he was teaching Greek - the presence of the Emperor in the city at the time making his capture easier - and brought back to Spain to face trial and execution in Toledo.[6] Eight or nine years later the Emperor was to repeat this move with a merchant of Burgos named Francisco de San Román who, based in Antwerp, became Protestant during a journey to Bremen. He spoke enthusiastically of reform when he returned to Antwerp, and wrote several letters to the Emperor. In Ratisbon (Regensburg) to confront the Emperor, he was taken prisoner and accompanied the court in chains via North Africa to Valladolid, where he was tried, condemned, and burnt alive in 1542. He thus became the first unequivocally Protestant Spaniard to be martyred: that is, the first whose beliefs had been consciously accepted as an alternative system of Christianity.[7]

In Antwerp at the time of San Román there were others from Burgos, the brothers Diego and Francisco de Enzinas, who also became Protestants.[8] After studying at Louvain, their ways separated. Diego went to study in Paris, and then to Rome - not a wise move. He wrote from there to Luther on 24 December 1545, and in the end was burnt at the stake for heresy in the same city in March 1547.[9] As early as 1540, Francisco had produced in Antwerp a small booklet with extracts from the work of Luther and Calvin in Spanish translation, with his own introduction and a Spanish version of the seven

---

[5] For Juan de Valdés, see José C. Nieto, *Juan de Valdés and the Origins of the Spanish and Italian Reformation* (Geneva: Droz, 1970); extensive documentary and bibliographical information in A.G. Kinder, 'Juan de Valdés', *Bibliotheca Dissidentium*, 9 (1988), 111-195, especially 119-20 which give reference documents indicating a trial of Valdés.

[6] M. Bataillon, *Erasmo y España* (Mexico City: FCE, 1966), 183-189, 475-483, and *passim*.

[7] J. I. Tellechea Idígoras, 'Francisco de San Román: un mártir protestante burgalés (1542)', *Cuadernos de Investigación Histórica*, 8 (1984), 233-260.

[8] E. Boehmer, *Bibliotheca Wiffeniana: Spanish Reformers of Two Centuries* (hereinafter *BW*), 3 vols (London: Truebner, 1874-1902), I, 131-184.

[9] Gottfried Buschbell, *Reformation und Inquisition in Italien um die Mitte des XVI Jahrhunderts* (Paderborn, 1890), 292-293.

penitential Psalms: *Breve y compendiosa institución de la religión christiana.*[10]
After graduation, he went to study Lutheran theology in Wittenberg, staying in
the home of Melanchthon. Already an accomplished classical scholar, he was
encouraged to make a Spanish version of the New Testament direct from the
Greek, the first translation into modern Spanish of a substantial part of the
Bible. In 1543, when this was ready, he took it to Antwerp for printing. As it
happened, the Emperor was in Flanders at the time, and Francisco decided to
dedicate the work to him, going to Brussels to present a copy. Before long he
was in prison, and most of the copies of his New Testament were destroyed,
meaning that copies are very rare. During his confinement, he witnessed the
sufferings of numbers of local Protestants. It is clear that if he had stayed there,
he would have died as horribly as them, so, when he mysteriously found his
prison-doors unlocked, he took the opportunity and escaped, running post-haste
back to Wittenberg. Melanchthon asked him to write down his experiences.
The Latin version of this work remains in manuscript, but a French version
eventually appeared in 1558, printed in Strasburg: *Histoire de l'estat du Pays
Bas et de la religion d'Espagne,* usually referred to as his *Mémoires.* After
travels in Switzerland, where he had some of his works printed in Basle by
Oporinus, having been warned that there were plots to recapture him and return
him to Spain to appear before the Inquisition, he accompanied Bucer to England
with a recommendation by Melanchthon to Archbishop Cranmer. So it was that
he became one of the cohort of foreign Protestants appointed to English
Universities to strengthen the evangelical cause, becoming professor of Greek at
Cambridge in 1548. It is also reported that he took part in the discussions
leading to the compilation of the second Book of Common Prayer and the first
Ordinal of the Anglican Church. He left England in 1550 to go to Basle to have
other books printed. In Strasburg in that same year to have yet more works
printed (which, according to Gilly, included Spanish versions of Ecclesiasticus,
Job, Proverbs, and the Psalms), he fell ill.[11] His wife and children left England
to join him, but ill as he was, an outbreak of the plague brought his life to an
end during the last days of 1552.

Another classical scholar, Juan Díaz, from Cuenca, also became Protestant in
northern Europe.[12] Whilst studying theology in Paris, he was persuaded of
evangelical truth by Diego de Enzinas around 1540. In 1545 he went to Geneva

---

[10] See M. Bataillon, *El hispanismo y los problemas de la espiritualidad española (al
propósito de un libro protestante olvidado)* (Madrid: FUE, 1977).
[11] See C. Gilly, *Spanien und der Basler Buchdruck bis 1600* (Basle: Helbing &
Lichtenhahn, 1985), 510-511, who claims that all these versions were made from the Latin of
Sebastian Castellio. There is nothing in the books themselves to connect them with Enzinas,
although the subject, date, and printer give strong indications in that direction.
[12] For Juan Díaz, see *BW*, I, 187-216.

to confer with Calvin, and then took up residence in Strasburg, where he made his confession of faith before a Protestant congregation. Unfortunately, this was witnessed by another (unconvinced) Spaniard, who went and spread the news. At the end of 1545, Bucer went as the representative of Strasburg to a Colloquy in Ratisbon, and asked that Díaz should accompany him. On the opposing side there was another Spaniard, Pedro Maluenda, who was much irritated by Díaz's presence and vainly tried to persuade him to change his opinions. The news of Juan Díaz's participation in the Colloquy reached Rome, where his brother, Alfonso, was a lawyer at the papal law-court, the Rota. He set off as fast as he could with a companion and came to Ratisbon, finding that Juan had left for Neuburg-on-Danube, where he was supervising the printing of a book by Bucer, and also one by himself, *Christianae religionis summa* (Kilian, 1546). When Alfonso arrived, the unsuspecting Juan welcomed him, and they discussed the Protestant interpretation of religion. Feigning interest, Alfonso took Juan's attention, allowing his accomplice to drive an axe into Juan's skull, causing a slow, painful death. The two murderers fled, being apprehended by Catholic authorities, then transferred to the Pope's jurisdiction, and finally released without trial.[13] The indignation caused by this fratricide and the failure to bring the perpetrators to trial gave rise to numbers of Protestant pamphlets, which are at the root of the European version of the so-called Black Legend.[14]

A brief flurry of anxiety was aroused in Seville around 1550, when the cathedral canon, Juan Gil (alias Dr Egidio), was brought before the Inquisition and forced to recant his evangelical views. At that time, several people felt it would be prudent to leave Spain. Among their number were two priests teaching at the city orphanage, the Colegio de los Niños de la Doctrina, Juan Pérez de Pineda and Diego de la Cruz, a printer named Gaspar Zapata, and Luis Hernández del Castillo. Zapata later appeared in London, helping to produce the first Spanish version of the whole Bible, before negotiating his return to Spain without penalty, despite having been burnt in effigy on 26 October 1562. The other three went to Paris, where with Juan Morillo they kept open house for Protestant sympathizers. It was reported that in Paris Juan Pérez de Pineda had been making use of a copy of Francisco de Enzinas's New Testament in the

---

[13] Franz Bernhard von Bucholtz, 'Päpstliche Avokation des Processes gegen Alphonsus Diaz und Johann Prieto, 28 September 1546' in his *Geschichte der Regierung Ferdinand des Ersten* (Vienna: C. Schaumberg, 1936), IX, 388-389. See below for titles of pamphlets.

[14] Claude Senarclens, *Historia vera de morte sancti viri Joannis Diazij Hispani, quem eius frater germanus Alphonsus Diazius...nefarie interfecit...* [Basle: Oporinus], 1546, and others in German (below).

preparation of his own version. When they were denounced to the French authorities, the group dispersed.[15]

A similar case to that of Juan Díaz happened ten years after his. A priest named Juan Morillo, who had been a theologian in the entourage of the English cardinal, Reginald Pole, at the Council of Trent, disappeared from view after the first session of the Council until he resurfaced in Paris, in the early 1550s, consorting with others of Protestant persuasion. Then he went to Antwerp, where he was ordained as a Calvinist minister in a French-speaking congregation. Life in Antwerp was not easy for them, so they decided that the whole church would seek a new place to reside. Morillo was sent off into Germany to find a likely town, eventually deciding that the right conditions were afforded by Wesel on the northern Rhine. Soon the Lutheran town-council tried to interfere with their ways of worship, and they decided to seek another resting-place. Again Morillo went off to search, and was able to get permission for them to settle in Frankfurt-on-Main. Another trek was needed, and all established themselves in their new home just in time to be of assistance to the English exiles who were fleeing the persecutions of Mary Tudor's reign. Disaster struck Morillo in 1555 when he was on a journey for unspecified reasons in Nürtingen, near Stuttgart. Having successfully evaded an ambush by Spanish agents, he died mysteriously. This death was confidently attributed to poison in a letter sent in 1555 by the Italian Protestant exile, Pier Paolo Vergerio, to Bullinger in Zurich.[16]

After leaving Paris, Diego de la Cruz set himself up in business in Frankfurt-on-Main, and kept up a communications network with exiled Spaniards as he made his mercantile journeys. He was able to give shelter in his home to Casiodoro de Reina when he turned up in Frankfurt. Luis Hernández also ended up in Frankfurt, having perhaps kept company with Morillo before arriving there. Both he and Morillo were officeholders of the French-speaking Protestant Church there, and their names appear at the end of that church's prayer-book, printed in 1554. Morillo's name is significantly missing from the edition of 1555, confirming his death in that year, whether from poison or not.

Juan Pérez arrived in Geneva, where he was instrumental in the printing by Jean Crespin of a number of Protestant works in Spanish, including the New Testament (1556), the Psalms (1562), and various doctrinal tracts, copies of which were carried overland across the full length of France and Spain to Seville, by an associate, Julián Hernández. This was not the first journey

---

[15] J.I. Tellechea Idígoras, 'Españoles en Lovaina en 1551-8', *Revista Española de Teología,* 23 (1963), 21-45.

[16] See A.G. Kinder, 'A Hitherto Unknown Centre of Protestantism in Sixteenth-Century Aragon', *Cuadernos de Historia de Jerónimo Zurita,* 51-52 (1985), 131-160. Vergerio was the former bishop of Capodistria who entered the service of the Duke of Württemberg.

Hernández had made as a courier between Spanish religious exiles and their families and sympathizers inside Spain, but it was his last.   An incautious delivery of books in Seville alerted the Inquisition to the presence of Protestants in the city, and almost the last order given by Charles V was for the movement to be rooted out in an exemplary manner.   Philip II was in his northern dominions at the time, but was doubtless in agreement.   Julián Hernández was captured hiding in the Sierra, and a wholesale hue and cry was set in motion, not only in Seville, but all over Spain.   Of the many believers in Seville, some few escaped, helped by the fact that it is a port and, apparently, by someone giving warning to the monks of San Isidoro del Campo.   Several of these went on to become well known in their day in countries where they sought refuge: Casiodoro de Reina, whose life was made difficult by Spanish agents attempting to manoeuvre him into their grasp.   He eluded them more than once, often only by a narrow margin, as did Cipriano de Valera, who taught in Cambridge, and Antonio del Corro, who eventually became a teacher in Oxford.

As far as Seville goes, the University of Alcalá de Henares had an important role in the trend towards Protestantism.   Valladolid and Aragon seem to have been more influenced by individual contact with foreign influences.   By 1550 or so there was a growing body of people in Spain holding Protestant ideas, and increasingly these were consciously held as an alternative system to what was on offer in the Roman Catholic Church.   It is well enough known that Seville and Valladolid were the main centres: in the former there were representatives of a large number of people from a wide variety of classes, as well as clerics, monks, and nuns; the latter a smaller and more homogeneous group of well-connected people.   A smaller nucleus existed in Aragon, unsuspected until about ten years ago.

Before the late 1550s, individual Spanish Protestants were brought before the Inquisition in various towns and some were executed, but the majority received less extreme treatment.   When, however, the news reached Charles V in retirement in the monastery of Yuste (Philip II being out of the country) that it had been discovered that Seville contained a large number of Protestants, slowly, but thoroughly, the Inquisition moved into action.   With one person incriminating another, the connections were revealed, until prisons and other places of confinement were overflowing with the accused.   In due course over 125 leading believers were identified, and many more who had had some dealings with them.   After the due processes of the law had been gone through, from 1559 onwards Spanish Protestants appeared in *autos de fe* in various towns.   In Seville, large set-piece *autos* were held on 24 September 1559, 22 December 1560, 26 April and 28 October 1562 in the Plaza de San Francisco, before those to be punished by the secular authority were handed over: some to be burnt alive, others to be garrotted and then burnt on the *quemadero* (more or less where the main railway station used to be before the 1992 Exhibition), others went to be whipped through the streets, to serve in the galleys, and so on. All those sentenced, however light their punishment, had to wear in perpetuity the overall of shame known as the *san benito* and were forbidden to wear jewellery or clothing of expensive materials, to carry swords, or to ride on horses (only mules or asses being permitted).

The threads of investigation led in some months to Valladolid, where there was a smaller but more patrician group in existence, many connected to the court. Its principal member was the chaplain royal, Dr Agustin de Cazalla. The influence of Juan de Valdés seems to have been reintroduced into Spain by an Italian member of this group, Carlos de Seso, the *corregidor* of Toro. There was a rivalry between Valladolid and Seville as to whose Inquisition was to stage the first anti-Protestant *auto de fe*. As the capital of Castile, Valladolid won, and held its *auto* in the presence of royalty on Sunday, 20 May 1559, followed by others on 8 October 1559, and 28 October 1561. The *autos* took place in the Plaza Mayor, and the *quemadero* was in the Campo Grande, now a park near the railway station. About 55 persons were accused and punished.

The search went on. In Aragon the much smaller group was dealt with at *autos* in Zaragoza on 17 May 1560 and 20 November 1562, at which Spaniards appeared. Other *autos* had no more than the occasional Spaniard, for a number of French Protestants was found in this area. The French featured largely in later *autos* and seem in general to have been dealt with more severely than the native Aragonese.

Elsewhere, Spanish Protestants, as opposed to foreigners of various kinds, were found in ones and twos and dealt with in various ways. The search went even beyond the grave to exhume the bones of those already dead, and beyond the frontiers of Spain. Those out of reach were sentenced and burnt in effigy. Right up to 1570, one Spanish Protestant or another appeared in an *auto de fe*: in Toledo, Logroño, Barcelona, Valencia, Cuenca, apart from the three main centres mentioned, without counting the many foreigners who suffered. By that date the country seemed to have been cleared of evangelical belief by coercion, by martyrdom, by the accused fleeing abroad, or by suspects merely remaining abroad if their conversion had taken place outside Spain.

Besides the monks of San Isidro, a number of other Protestants were able to escape from Seville by sea. For would-be fugitives, the land-locked situation of Valladolid was, geographically, a less fortunate one than Seville. Only one, Juan Sánchez, managed to escape to apparent safety abroad; he was captured in Flanders as he awaited passage to England, and returned to Valladolid for trial and execution with the rest. However, the latter is the only group for which we have a detailed statement of beliefs. Even though this is merely the record of what the Inquisition scribes took down during the interrogation of its members, it is extremely useful, if only because there is still a perverse tendency amongst many Spanish scholars to claim that these manifest Protestants were something - anything - other than what they really were. As Tellechea has stated, after the publication of this document there is no room for denying that Protestantism in Spain was not the same as that further north.[17] The efficacy of the Inquisition, and the fact that for at least four centuries there was no Protestant presence in Spain, has led many to read back into the situation in the mid-sixteenth century the idea that every Spaniard offered a unanimous and sturdy refusal to the evangelical interpretation of Christianity.[18]

The group in Zaragoza and its region remained unknown until a few years ago when I was very fortunate in being able to reveal its existence after a serendipitous discovery in the Archivo Histórico Nacional. It was much less closely organized than the other two, but one of its products was the above-mentioned Juan Morillo. Youngsters from Spain were sent to him in Paris to be instructed in the evangelical faith. Another was the rector of the Estudio Mayor of Zaragoza, Miguel Monterde, who kept up correspondence with religious exiles, including Juan Pérez de Pineda. In fact, the only letters of Pérez that have survived are two found amongst Monterde's papers, of which we have notarial copies. Family members of the man we saw in Seville, Juan Gil, who originated from Olvera, in the region, were also implicated in this network of dissidents. One young man tried at the time, Jaime Sánchez, had been educated in Paris by the Morillo group, and then, apparently in all innocence, returned to Spain to live. Sentenced not to leave Zaragoza, and report daily to the Inquisition headquarters in the Aljafería castle, one day he did not appear, and seems to have got clean away with the help of sympathizers who provided the arms and horse forbidden to anyone condemned by the Inquisition, and the clothing to replace the *san benito*, which they disposed of for him.

The hunt was not confined to Spain: Spanish dominions were also subject to inquisitiorial pressure. Sicily, Naples, Sardinia, and Mexico had their *autos*. In Flanders there was assiduous activity of agents, who had some success in catching their prey, and occasional success in persuading those who were safe from capture to accept pardon in exchange for return to Spain with a lucrative position. Felipe de la Torre and Fadrique Furió Ceriol were two who took advantage of this, even though there is evidence that the former had been closely associated with Morillo, Juan Pérez, and the others in Paris, and the

---

[17] J.I. Tellechea Idígoras, 'Perfil teológico del protestantismo castellano del siglo XVI: un memorial inédito de la inquisición (1559)', *Cuadernos de Investigación Histórica*, 7 (1983), 79-111.

[18] For example, J. Contreras, 'The Impact of Protestantism in Spain 1520-1600', in S. Haliczer (ed.), *Inquisition and Society in Early Modern Europe* (London: Croom Helm, 1986), 47-63.

latter had actually been ordained as a Protestant minister. The spies based in Flanders spread their tentacles into England, France, and Germany, in their attempts to capture or entice exiles, with some success, as one document reveals.[19]

Those who managed to escape from Spain when the persecution started in earnest produced a whole body of literature, only a small part of which actually ever reached Spain, but, like the seed that fell along the wayside and was immediately lost, in this case, the vigilance of the Inquisition consigned it to the fire. After a short period in Geneva, Casiodoro de Reina, Cipriano de Valera, and several other monks from Seville got to England. Casiodoro's overriding interest was to provide a complete Bible in Spanish, on which he might possibly have been working even before leaving Spain. He managed to gather a number of Spaniards in London into a Protestant church, alongside French, Italian, and Dutch churches that already existed. It has been pointed out that the ease with which he could do this must have meant that there were already Protestant Spaniards in London, many of whom may well have come from the Spanish Low Countries. Spanish agents made his life difficult, if not impossible, for him, and he fled to Antwerp. Narrowly missing being caught there, he risked passing through Paris and on to Béarn in southern France, where at that time there was much Protestant activity. He joined there his fellow-monk, Antonio del Corro, whose route had taken him from Geneva to the same part of France. Soon all foreign Protestant pastors were expelled from office, but these two had the good fortune of being taken into the service of Renée de France, the sister of the King of France, and dowager Duchess of Ferrara, who took them to her castellany of Montargis, about 50 miles south of Paris, where she maintained a Protestant enclave, protected by her royal status. Corro was one of her domestic chaplains, soon to be joined by another Spaniard, Juan Pérez de Pineda who, having resigned his post as the pastor of a Spanish congregation in Geneva on grounds of ill-health, had responded, on recovering, to a call for pastors to go to the leaderless congregations in France. After some service in that capacity, he had been taken in by Renée as another domestic chaplain. Casiodoro left to join his wife in Frankfurt-on-Main, all the time keeping uppermost the goal of producing a Bible in Spanish. Trading in silk and books along the rivers Rhine and Main, he almost succeeded in obtaining a post as pastor in Strasburg, but his great success, in spite of his life of continual movement, was to get his Bible finally completed and published in Basle in 1569, the first complete Bible directly translated from the original tongues,

[19] R.W. Truman & A.G. Kinder, 'The Pursuit of Heretics in the Low Countries: The Activities of Alonso del Canto, 1561-1564', *Journal of Ecclesiastical History*, 30 (1979), 65-93.

rather than from the Latin Vulgate, and the Bible that has remained, with various revisions, the standard text for Protestant Spanish-speakers until this day. Casiodoro was eventually fortunate in being appointed pastor to a French-speaking Lutheran congregation in Antwerp in 1579, but the arrival of Spanish troops and the ultimatum to Protestants to leave the city within four years forced another move. This he made by taking his congregation with him to Frankfurt and re-establishing the church there. He died in 1594 as its pastor, and his son succeeded him in the post.

Meantime Cipriano de Valera had moved on to England, where he was first for eight years a fellow and teacher of theology at Magdalen College, Cambridge. After a move to London, where his occupation is not known with any degree of certainty, he came into prominence in the year of the Armada, 1588 when, at the instigation of important politically-minded Englishmen, he began to produce a number of theological and polemical works to be used in the ideological side of the war with Spain.[20] Well past the age of sixty, he travelled to Amsterdam in 1602 to have printed his revision of the Bible that his companion, Reina, had produced. This was financed by a German prince, and the major revision was to rearrange the order of the books, gathering the Apocrypha together between the Old and New Testaments, rather than having the books scattered amongst those of the Old Testament, together with the change of the name *Iehova* for God to *Señor*.[21]

Antonio del Corro had been on the move too. From Montargis he had decided to offer himself as a French-speaking Calvinist pastor in Antwerp. The congregation there had sent the call to Juan Pérez de Pineda, who was too ill to accept. Nevertheless he had busied himself preparing in Paris reprints of various works of his own, including the New Testament. His illness worsened, and Corro arrived in 1566, just in time to be with him on his deathbed. All the books being printed were confiscated by the French authorities and destroyed; not a single copy of any of them seems to have survived. On went Corro to Antwerp, where he found that, being a Spaniard, he was not allowed to function as a pastor there. Within a year he had left, but not without publishing two books in French in 1567, one of which, addressed to King Philip II, gives the detailed story of his conversion to Protestantism, and makes an impassioned plea for understanding and tolerance of the Protestant point of view.[22] His final

---

[20] A.G. Kinder, 'Religious Literature as an Offensive Weapon: Cipriano de Valera's Part in England's War with Spain', *Sixteenth Century Journal*, 19 (1988), 223-235.

[21] A.G. Kinder, 'Cipriano de Valera (?1530-?1602)', *Bulletin of Hispanic Studies*, 46 (1969), 109-119.

[22] *Lettre envoyée a la majesté du roy des Espaignes, &c. Nostre Sire. Par laquelle un sien tres-humble subject lui rend raison de son departement du Royaume d'Espaigne, & presente à sa Ma. la confession des principaux poinctz de nostre religion chretienne: luy monstrant*

refuge was England: first in London, where he made a fruitless attempt to gather together the Spanish Church, left leaderless when Casiodoro de Reina had fled in 1563, and then he threw in his lot first with the Italian Church, and, when the foreign Protestants found fault with him, with the Church of England as a theology lecturer at the Inns of Court, and then at Christ Church, Oxford, with lectureships at various other colleges, and prebends at St Paul's Cathedral and Lichfield Cathedral.[23]

The title of this conference is *Fervor y Fanatismo*: in the light of what has gone before, it is a question, therefore, as to whether those Spaniards who became Protestants were fervent or fanatical. Only one or the other epithet can be used to denote so strong an adherence to beliefs as to lead some to go to their deaths rather than recant, and others to endure exile from their homeland. The decision as to which designation to use depends on one's point of view. My interest in this subject doubtless reveals my own judgement. But what of the institution that was in the main responsible for the suppression of this movement? The Spanish Inquisition was originally designed on behalf of the Catholic Monarchs to keep converted Jews and Muslims within the Christian fold, whatever the reason for their baptism - and one must always bear in mind that there were many (Jews especially) whose baptism was the result of coercion, and not accepted as a result of a free-will decision. It is not surprising, therefore, that there were many Jews who were liable to attract the attention of the Inquisition; since they had been unwillingly baptized under duress, such so-called conversion, naturally, did little to the inner convictions of the forced converts, and they continued to practise covertly what they could of their former religion, thus bringing them to the notice of the Inquisition. Both Jews and Muslims had a tenet that to avoid death they could pretend to convert, so long as they were true to their religion in their hearts, and carried out what they could of it in secret. The strict Catholic interpretation says that baptism carried out by coercion is not valid: the official view of the Spanish Inquisition, formulated for reasons of state, contrary to standard Catholic teaching, was that once baptism has been accepted, even under violence or the threat of it, a person was obliged to be and remain a Christian, rather like the present-day Muslim rule which does not allow the possibility of leaving that religion. Thus all baptisms were considered to be legally indelible and therefore enforceable. So, already, before the arrival on the scene of heterodoxy or heresy amongst so-called Old Christians, the question is writ large over the sufferings of *conversos* and *moriscos*: who were the fanatics, who were the fervent? There is no doubt

---

les grieves persecutions, qu'endurent ses subjects des Pais bas pour maintenir ladite religion, & le moyen duquel sa Ma. pourroit user pour y remedier [...].

[23] For Antonio del Corro, see A. G. Kinder, 'Antonio del Corro', *Bibliotheca Dissidentium*, 6 (1986), 121-176.

that the Spanish Inquisition was set up for political reasons, that is, the desire to eliminate elements from Spanish society that were seen to be threats to its coherence. The tragedy was that the Inquisition, although set up for political reasons, was operated as a religious tribunal by religious personnel apparently convinced of its rightness and usefulness. The Inquisition was there to supervise converts to make sure they remained within the flock and did not deviate. It had no brief to convert those who were not Christians, only to keep Christians on the straight and narrow, and had the duty of rooting out heresy, seen at first as Judaic or Islamic beliefs and practices persisting in the converted. After the decrees of 1492 and later, which presented the choice of conversion or expulsion, all former Jews and Muslims remaining in Spain were, by definition, Christians anyway, and all evidence of continuing Jewish or Muslim practice was ground for prosecution. Although lengthy imprisonment before trial and the use of torture to extract information and confession were standard practice in all tribunals, and despite the fact that within the limits of its rules the Inquisition operated in strict fairness, the idea of clerics sitting in judgement and deciding on punishments, of their keeping people in secret prisons without revealing what the charges against them were, or who the accusers were, and operating the public humiliation of the *auto de fe*, where the guilty were paraded through the streets dressed conspicuously, exhibited on stands as miscreants and sentenced in that situation, and then handed over to the secular authorities for their punishments to be carried out, is very distasteful. Add to that the fact that the secular authorities were solemnly asked to deal with the victims with Christian love in the full knowledge that some were to be burnt alive at the stake, others garrotted and then burnt, some to be sent to row in the galleys, where few survived for long, some to be whipped through the streets, and so on. Even the burning was a hypocritical process in itself, for burning was conceived as a way of not shedding blood, something forbidden in Scripture. It took place outside the town for practical reasons of fire safety, as well as for symbolic reasons that it happened outside society as befitted an outcast and blasphemer.[24] (As an aside, it is pointed out that both Protestant and Catholic nations further north, having decided that Anabaptists were worthy of punishment, decided that drowning was appropriate, partly because blood was not shed, but also in parody of their rebaptizing Christians who had already been baptized in infancy.) What had, in the end, been put into place by the setting up of the Inquisition was capable of being adapted to offenders other than those originally envisaged, so taking in all those who criticized or wished to change the Catholic Church. So it was that, when the views of the Reformation came on the horizon, there was no difficulty in widening the scope

---

[24] Lev. 24: 14.

of the Inquisition to include not just converts, but any Christian who was deviating from what was seen as orthodoxy.

Some few Spaniards were at first courageous enough to speak out against the Inquisition, but the clerics who operated it seemed to be oblivious to or unconcerned by the huge contradiction between the practice of the institution and the Gospel of the Prince of Peace, who preached love and tolerance. Christ may have been angry against those who offended (he had hard things to say about certain Pharisees of his day, and he overturned the money-changers' tables) but he restrained those who wished to carry out physical punishment on the adulteress by pointing to their own sin.

The Protestant nations of northern Europe were quite aware of who in their view was the fanatic, and they set about deliberately creating an attitude to the Inquisition, and ultimately to all Spaniards, which is usually referred to as the Black Legend. This term is of surprisingly recent vintage, seeing that it describes an attitude that had been a feature of northern European thinking ever since the second half of the sixteenth century, moving early into North-American ideas. The invention of the term 'Black Legend' is generally accredited to Julián Juderías, in an essay first published in 1913, in protest against the antipathy of northern Europe and North America towards Spain.[25] The expression quickly caught on as a convenient way of describing the amalgam of ideas which make it up. In common with all legends, it is erected on a foundation of facts, which in this case were quite deliberately publicized by the Dutch as part of their efforts to wrest their independence from Spain, and taken up by the English, because it was understood that, when the question of Holland was settled, Spain would then direct its attacks towards England. Hence the blackest facts about Spain, and notably the Inquisition, were presented as scare-tactics to alert people of the fate that might await them if Spain were to emerge victorious, denigrating the character of Spaniards and their rulers so thoroughly that Spain became synonymous with all forms of repression, brutality, religious and political intolerance, and intellectual and artistic backwardness. An American version of the Black Legend includes the

---

[25] He wrote a prize-winning essay in 1913 for the magazine *La Ilustración Española y Americana,* which was published in that periodical in the following year (8, 15, 22, and 30 January, and 8 February), and in augmented form as a book *La Leyenda negra y la verdad histórica* (Madrid: Tip. de la Rev. de Arch., Bib., y Museos, 1914); 2nd edn (Barcelona: Araluce, 1917). See also W. S. Maltby, *The Black Legend in England: The Development of Anti-Spanish Sentiment, 1558-1660* (Durham, NC: Duke University, 1971); E.S. Arnoldsson, *La Leyenda Negra: Estudios sobre sus orígenes,* Göteborgs Universitets Årsskrift, 67:3 (Gothenburg: Elanders boktr. aktiebolog; distr. Almqvist & Wiksell, 1960); H. Kamen & J. Pérez, *La imagen internacional de la España de Felipe II: 'Leyenda negra' o conflicto de intereses* (Valladolid: University of Valladolid, 1980); A.G. Dickens et al., *The Reformation in Historical Thought* (Cambridge: MA, 1985), 130-154.

writings of Bartolomé de las Casas which tell of the shameful treatment of the native Americans by the conquistadors, happily ignoring the equally disgraceful activities of northern European nations against native populations. This attitude to things Spanish took a long time to die if, indeed, it ever did. It may well still be lurking in many minds.

As far as the European version of the Black Legend goes, in the strategy of its creation the information supplied by native Spanish Protestants was particularly useful as ammunition for the northern Low Countries and England in the ideological struggle, since these countries saw themselves as bastions of evangelical truth in much the same way as Spain assumed the role of champion of Roman Catholicism. The Spanish refugees' revelations about the way in which their homeland treated its own Protestant subjects provided much of the hard core of fact on which the Legend was constructed. To augment the picture, there were disclosures by non-Spanish authors on the cruel treatment of foreign Protestants by the Spanish Inquisition: of those written in English, William Lithgow's harrowing account of his own sufferings in Spain and Robert Tomson's less painful encounter with the Mexican Inquisition spring to mind.[26] However, it owes a great deal of its origin to one or two things written by or about Spanish Protestants.

The pamphlets that were written in Latin and German to publish the news of the murder of Juan Díaz raised hair on the necks of many in the north of Europe. In addition to Senarclens's work, already referred to, Melanchthon wrote an account of the murder in German in a tract which appeared in three different editions in 1546.[27] Another similar but anonymous tract was printed in Erfurt in the same year, and the matter was mentioned widely in other publications and letters.[28] The report was taken up by Johann Philippson Sleidanus in Book 17 of his *De statu religionis et reipublicae, Carolo quinto Caesare, commentarii* (Strasburg, 1555), which went through numerous

[26] *The Rare Adventures and Painful Peregrinations of William Lithgow* (1632); Robert Tomson, *The Voyage of Robert Tomson, Marchant, into Nova Hispania in the yeere 1555*, published by Hakluyt in 1599, and more recently by C. G. R. Conway, *An Englishman and the Mexican Inquisition* (Mexico City, 1927).

[27] *Ware Historia, Wie newlich zu Newburg an der Tonaw ein Spanier, genant Alphonsus Diasius, oder Decius, seinen leiblichen bruder Johannem, allein ausz hasz wider die einige, ewige Christliche lehr, wie Cain den Abel, grausamlich ermördet habe* (n.p.: n.pub., 1546). The others have similar titles.

[28] *Ein erbermlich geschicht, wie ein Spaniölischer, und Rhömischer Doctor, umb des Evangelions willen, einen leiblichen bruder ermordt hat. Mit einer vorrede Doctor Johan Langen zu Erfurt Ecclesiasten* (Erfurt: Merten von Dolgen, 1546). For quotations from other sources, *BW*, I, 201-202.

editions,[29] and was translated into German twice in 1557 and again in 1567 (reprint 1581);[30] into French also in 1557 and once more in 1767; into English in 1560 and again in 1689;[31] in addition Dutch and Italian versions are mentioned, but these have not been identified. The account was included by Jean Crespin in the French and Latin editions of his Geneva Martyrology of 1556,[32] of which eight reprints were made between 1560 and 1619, and a German version by Christoph Rab appeared in Herborn in 1590.[33] The latter was several times reprinted: Herborn (1595 and 1608); separately in Basle and Siegen (1597); Hanover [c. 1600]; Hanau (1606 and 1617). in both Bremen and Schmalkalden (1682); and even translated into Rhaeto-Romansch (1718), and back into Latin (Basle, 1597).[34] Leonhardt Meyer repeated the story of Díaz in his *Geschichten der Märtyrern* (Schaffhausen: J. K. Sutern, 1614), as did Heinrich Pantaleon in *Martyrum historia [...] pars secunda* (Basle: N. Brylinger, 1563), and an anonymous Dutch *Historie der vromer martelaren* (Dordrecht: Hendrik van Esch, 1643).[35] Vitus Ludwig von Senckendorff gives it in his *Commentarius de Lutheranismo* (Frankfurt/ Leipzig, 1692) and (Leipzig, 1694), which came out in German (Leipzig, 1714), Dutch (Delft, 1730), and French (Basle, 1785) versions; as did Christian August Salig in *Vollständige Historie der Augspurgischen Confession (Halle:* Renger, 1733).   Rather surprisingly, John Foxe passes Díaz over unmentioned in his *Book of Martyrs,* although he does retell the story of the deaths of Jaime Enzinas and Francisco de San Román from Dryander's *Mémoires,*[36] referring the reader to the latter

---

[29] Geneva: P. J. Polanus & Antoine Rebulus, 1557; Strasburg, 1558; Geneva: C. Badius, 1559 and T. Courteau, 1559; Frankfurt: Petrus Fabricius, 1568; Strasburg, 1572; Geneva: Jacques Stoer, 1580; Frankfurt, 1610 and 1785.

[30] *Chronica* (Pforzheim: G. Raben, 1557); *Warhafftige Beschreibung* (n. p., 1557); a new version of *Warhafftige Beschreibung* (Frankfurt, 1567; 2nd edn, 1581).

[31] *A Famouse Chronicle of oure Time* [...] (London: John Day, 1560); *The General History of the Reformation of the Church* (London, 1689).

[32] *Recueil de plusieurs personnes, qui ont constamment enduré la mort pour le nom du Seigneur* (Geneva: Crespin, 1555), 275-323; *Acta martyrum* (Geneva: Crespin, 1556), 268-316.

[33] *Märtyrbuch: Darinnen merckliche denckwürdige Reden und Thaten viler heiliger Märtyrer beschriben werden* [...] (Herborn: C. Corvinus, 1590).

[34] *Martyrologium magnum, oder il Cudesch grand dels martyrs,* trans. Conradino Riolano (Strada: Janet), which, according to the BL Catalogue, was translated from the German version of Paulus Crocius.

[35] On 89b-93b. This work contains in addition: the execution of Jaime Enzinas in Rome (93b); of Francisco de San Román (80a-80b, wrongly said to have happened in Ratisbon); Jan Aventrot (454b-455b); the Valladolid martyrs (260a-262b); and the martyrs of Seville (289a-293a).

for fuller information.[37] Portraits of Juan Díaz, with brief information regarding his death are to be found in Beza's *Icones* and its French version *Vrays pourtraits* (both Geneva: Jean de Laon, 1580); in Jacob Verheiden's *Praestantium aliquot theologorum, qui Rom. Antichristum praecipue oppugnarunt, effigies* (The Hague: B. C. Nieulandius, 1602), second edition 1725; and in Sebastian Furck's *VI pars bibliothecae chalcographicae: id est continuatio prima, iconum virorum [...] illustrium [...]* (Frankfurt: Johann Ammonius, c. 1650).

The work which had most influence, however, was the *Sanctae Inquisitionis Hispanicae Artes aliquot detectae, ac palam traductae [...]*, by the pseudonymous author Reginaldus Gonsalvius Montanus.[38] The identity of this man remains a mystery, despite several categorical claims to have got behind the mask.[39] Whoever the writer was, there is no doubt that he was a Protestant Spaniard, and the fact that the work was published in Latin made it accessible to educated people of the day, making it an immediate success in Protestant lands. A second edition was prepared by Joachim Beringer (Ursinus), and printed by Johannes Schönfeld at Amberg in 1611, with the intention, stated on the title-page, of combating the proposals of the Jesuits to introduce an Inquisition of the Spanish type into Germany and Bohemia.[40] An abridged version had appeared eight years earlier, printed in Heidelberg by Vögel, and perhaps

---

[36] See below. Dryander's account of San Román was for long the only substantial contemporary source of evidence for this man's sufferings, but recently more has come to light, and has been published by J. I. Tellechea Idígoras (note 7 above).

[37] Foxe's use of Spanish Protestant sources is discussed at length in A. G. Kinder, 'Spanish Protestants and Foxe's Book: Sources' at present with *The John Foxe Society Journal*.

[38] *Sanctae Inquisitionis Hispanicae Artes aliquot detectae, ac palam traductae. Exempla aliquot, praeterea quae suo quaeque loco in ipso opere sparsa sunt, seorsum reposita, in quibus easdem Inquisitorias artes veluti in tabulis quibusdam in ipso porro exercitio intueri licet. Addidimus appendicis vice peorum quorumdam martyrum Christi elogia, qui cum mortis supplicium ob fidei confessionem christiana constantia tulerint, Inquisitores eos suis artibus perfidiae ac defectionis infamarint* (Heidelberg: Michael Schirat, 1567) (hereinafter *Artes*).

[39] B. A. Vermaseren, 'Who was Reginaldus Gonsalvius Montanus?', trans. A. G. Kinder, *Bibliothèque d'Humanisme et Renaissance*, 47 (1985), 47-77, enters a claim for Antonio del Corro, whilst C. Gilly, *Spanien und der Basler Buchdruck bis 1600* (Basle: Helbing & Lichtenhahn, 1985), 373-385, plumps for Casiodoro de Reina.

[40] *Hispanicae Inquisitionis ex carnificinae secretiora. Ubi, praeter illius originem; processus tyrannicus, in Fidelium religionis reformatae confessorum, Comprehensione [...] Per Joachimum Ursinum, Anti-Jesuitam, de Jesuitis, qui inquisitionem Hispanicam in Germaniam & Bohemiam vicinam introducere moliuntur, praefantem.*

prepared by Simon Stenius, a professor in the same city. Translations into various vernaculars followed much closer on the heels of the original.[41]

The English version of the *Artes* came out in 1568, translated by Vincent Skinner and printed in London by John Day. The following year a second edition with corrections was issued, perhaps indicating good sales during the previous year. Two other editions appeared in 1625, one printed by Benjamin Fisher and the other for J. Bellamy. In 1714, the biographical parts of this work were published by Michael Geddes in his *Spanish Protestant Martyrology*.

A French translation, too, appeared in 1568, without imprint, but probably produced in Geneva. A Dutch rendering of this was made by Joris de Raedt, elder of the Flemish Church of Frankfurt. It is dated 1569, but gives no place or printer.

In the same year, two other Dutch versions appeared, both translated from the Latin: one was produced in London by Maulumpert Taphaea and printed by John Day; the other has no indication of printer or place, but was evidently made by Jacobus van Wesembeke, a former pensionary of Antwerp. A second edition of the latter was published by a man of Spanish descent living in Flanders, Joan B. Aventrot, and printed in The Hague by Aert Meuris in 1620 and again in 1621 with a differing title-page.[42] Once more, one supposes that printings in successive years means that the original printing was quickly sold out.

Two German versions of the *Artes* were published in 1569: one was translated by an unnamed theologian, who may be indicated by the initials E.F.G., and was printed by Johan Mayer in Heidelberg with two variant title-pages; the other also occurs with two variant title-pages, and was apparently translated by Wolfgang Kaufmann and Benedict Taurer, and printed in Eisleben by Andreas Patri. A second edition of the Heidelberg German version was published at Amberg in 1611 by Johan Schönfeld. Michael Geddes's martyrology was taken up in Latin translation into J. L. von Mosheim's *Ecclesiastical History* of 1733.[43]

---

[41] F. L. Hoffmann , 'Zur Bibliographie des Buchs Sanctae Inquisitionis Hispanicae Artes', *Serapeum,* 27 (1866), 161-170; *B W,* II, 13-142.

[42] Aventrot also published *Epístola a los Peruleros* (Amsterdam: Jores van Heughel, 1627) and a Spanish version of the Heidelberg Catechism (Amsterdam: Jores van Heughel, 1628). He died at the stake as a result of the Inquisition *auto de fe* at Toledo in 1632.

[43] *Dissertationum ad Historiam Ecclesiasticam pertinentium volumen accedit Mich. Geddesii Martyrologium Protestantium Hispanorum Latine versum ex Anglico* (Altona).

In 1570, a large part of the *Artes* was even published in Hungarian by the Protestant printer Gáspár Heltai of Kolozsvár, especially the sections referring to the individual sufferings of named Spanish Protestants.[44]

Sections from the *Artes* were extracted for inclusion in several often-reprinted Protestant martyrologies: Jean Crespin's *Histoire des vrays tesmoins de la vérité de l'Évangile* (Geneva, 1570); the anonymous *Märtyrbuch* (Herborn, 1590); and the augmented version of Adriaan Haemstede's *De geschiedenis der martelaeren* (Amsterdam, 1671). Thus widely and repeatedly disseminated in whole or in part, the *Artes* was a major contributory element to the rise of the Black Legend and its persistence.

Cipriano de Valera published in London in 1588 a violently anti-catholic and anti-papal tract, *Dos tratados: el primero es del papa [...] el segundo es de la missa [...]* (Arnold Hatfield). Since this was in Spanish, it seems to be no accident that it was published in the year of the Invincible Armada; very likely it was intended as a piece of propaganda in the war between England and Spain. A greatly augmented version followed in 1599.[45] The Spanish original is unlikely to have had an extensive circulation - and there is no guarantee that even one copy entered Spain, beyond an Inquisition 'file-copy', but a wider dissemination was achieved by its translation twice into English: by John Golbourne in 1600, and by J. Savage in 1704.[46] Although composed in a popular style, with a reliance on heavy puns, it bears evidence of erudition based on wide reading in the pagan classics, the Fathers, and mediaeval, Catholic, and Protestant theologians and historians. Amongst the anti-Roman polemic there is a considerable amount about the treatment of the Protestants in Seville.

---

[44] *Háló: mellyel á meg testessült ördeg, á Papa Antichristus Hispaniaba az együgü iambor Keresz tyéneket az Evangeliomnac követöit [...]*. Full text in Zoltán Trócsányi (ed.), 'Heltai Gáspár: Háló', *Régi Magyar Könyvtár*, 36 (1915), 1-192. See also László Szörényi, 'La traduzione anti-trinitaria fatta di Gáspár Heltai del manifesto contro l'Inquisizione di Reginaldo Gonsalvio', in R. Dán & A. Pirnát (eds), *Antitrinitarianism in the Second Half of the 16th Century* (Budapest: Akadémiai Kiadó, 1982), 243-251.

[45] *Dos tratados: el primero es del papa y de su autoridad colegido de su vida y dotrina, y de lo que los dotores y consilios antiguos y la misma sagrada Escritura enseñan. El segundo es de la missa recopilado de los doctores y concilios y de la sagrada Escritura* ([London]: Arnold Hatfield, 1588); *Dos tratados: el primero es del papa y de su autoridad colegido de su vida y dotrina, el segundo es de la missa: el uno y el otro recopilado de lo que los doctores y consilios antiguos, y la sagrada Escritura enseñan [...]* ([London]: Richard Field, 1599).

[46] *Two treatises: the first, of the lives of the Popes, and their doctrine. The second, of the Masse: the one and the other collected of that which the doctors, and ancient councels and the sacred Scripture do teach [...]* (London: John Harrison, 1600); and *A full view of popery in a satirical account of the lives of the Popes, &c, from the pretended succession of St Peter, to the present Pope Clement XI [...] To this is added a confutation of the Mass, and a vindication of reformed devotion [...]* (London: for Bernard Lintott, 1704).

Certainly, as a former monk in San Isidro, quite near the city, Valera was a man with undoubted authority to speak about the situation in Seville, but his treatment of the parallel circumstances in Valladolid is no less damning. He also accuses the Roman Catholic priesthood of abusing the confessional for personal and political ends, a commonplace element of the Black Legend.[47]

In spite of the sympathies and interests already made clear in this paper, and without any wish to perpetuate the Black Legend into the present day, it can nevertheless be said that it is not long since, well within living memory, that we saw in the driving-seat in Spain an attitude not dissimilar to that which brought about the Inquisition. There were not a few Protestant victims of Franco's fanatical Roman Catholicism: several pastors were murdered, churches had their books and furniture destroyed and their land confiscated; the number of Protestants in Spain before Franco was reduced to about ten per cent of that number by the time he went to his eternal reward. He is just one recent illustration, of many possible ones from various countries, of how easily religious or political fervour can become fanaticism, which only eternal vigilance can prevent.

Bibliography

Arnoldsson, Erik Sverker, *La Leyenda Negra: Estudios sobre sus orígenes,* Göteborgs Universitets Årsskrift, 67:3 (Gothenburg: Elanders boktr. aktiebolog; distr. Almqvist and Wiksell, 1960)

Bataillon, Marcel, *Erasmo y España* (Mexico City: Fondo de Cultura Económica, 1966)

----------, *El hispanismo y los problemas de la espiritualidad española (al propósito de un libro protestante olvidado)* (Madrid: Fundación Universitaria Española, 1977)

Boehmer, Eduard, *Bibliotheca Wiffeniana: Spanish Reformers of Two Centuries from 1520*, 3 vols (London: Truebner, 1874-1902)

Bucholtz, Franz Bernhard von, 'Päpstliche Avokation des Processes gegen Alphonsus Diaz und Johann Prieto, 28 September 1546' in his *Geschichte der Regierung Ferdinand des Ersten* (Vienna: C. Schaumberg, 1936), IX, 388-389

Buschbell, Gottfried, *Reformation und Inquisition in Italien um die Mitte des XVI Jahrhunderts* (Paderborn: 1890)

---

[47] *Dos tratados* (1599), 189-90; *Artes,* 184-186.

Contreras, Jaime, 'The Impact of Protestantism in Spain 1520-1600' in S. Haliczer (ed.), *Inquisition and Society in Early Modern Europe* (London: Croom Helm, 1986), 47-63

Donald, Dorothy and Elena Lázaro Corral, *Alfonso de Valdés y su época* (Cuenca: Diputación Provincial, 1983)

Gilly, Carlos, 'Juan de Valdés, traductor y adaptador de escritos de Lutero en su *Diálogo de doctrina christiana*' in Luis López Molina (ed.), *Miscelánea de estudios hispánicos: Homenaje de los hispanistas de Suiza a Ramón Sugranyes de Franch* (Montserrat: Abadia, 1982), 85-106

----------, *Spanien und der Basler Buchdruck bis 1600* (Basle: Helbing & Lichtenhahn, 1985)

Hamilton, Alastair, *Heresy and Mysticism in Sixteenth-Century Spain: The 'Alumbrados'* (Cambridge: Clarke, 1992)

Hoffmann, F.L., 'Zur Bibliographie des Buchs Sanctae Inquisitionis Hispanicae Artes', *Serapeum,* 27 (1866), 161-170

Kamen, Henry & Joseph Pérez, *La imagen internacional de la España de Felipe II: 'Leyenda negra' o conflicto de intereses* (Valladolid, University of Valladolid, 1980)

Kinder, A.G., 'A Hitherto Unknown Centre of Protestantism in Sixteenth-Century Aragon', *Cuadernos de Historia de Jerónimo Zurita,* 51-52 (1985), 131-160

----------, 'Antonio del Corro', *Bibliotheca Dissidentium,* 6 (1986), 121-176

----------, 'Cipriano de Valera (?1530-?1602)', *Bulletin of Hispanic Studies,* 46 (1969), 109-119

----------, 'Juan de Valdés', *Bibliotheca Dissidentium,* 9 (1988), 111-195

----------, 'Le Livre et les idées réformées en Espagne', in J-F Gilmont (ed.), *La Réforme et le livre: L'Europe de l'imprimé (1517-v. 1570)* (Paris: Cerf, 1990)

----------, 'Religious Literature as an Offensive Weapon: Cipriano de Valera's Part in England's War with Spain', *Sixteenth Century Journal,* 19 (1988), 223-235

----------, 'Spanish Protestants and Foxe's Book: Sources' at present with *The John Foxe Society Journal*

Maltby, W. S., *The Black Legend in England: The Development of Anti-Spanish Sentiment, 1558-1660* (Durham, NC: Duke University, 1971)

Nieto, José C., *Juan de Valdés and the Origins of the Spanish and Italian Reformation* (Geneva: Droz, 1970)

Szörényi, László, 'La traduzione anti-trinitaria fatta di Gáspár Heltai del manifesto contro l'Inquisizione di Reginaldo Gonsalvio' in Robért Dán & Antal Pirnát (eds), *Antitrinitarianism in the Second Half of the 16th Century* (Budapest: Akadémiai Kiadó, 1982), 243-251

Tellechea Idígoras, José Ignacio, 'Españoles en Lovaina en 1551-8', *Revista Española de Teología,* 23 (1963), 21-45

----------, 'Francisco de San Román: Un mártir protestante burgalés', *Cuadernos de Investigación Histórica,* 8 (1984), 233-260

----------, 'Perfil teológico del protestantismo castellano del siglo XVI: Un memorial inédito de la inquisición (1559)', *Cuadernos de Investigación Histórica,* 7 (1983), 79-111

Trócsányi, Zoltán (ed.), 'Heltai Gáspár: Háló', *Régi Magyar Könyvtár,* 36 (1915), 1-192

Truman, R.W. & A.G. Kinder, 'The Pursuit of Heretics in the Low Countries: The Activities of Alonso del Canto, 1561-1564', *Journal of Ecclesiastical History,* 30 (1979), 65-93

Vermaseren, B.A., 'Who was Reginaldus Gonsalvius Montanus?', trans. A.G. Kinder, *Bibliothèque d'Humanisme et Renaissance,* 47 (1985), 47-77

5

Did Spanish Crypto-Jews desecrate Christian Sacred Images and why?: The Case of the *Cristo de la Paciencia* (1629-32), the *Romance* of 1717 and the Events of November 1714 in the *Calle del Lobo*

Michael Alpert

On 4 July 1632 an impressive *auto de fe* was held in Madrid.[1] This was a day-long ceremony of processions, sermons and masses, where those who had admitted their heretical or other religious crimes to the Inquisition solemnly abjured their sins, were absolved, heard their sentences read and were returned to the Inquisition gaol to serve their sentences, or were taken to be burnt at the stake. Among the penitents was a group of crypto-Jews, *judaizantes* or *observantes de la Ley de Moisés,* poor Portuguese migrants who had preserved their Judaism throughout several generations, since their ancestors, Portuguese Jews or exiled Spanish Jews, had been forcibly baptized in 1496.

In addition to attempting to observe Saturday as the Sabbath, respect the Jewish dietary laws and marry other Jews, this group had confessed under torture to having, two years earlier, verbally and physically mistreated a carving of Jesus on the cross by whipping and attempting to burn it.

Furthermore, in the early morning, a few hours before leaving the Inquisition prison for the *auto de fe,* one of the victims confessed that the carving had bled and had spoken to them, saying that it was their God and asking why they were mistreating it. According to this prisoner, the *judaizantes* had answered 'no eres más que un pedazo de madera'.[2] It is noteworthy that the opprobrious term

---

[1] I am grateful to Professor Haim Beinart, Professor Yosef Kaplan and Dr Ada Rapoport-Albert for their valuable comments on this article.

[2] For further details of the *auto* and an analysis of the evidence, see British Library 593 h. 17 (110), *Relación del auto de la fe del 4 de julio de 1632 celebrado en Madrid etc* (Granada: 1632); Julio Caro Baroja, *Los judíos en la España moderna y contemporánea, 2nd edn* (Madrid: ISTMO, 1978), II, 445-448; Yosef Hayim Yerushalmi, *From Spanish Court to Italian Ghetto: Isaac Cardoso; A Study in Seventeenth-Century Marranism and Jewish Apologetics* (New York: Columbia University Press, 1971); Archivo Histórico Nacional, Sección de Inquisición (Toledo: Legajo, 1272), cited by M. Escamilla-Colin, *Crimes et*

'*marranos*' by which these Jews are known even in Jewish history, is not found in Inquisition documents.

Cases of judaizing which came before inquisitorial courts occasionally mentioned such sacrilege. However, probably because the image was reported to have spoken, a great deal was made of this case in the published accounts of the *auto* and it became part of popular legend.

The British Library possesses an anonymous printed ballad, sections of which are reproduced in an appendix below, about the case, which became known as that of the *Cristo de la Paciencia*. Nothing in the ballad mentions the seventeenth-century date, though reference to the friary that was built in 1639 on the site of the house where the supposed events took place provides the earliest date of composition.

The ballad, however, claims, in one of its lines, to have been composed in 1717. Since there was also a case of desecration of a crucified image of Jesus among the many trials of Judaizers in the early eighteenth century, one might think that the ballad was composed to illustrate it. However, none of the depositions regarding this latter case is dated as early as 1717. Moreover, Inquisition evidence was strictly confidential until the guilty parties had undergone the *auto de fe*. Since the relevant one did not take place until 1721, it seems unlikely that the ballad refers to the same events, even indirectly. Nevertheless, the ballad states that the events had happened on 15 July 1717. One might then conclude that the composition of the ballad in 1717 possibly reflected some rumours or suspicion that such desecrations of sacred images were still taking place nearly ninety years after the case of the *Cristo de la Paciencia*. The contemporaneity of the ballad with the eighteenth-century reports of desecrations of images may, on the other hand, be entirely coincidental. In any case, the details of the ballad, that is the location of the house and the miraculous utterance of the image, obviously describe the events which led up to the 1632 *auto de fe*. That the story of the *Cristo de la Paciencia* was still popular is demonstrated by the publication, in 1709, of an account of the case by Fray Matheo de Anguiano: *La nueva Jerusalén en que la perfidia hebraica reiteró con nuevos ultrajes la passion de Christo, salvador del mundo, en su sacrosancta imagen del Crucifixo de la Paciencia en Madrid...etc.*

In 1630, the secret Jews were already under arrest when evidence, based on children's gossip, came to the Inquisition's notice that in addition to the usual judaizing acts, the accused had whipped, insulted and tried to burn a figure of the crucified Jesus. Only under the extremes of torture did the Inquisitors extract a confession from some, though not all, of them. The ballad account, in contrast, paints a picture of the crypto-Jews being so impressed by the words which the figure

châtiments dans l'Espagne inquisitoriale (Paris: Berg International, 1992), I, 109. Inquisition documentary references will hereinafter be cited as L.

uttered, that they spent the night in prayer and hastened next morning to confess to the Inquisition, which immediately pardoned them.

The convicted secret Jews who appeared at the *auto* of 4 July 1632, Beatriz Rodríguez, Fernán Baez and his wife, Leonor Rodríguez, Miguel Rodríguez and his wife, Isabel Núñez Alvarez, and Jorge Quaresma, were burnt at the stake at the *quemadero* outside the *Puerta de Alcalá*. Several others received sentences of flogging, penitential prison and wearing the penitent's robe.

The *auto* of 1632 made a great impression on Spanish Jews who lived outside the Peninsula. Forty-seven years later, in his *apologia* for Judaism, *Las Excelencias de los Hebreos,* Isaac Cardoso, who rarely refers to his life as a secret Jew in seventeenth-century Spain, denied the sacrileges:

> Vinieron de Portugal unos Judíos Portugueses a la Corte con sus mujeres e hijos pequeños, que enviándolos a las escuelas y conversando con los otros muchachos, éstos les daban confites y golosinas, y los iban inquiriendo si eran Judíos, y si sus padres en casa maltrataban o azotaban un Cristo. Negaban ellos al principio, mas persuadidos de las golosinas que les daban, y del maestro, poco afecto a esta Nación[...] vinieron a confesar lo que les imputaban[...] Prenden los padres[...] ponenlos a tormento viejos, pobres y enfermos, y exhortándolos a que confesasen y se usaría con ellos de piedad,[...]confesaron cuanto les acusaban y quemaron seis o siete personas (Yerushalmi, 70).

Yosef Hayim Yerushalmi, Cardoso's biographer, who read the trial evidence, believes that the whole account of the maltreatment of the crucified figure is untrue. Juan Antonio Llorente, the ex-Secretary of the Inquisition, who wrote the first scholarly account of the Holy Office, based on documents which were available to him, suggests that the account of the image speaking 'no es tan cierto'.[3] The anthropologist, Julio Caro Baroja, who read the documents of the eighteenth-century trials, suspends judgement on the question of whether the crypto-Jews committed such acts:

> Dejo al lector en libertad de pensar si estas gentes dislocadas fueron o no capaces de cometer todo lo que se les atribuyó. Bien sé que los hombres de fe mosaica consideran la acusación de sacrilegio como calumniosa y que algunos de fe cristiana la darán como segura (Caro Baroja, III, 80).

Turning to the trials of Madrid crypto-Jews in the early eighteenth century, one of the most important witnesses, Francisco de Torres, testified that one winter morning in 1714, he was standing outside his business premises, when he was approached by

---

[3] José Antonio Llorente, *Historia crítica de la inquisición en España*, 4 vols (Madrid: Hiperión, 1981), IV, 110.

Isabel de Aragón and Mariana Pacheco, two elderly members of the crypto-Jewish group, whom Torres habitually aided financially. They said they had found a wax figure of the Christ-child with pins stuck into it, in a house occupied by Isabel's niece, María Feliciana Hurtado de Mendoza Pimentel. Isabel had protested to María Feliciana, who said the old woman was too inquisitive and threw the wax figure into the burning brazier. By the time of his arrest and trial, Torres was trying hard to curry favour with the Inquisition, because he was in serious trouble himself, having been once before 'reconciled' with the Church and, thus, in danger, as a relapsed Judaizer, of going to the stake. In his evidence, he claimed to have been horror-struck when María Feliciana said that the only explanation of the Virgin Birth was that Mary was 'una puta', who deceived her husband, Joseph. Torres added that María Feliciana, her sister, Manuela, and her daughter Agustina had tongues like scorpions.[4] A degree of personal antagonism emerges quite clearly from the evidence.

On 12 December 1719, Torres began to tell the inquisitors about a meeting of the crypto-Jewish group one day in November 1714. The group had been addressed in Torres's house in the Calle de Lobo (now Calle de Echegaray) by Miguel de Robles, who had been brought up in the ex-Iberian Jewish community in Bayonne which practised Judaism without hindrance, though still ostensibly composed of 'New Christian Portuguese merchants'.

As Robles finished, he took a statuette of the crucified Jesus from his pocket and said: 'este es el embustero que dice que es el verdadero Mesías, y no lo siendo, andamos por él arrastrados'. María Arias, the wife of the wealthy tax-farmer Francisco de Miranda, rose and took some pieces of straw, lit them at the brazier, and whipped the image. Her daughter, Luisa, did likewise with esparto-grass drawn from the mats. Francisco de Miranda himself confirmed the account in evidence at another trial.[5]

On another occasion, Agustina Pimentel said that her aunt, Manuela, had claimed that, once the clothes were stripped from holy images, only wood was left ('no quedaba más que un palo').[6] She also said that Mary had deceived Joseph, which was the origin of the story of the Virgin Birth. Torres's wife, Isabel de Ribera, in her evidence at her husband's trial, recalled another occasion on which the virginity of Mary had been denied. Jesus had been called 'the blacksmith's son' ('O filho do ferreyro'), in a Portuguese expression that had probably been preserved since the crypto-Jews' grandparents had come into Spain from Portugal, like so many in the early seventeenth century.

---

[4] L157/12, trial of María Feliciana Hurtado de Mendoza Pimentel.
[5] Ibid. and L157/11, trial of Manuela Hurtado de Mendoza Pimentel.
[6] L157/12.

Other witnesses recalled statements which were more fundamental denials of Christianity. Rodrigo de la Peña testified that some crypto-Jews had spoken of Christians as worshippers of wooden idols. They had said that the Messiah had not come; there were no saints; there was no sacrament in the mass. Jesus was merely a good man who could do magic.[7] For another crypto-Jew, Manuel de Balcárcel, the Law of Moses was the only one in which they could be saved (an opinion expressed in the Christian discourse, which they inevitably used to speak of religion, and a view which is notably non-Jewish). This was because, he said, the Prophets of Israel were more likely to be right than the Apostles, who were only fishermen.[8]

Asked why they had committed the sacrilegious act of whipping and burning the figure of Jesus on the cross, Francisco de Miranda, a worldly man, able to look at the issues involved with some detachment, said that they had done it in the belief that Jesus was not the Messiah and that the figure on the cross was no more than a piece of matter, of no spiritual import.

Miranda's statement reveals the real reason for the desecration. However, to explain the events rationally assumes that they did in fact take place. It is to contest the view of Cardoso, who had lived as a secret Jew in Spain, probably witnessed the *auto de fe* of 1632, and who disbelieved the whole story. It means accepting the broad truth of the ballad of the *Cristo de la Paciencia*, which reflected the popular view of the time, invented an immediate confession and suggested that the Jews were re-enacting the Crucifixion when they mistreated the image. The prose account of the *auto de fe*, published in August 1632, is different. It claims that, when the image spoke, it said: 'Malditos, porque me açotays? sabeys que soy vuestro Dios' to which the *marranos* replied, 'Pues por esso', (an even less convincing story). The account given by Miguel Rodríguez and his wife, at dawn, hours before their last day on earth, claimed that they had told the image it was merely a piece of wood. Given Francisco de Miranda's explanation above, Rodríguez probably had said something like that, but it would have been before the supposed utterances of the image, hardly afterwards. Perhaps Rodríguez and his wife hoped to save their lives by this last-minute confession.

How the writers of accounts of the *auto* got to know of the offences that the *marranos* had committed remains a grey area. The prose account says that the 'sentences' were read out. This probably means the heads of the accusations, such as are to be found in the *relaciones de causas* which were sent up by the local Inquisition courts to the *Suprema*. It would be useful to know how detailed a public account was given of the offences. One must assume that the inquisitors did read out details of the maltreatment of the carving. Whether they announced that it bled

---

[7] L186/3, trial of Francisco de Torres.
[8] L157/11, Francisco de Torres at trial of Manuela Hurtado de Mendoza Pimentel.

and spoke, however, is uncertain, given especially that the words it was supposed to have said differ in two of the accounts.

It is understandable that Jews and liberal historians should deny accusations that the former maltreated Christian images or sacred objects.[9] Yet one may disbelieve, as the inquisitors probably did, though they allowed the story to be published, that the image bled and spoke, without necessarily denying the rest of the events.

Such sacrilegious acts are not impossible, if understood in the context in which they were said to have occurred in the seventeenth and early eighteenth centuries. The object of the whipping and burning of the figure was not to harm what it represented. It was not like a black magic ritual, which may demand the use of sacred objects for its purposes because it recognises the Christian power that they represent. The crypto-Jews, however, as Francisco de Miranda clearly explained to the inquisitors, were demonstrating the absolute materiality, the absence of spiritual meaning of the objects they 'desecrated'. However, they were not doing this as a public revolutionary statement, as was the case with anti-clericals who destroyed images in the Spanish Civil War, or the iconoclasts of the English Revolution.

The crypto-Jews committed those acts because of the nature of their predicament in the context of Spanish life. While some of the eighteenth-century group, such as Francisco de Torres and Francisco de Miranda, were mature men, who read and who knew something of normative Jewish life outside Spain, others, mostly women, were so illiterate that they did not sign their names to their depositions, and some of the seventeenth-century group were itinerant hawkers. They needed tangible and visible, rather than intellectual, explanations of what being Jewish meant, given that they lived in a world of mental and verbal discourse that was entirely Catholic. To understand that they were not Christians presented an intellectual challenge which they were ill-equipped to face. The daily and weekly round of religious service, the rosary, confession, communion, mass, *romerías*, their daily vocabulary, their calendar, and the decorations of their houses were replete with expressions of Catholicism. How could they be anything but Catholics? It was coterminous with being Spanish. Yet, they were secretly Jews, observers of the Law of Moses, as they said. Miranda and Robles might well explain to them that Jesus was not divine, but a physical demonstration of the impossibility of being Jewish and Christian at the

---

[9] See Haim Beinart, *Records of the Inquisition in Ciudad Real*, 3 vols (Jerusalem: Israel Academy of Science, 1974-1981), I, 570 (...'e tenia un crucifixo en su cassa y lo açotava los viernes en las tardes...'). Beinart, who has published many Inquisition trials, generally accepts their accuracy, but cf. Yitzhak Baer's famous *History of the Jews in Christian Spain*, 2 vols (Philadelphia: Jewish Publication Society of America, 1978), II, 362, who writes: 'True, Jews and *conversos* were capable of at times breaking crucifixes or trampling them underfoot, but scourging is unthinkable'. Baer does not explain why he believes his last statement.

same time would be far more effective than any amount of theological argument which, in the absence of even Spanish texts of Scripture, could not be sustained.

It is not unlikely, then, that the events of the affair of the *Cristo de la Paciencia* in 1629-1630, discounting the miraculous speech of the crucified Jesus, did indeed take place, and were reproduced in the house in the *Calle del Lobo* in Madrid nearly a century later.

Appendix

The ballad of the case of the 'Cristo de la Paciencia'

Title
Romance nuevo del portentoso caso que ha sucedido en la Corte de Madrid. Dase cuenta como unos Judios, açotando, arrastrando, queriendo quemar en un bracero à un Santissimo Christo, su Divina Magestad les habló, y fue bastante para que se convirtieran.

Date
The British Library Catalogue (11451. bb. 52) suggests 1720 as publication date. The colophon reads 'Con licencia Madrid Juan Sanz'

Illustration
The ballad is prefaced by a coloured picture. There is a floor with a pattern of red and black tiles, and a burning brazier. There are four people. From left to right, these are: a man, wearing a high-crowned black hat, a red and black doublet and breeches, and blue hose. He is dragging a green cross with a crucified Jesus saying, 'porque me açotais - siendo vuestro Dios?' Another figure without hat or beard, wearing a blue robe with slashed sleeves, is standing over the crucifix with a whip. A woman in a yellow dress comes next, also brandishing a knotted whip. Lastly there is a man like the first, but wearing blue, also holding a whip. The costumes are seventeenth century.

The ballad is composed of 277 lines of which the most relevant to the case are copied here:

El mundo se atemorize/llore todo el universo,
hoy se quebranten las peñas/Silven con aire los vientos.
aviven con furia el fuego./El Sol y sus resplandores
vistanse de lutos luego/ y en otro segundo eclipse

repitan su sentimiento.................................
....

pues su Criador inmenso/segunda vez hoy padece/
la crueldad de los Hebreos./Lloren plantas y animales
y los hombres con estruendo/de que pueda en estos tiempos
verse infamias tan atrozes/como la que estamos viendo
....
O tirana gente infame/vil canalla, ingrata [sic] pueblo,
Judios endemoniados,/tizones que en el infierno/
aveis de arder en vorazes/chispas de aquel horno fiero!
....
Lo que en tres dias hizisteis/padecer à este Cordero,
es imposible se sepa [...].
....
En este año en que estamos, que es de mil y setecientos
y diez y siete, segun/en los anales del tiempo
se cuenta puntualmente/desde el santo Nacimiento,

a quinze del mes de Julio/sucedió, que en el portento
de la Villa de Madrid,/Corte insigne y cielo bello
en que el Monarca mayor/tiene la Silla, y el Cetro,
vivian unos Judios/cerca del regio Convento
de los Padres Capuchinos/de la Paciencia, y à tiempo/
que la noche con sus lutos/todo lo dexó en silencio
en un quarto de la casa,/en que vivian los perros,
arrastravan una imagen/del dulce, y manso cordero,
que pendiente en una Cruz/nos rescato del infierno,
y con crueles açotes,/y salivazos le hizieron
mil repetidas injurias;/y previniendo un brasero
intentaron el quemarle/con furia, y atrevimiento,
Dezianle mil aprobios,/tratandole de embustero [...].
....
Luego que estos fieros brutos/al Señor del Universo
le arrastaron, y açotaron,/por sus labios tan del cielo
le oyeron estas palabras:/
Porquè me açotais siendo/vuestro Dios ? y luego
que oyeron estas razones,/con pasmo y desassosiego,
exalando por los ojos/agua de arrepentimiento,
postraronse de rodillas,/ y con grande rendimiento
dezian: O gran Jesus,/ y Messias verdadero!

bien conocemos, Señor,/que nuestros continuos yerros
te ocasionaron gran Dios,/el verte en aquesse leño, [...]
....
Passaron aquella noche/en continuos rendimientos,
confesando a nuestro Dios/por unico y verdadero:
y llegando al otro dia/todos juntos se partieron
a la Santa Inquisicion, / y audiencia luego pidiendo,
postrandose de rodillas/a los pies de aquellos rectos
Señores, les confessaron/la verdad de aquel sucesso,
y piden misericordia/de sus repetidos yerros.
Absolvieronles al punto
de sus crimines, y excessos,/ y les dieron penitencia,
y luego fueron cumpliendo,/ viviendo tan convertidos,
que à todos les dan exemplo [...].
....
Escarmentad, vil canalla,/Judios, que tan protervos
estais en la ceguedad/de que el Messias supremo
no ha venido todavia [...].

Bibliography

Alcalá, A., *Inquisición española y mentalidad inquisitorial* (Barcelona: Ariel, 1984)

Archivo Histórico Nacional, Sección de Inquisición (Toledo: Legajo, 1272)

Baer, Yitzhak, *History of the Jews in Christian Spain*, 2 vols (Philadelphia: Jewish Publication Society of America, 1978)

Beinart, Haim, *Conversos on Trial: The Inquisition in Ciudad Real* (Jerusalem: Magnes Press, the Hebrew University, 1981)

Beinart, Haim, *Records of the Inquisition in Ciudad Real*, 3 vols (Jerusalem: Israel Academy of Science, 1974-1981)

Caro Baroja, Julio, *Los judíos en la España moderna y contemporánea*, 2nd edn (Madrid: ISTMO, 1978)

Domínguez Ortiz, A., *La clase social de los conversos en Castilla en la edad moderna* (Madrid: CSIC, 1985)

Edwards, John, 'The Conversos: A Theological Approach', *Bulletin of Hispanic Studies*, 62 (1985), 39-49

Escamilla-Colin, M., *Crimes et châtiments dans l'Espagne inquisitoriale*, 2 vols (Paris: Berg International, 1992)

Kamen, Henry, *The Spanish Inquisition* (London: Weidenfeld and Nicolson, 1965)

Kaplan, J., *Jews and Conversos: Studies in Society and the Inquisition* (Jerusalem: Magnes Press, the Hebrew University, 1985)

Lea, H., *A History of the Inquisition of Spain,* 4 vols (New York: Macmillan, 1906-1907)

Llorente, José Antonio, *Historia crítica de la inquisición en España,* 4 vols (Madrid: Hiperión, 1981)

Pérez Villanueva, J. (ed.), *La inquisición española: nueva visión, nuevos horizontes* (Madrid: Siglo XXI, 1980)

---------- and B. Escandell Bonet, *Historia de la inquisición en España y América,* 2 vols (Madrid: BAC, 1984)

Relación del auto de la fe del 4 de julio de 1632 celebrado en Madrid etc. (Granada: 1632), in British Library 593 h. 17 (110)

Révah, I., 'Les Marranes', *Revue des Etudes Juives,* 118 (1960), 29-77

Roth, C., *A History of the Marranos* (Philadelphia: JPS, 1932)

Yerushalmi, Yosef Hayim, *From Spanish Court to Italian Ghetto: Isaac Cardoso; A Study in Seventeenth-Century Marranism and Jewish Apologetics* (New York: Columbia University Press, 1971)

6

Popular Religious Scepticism and Idiosyncrasy in Post-Tridentine Cuenca

Nicholas Griffiths

It has become axiomatic that, in the second half of the sixteenth century, under the impetus of the Council of Trent, the Spanish Church undertook a massive programme of religious indoctrination which sought both to transform the understanding of doctrine among the Old Christian population, and to impose uniformity of belief and practice. There have been convincing demonstrations that, as a result of this programme, a basic minimum knowledge of doctrine was imparted (probably for the first time) to the *pueblo llano* (or the non-clerical section of the population) during the latter half of the sixteenth century and first half of the seventeenth century.[1] However, it is by no means clear that more systematic teaching and instruction guaranteed the imposition of conformity. Greater knowledge does not necessarily lead to greater commitment. Nor does more effective dissemination of an official norm guarantee more widespread adherence to it. Indeed, as I shall attempt to show here, there is considerable evidence that the sixteenth-century Christianization

I should like to thank the British Academy for funding the research on which this article is based. I should also like to express my gratitude to Dimas Pérez Ramírez, and his assistant Francisco Javier Triguero Cordente, for their kind assistance and attention at the Archivo Diocesano Conquense. I should also like to express my warmest thanks to Professor Trevor J. Dadson, Dr John Edwards, Dr Adelina Sarrión and Professor Chris Wickham for their invaluable comments on earlier drafts of this article.

[1] See Jean-Pierre Dedieu, 'Christianization in New Castile. Catechism, Communion, Mass, and Confirmation in the Toledo Archbishopric, 1540-1650' in Anne J. Cruz and Mary E. Perry (eds), *Culture and Control in Counter-Reformation Spain*, Hispanic Issues, vol. 7 (Minneapolis: University of Minneapolis Press, 1992), 1-24; Jean-Pierre Dedieu, *L'Administration de la Foi: L'Inquisition de Tolède (16-18 siècle)*, Bibliothèque de la Casa de Velázquez , vol. 7 (Madrid: Casa de Velázquez, 1989); and Sara T. Nalle, *God in La Mancha: Religious Reform and the People of Cuenca 1500-1650* (Baltimore and London: John Hopkins University Press, 1992).

programme reinforced religious deviance among the *pueblo llano* rather than imposing greater religious uniformity.

The critical study of religious deviance among the Old Christian population of early modern Spain may be undertaken thanks to the data bank furnished by the records of inquisitorial denunciations and trials. The archive of the Conquense Inquisition provides one of the richest sources for this study since, rarely among tribunals, it preserves detailed accounts of entire *procesos* (trials), rather than the summary *relaciones de causas* (case reports) on which researchers in many other tribunals have to rely. The most fruitful areas of inquisitorial activity for this purpose are cases of blasphemy (irreverent utterances about sacred things) and 'propositions' (erroneous statements about the faith which were not necessarily formally heretical but nevertheless did not conform to orthodoxy as defined by the Church). Investigation of these sources reveals that popular religious deviance among Old Christians took two principal forms: religious scepticism (lack of belief in a particular aspect of religion) and religious idiosyncrasy (the personal interpretation or independent reading of a religious concept, text or image, constituting an appropriation and distortion of doctrine rather than a lack of belief). The imaginative speculations of miller Andrés de Sepúlveda, who first appeared before the Conquense tribunal in 1659, accused of blasphemy, furnish a prime example of religious idiosyncrasy. Sepúlveda denied the existence of hell and purgatory, arguing instead that souls roamed among the thyme and broom fields where they expiated their sins by digging with a hoe; once they tired of digging, their suffering ceased and that was an end to it. Alternatively, those who were not banished to the thyme fields expiated their sins inside a doorjamb (*quicial*). Another defendant, tailor Alonso Gómez, tried by the tribunal in 1662 for 'heretical utterances', displayed a similar capacity for independent and idiosyncratic interpretations of received wisdom when he maintained that the 'form' of Christ was 'represented' or 'imprinted' on the consecrated host. On the other hand, his affirmation that the Holy Trinity did not exist, that images were mere lumps of wood which did not merit reverence and that the consecrated host was nothing but a bit of bread were characteristic of religious scepticism, the second form of popular religious deviance investigated here. Scepticism and idiosyncrasy were not mutually exclusive phenonema; the fact that they could co-exist in the same individual, as in Gómez, demonstrates their complexity.[2]

---

[2] See Leg 523, Exp 6742, Alonso Gómez (Campo de Criptana, 1662); Leg 512, Exp 6699, Andrés de Sepúlveda (Villanueva de la Jara, 1659); Leg 538, Exp 6820, Andrés de Sepúlveda, (El Picazo, 1671). Except where otherwise indicated, all the documents referred to in this article are to be found in the section *Inquisición* of the *Archivo Diocesano de Cuenca*. Folio numbers are given where they exist.

The recognition that ordinary people engaged in their own readings of religious doctrines owes much to the work of Roger Chartier, Carlo Ginzburg and Natalie Zemon Davis among others. Spiritual models provided by the clergy did not act as imperative conditioning; the faithful were not passive ciphers but often defied the dominant messages, subjecting them to what Chartier calls 'adaptations, trespassing and subversion'.[3] The consumption of religious phenomena was not dependent or submissive but creative, and entailed a process of re-working and revision. Religious experience, like any other, was a cultural artefact capable of diverse interpretations and appropriations which did not merely mimic the normative model. As Zemon Davis has observed, when a peasant read religious literature, he was not a blank sheet on which a literal message could be stamped; rather, he was an active user and interpreter of printed material.[4] The classic example is the Friulian miller, Menocchio, tried by the Inquisition in the 1580s and 1590s, who, as Ginzburg indicates, unconsciously 'placed a screen between himself and the printed page: a filter that emphasized certain words while obscuring others, that stretched the meaning of a word taking it out of context, that acted on his memory and distorted the words of the text'.[5] In this way, he created his personal reading of texts which reflected his own aspirations and expressed his own understanding of the world. The same was true for religious concepts which were communicated not through printed matter but by word of mouth, in sermons and preaching and day-to-day conversation. Many of the defendants in Conquense inquisitorial trials showed the same 'aggressive originality' with regard to religious doctrines, reformulating and reinventing them, translating them into versions that corresponded to their own experiences, aspirations and

---

[3] See Roger Chartier, 'Culture as Appropriation: Popular Cultural Uses in Early Modern France' in Steven L. Kaplan (ed.), *Understanding Popular Culture: Europe from the Middle Ages to the Nineteenth Century* (New York: Mouton Publishers, 1984), 229-253, 233. Chartier adheres to the school of thought which rejects the misleading distinction between 'elite religion' and 'popular religion'. For the debate on the usefulness of this distinction, see William A. Christian Jr., *Local Religion in Sixteenth-Century Spain* (Princeton: Princeton University Press, 1981); Kaspar von Greyerz (ed.), *Religion and Society in Early Modern Europe 1500-1800* (London: German Historical Institute, 1984); Robert Muchembled, *Popular Culture and Elite Culture in France 1400-1750* (London: Louisana State University Press, 1985); John Edwards, 'The Priest, the Layman and the Historian: Religion in Early Modern Europe', *European History Quarterly*, 17 (1987), 87-93; Bob Scribner, 'Is a History of Popular Culture Possible?', *History of European Ideas*, 10:2 (1989), 175-191.

[4] Natalie Zemon Davis, *Society and Culture in Early Modern France* (London, Duckworth, 1975), 190.

[5] Carlo Ginzburg, *The Cheese and the Worms: The Cosmos of a Sixteenth Century Miller*, trans. John and Anne Tedeschi (London: Routledge, 1980), 33.

fantasies.[6] Sepúlveda's notion of souls purging their sins in a thyme field or inside a doorjamb, for example, reveals the almost limitless possibilities for creative and imaginative variations on traditional Christian themes.[7]

Despite the advances of research in the field of mentalities, and scholarly interest in the interaction of normative and popular readings of religious doctrine, expressions of popular scepticism and idiosyncratic creativity have been largely overlooked by historians. This is unfortunate since these were important, defining aspects of popular religious experience. It would be a mistake to assume, as many historians often have, that these phenomena are isolated cases on the margins of meaningful religious experience, or mere curiosities, interesting as anecdotes, but hardly typical or significant. In fact, popular expressions of scepticism and idiosyncrasy were by no means infrequent. Indeed, on the contrary, these and related expressions of religious deviance were so common that the offences of blasphemy and propositions became the principal occupation of the Conquense inquisitorial tribunal, and most other Peninsular tribunals, in the seventeenth century and first half of the eighteenth century; the number of cases involving these offences outweighed

---

[6] Ibid., 112. Elsewhere Ginzburg has argued that the relations between high culture and the culture of subordinate classes implied circular exchanges, mediated through different sometimes opposite codes. See Carlo Ginzburg, 'The Dovecote has Opened its Eyes: Popular Conspiracy in Seventeenth-Century Italy' in Gustav Henningsen and John Tedeschi (eds), *The Inquisition in Early Modern Europe: Studies on Sources and Methods* (Illinois: Northern Illinois University Press, 1986), 191-95. I have also been influenced here by the observations of Rostas and Droogers about 'popular religion'. See Susanna Rostas and André Droogers (eds), *The Popular Use of Popular Religion in Latin America* (Amsterdam: Popular Uses, 1993), 1-5.

[7] Other defendants voiced similar convictions. Miguel de Chavarría denied the existence of hell and avowed that God let souls expiate where He saw fit, including under a doorjamb. For Cebrián Hernando, souls might go wherever God chose and could expiate under the doorjamb or under the stone slabs around the fire. Although he rejected a fixed location for hell and purgatory, and ridiculed the idea of sufferings in fire, he did not deny that God punished souls. Indeed, he argued that the torment to which they were subjected - inability to see the face of God - was far greater than merely being cast into flames. These defendants do not seem to have had any connection with each other; Chavarría's case, for example, antedated the other two by thirty years. The defendants were from different villages some distance one from the other: Sepúlveda's Villanueva de la Jara (in southern Cuenca) was about one hundred and thirty kilometres from Montiel (in south-eastern Ciudad Real) and about forty-four kilometres from Chavarría's San Clemente. However, the similar content of their deviant notions might suggest common origins in a popular gloss on the concept of purgatory. Leg 492, Exp 6572, Cebrián Hernando (Montiel, 1655), fols 40, 49, 55, 57^v, 69^v; Leg 412, Exp 5783, Miguel de Chavarría (San Clemente, 1624). For another example of idiosyncratic interpretations of the soul, see Ginés López who denied the existence of individual souls, arguing instead that 'the soul was the faith'. After all, had anyone seen a soul after death? Leg 445, Exp 6237, Ginés López (Olmedilla, 1633).

those for any other area of inquisitorial activity (see 114-115 below and the appendix). In other words, in the post-Tridentine world, popular scepticism and idiosyncrasy were not eliminated but, on the contrary, flourished; increased exposure to the official teachings of the Church seems only to have fuelled rather than eradicated their expression.

The significance of manifestations of these forms of religious deviance has been obscured in the past because debate has tended to revolve around the less meaningful issue of whether it was possible to be an atheist in the sixteenth (and early seventeenth) century. In order to appreciate how this debate has marginalized the wider question about popular expressions of religious scepticism and idiosyncrasy, the 'atheism' issue needs to be addressed here. Ever since Lucien Febvre's seminal work on Rabelais and the 'problem of unbelief', it has been axiomatic that atheism, in the modern sense of the term, was inconceivable in the sixteenth century; although the term *atheist* formed part of the vocabulary of learned men, it was used simply as a term of abuse.[8] Febvre's approach was limited by lack of data on the beliefs of ordinary people, something that Julio Caro Baroja attempted to remedy by reviewing the issue in the light of the evidence of inquisitorial trials. Noting the numerous prosecutions for 'incredulidad' in the tribunal of Cuenca throughout the sixteenth century, he classified as atheists those offenders who denied the immortality of the soul.[9] At the same time he demonstrated that the concept of atheism - in the sense of lack of belief in the existence of God - was recognized by the educated at this time. The words 'ateísmo', 'ateísta' and 'ateo' appear to have been introduced into Spanish at the end of the sixteenth century, and their use became more extended in the first half of the seventeenth century. One of the first texts in which the word atheist was used was Fray Luis de Granada's treatise *Del símbolo de la fe* (1582) where there is a discussion of the madness of the 'atheist epicureans' who attributed all creation to chance. Another authority, Fray Juan Bautista Fernández, discussed atheists in classical texts and the doubts of Aristotle about the immortality of the soul. If these men were able to conceive of the non-existence of God, then, argued Caro Baroja, so could others.[10] It is one thing, though, to recognize that the terminology of

---

[8] Lucien Febvre, *The Problem of Unbelief in the Sixteenth Century: The Religion of Rabelais*, trans. Beatrice Gottlieb (Cambridge, Mass.: Harvard, 1982).

[9] Julio Caro Baroja, *Las formas complejas de la vida religiosa: Religión, sociedad y carácter en la España de los siglos XVI y XVII* (Madrid: Akal, 1978), 200-202. The fact that inquisitorial questionnaires specifically asked subjects if they knew of anyone who had said that there was no paradise for the good or hell for the bad, or that life was nothing more than being born and dying, indicates that such statements were not uncommon.

[10] Ibid., 199-201. Elsewhere, Caro Baroja has discussed the use of the word 'atheist' in seventeenth-century Spanish literature, notably the works of Cervantes, Lope de Vega,

atheism may have formed part of the mental tools of a learned elite and quite another to assume that 'atheist' is an appropriate description of the ordinary people prosecuted by the Conquense tribunal. The terminology of atheism is inappropriate since it almost never appears either in the inquisitors' schema or in those of the accused.[11]

Even so, historians have continued to conceptualize the issue in terms of atheism, at the same time insisting that genuine scepticism was virtually non-existent. In his study of the Madrid inquisitorial tribunal, Juan Blázquez Miguel labelled as 'atheists' those offenders he found from the 1650s onwards who denied the immortality of the soul. He concluded, though, that the offence was rare, since denial of the after-life would be tantamount to denying God, something that remained, following Febvre, virtually inconceivable in the seventeenth century.[12] William Monter found that scepticism about the afterlife among victims of the Aragonese Inquisition was unusual. Cases such as that of the Valencian student, Miguel Pérez, who was formally reconciled in 1567 for saying that there was nothing except birth and death, while common in Sicily and the urban centres of mainland Italy, were almost never found in Spain (though Monter gave no explanation as to why Sicilians but not Spaniards should be capable of such expressions).[13] French historian Jean-Pierre Dedieu has taken issue with Caro Baroja's equation of Conquense 'irreligion' with

---

Quevedo and Calderón de la Barca. See Julio Caro Baroja, *De la superstición al ateísmo: Meditaciones antropológicas* (Madrid: Taurus, 1974), 257-280. Kamen has agreed that the vocabulary of irreligion was to be found among educated people in Europe from at least the 1580s. See Henry Kamen, *The Phoenix and the Flame: Catalonia and the Counter-Reformation* (New Haven and London: Yale University Press, 1993), 89-90. For the issue of learned denials of the existence of atheism in another context, see David Berman, 'The Repressive Denials of Atheism in Britain in the Seventeenth and Eighteenth Centuries', *Proceedings of the Royal Irish Academy,* 82C (1982), 211-245.

[11] It is however worth noting that, in 1639, Julio César Lissardo, a violinist from Pavia in Italy, was accused by the inquisitors of Toledo of being a 'heretical atheist' since he had denied the existence of hell, demons and the afterlife. The term 'atheist' appeared in the prosecution's accusations, in the testimony of witnesses and in the sentence imposed. See Archivo Histórico Nacional, Inquisición, Toledo, Heregía, Leg 100, Exp 6. There are also examples among the documentation for the tribunal of Murcia. See Archivo Histórico Nacional, Inquisición, Murcia, Leg. 2827, Relación de Causas de 1667, Thomas Castellano. It is extremely rare, though, to find the term employed in inquisitorial documents.

[12] Juan Blázquez Miguel, *Madrid: Judíos, herejes y brujas. El Tribunal de Corte (1650-1820)* (Toledo: Arcano, 1990), 163.

[13] William Monter, *Frontiers of Heresy: The Spanish Inquisition from the Basque Lands to Sicily* (Cambridge: CUP, 1990), 129 and 173-174.

atheism.[14]   However, he too was unable to find in Toledo any indications of the beginnings of an ontological denial of the existence of God.[15]

The attention that has been directed to the issue of 'atheism' has concealed the diversity of expressions of religious 'unbelief' in a wider sense and has made it more difficult to ask whether they might more profitably be called something else.   Caro Baroja already noted that sixteenth- and seventeenth-century commentators applied the term atheist to a broad range of manifestations of unbelief, including not only those who denied the existence of God or the immortality of the soul but also blasphemers, Epicureans, Libertines and Machiavellians.[16]   Preoccupation with the issue of atheism has tended to obscure the fact that an individual can experience varying degrees of scepticism without necessarily being an atheist in the modern sense.   As John Edwards wrote in an important article on religious doubt in medieval Soria: 'even if Febvre was right to argue that atheism in the modern sense was not an option in the sixteenth century or earlier, it does appear that there was genuine religious scepticism in late medieval and early modern Europe'.   Edwards concludes that 'virtually every theological and philosophical option so far available to humankind was espoused by someone in this region of Spain in the late fifteenth century'.[17]   Henry Kamen has agreed that popular scepticism was frequently

---

[14] Whereas Caro Baroja asserted that the category of 'incredulidad' appeared far more frequently among trials in Cuenca than in Toledo, a fact which he attributed to differences in the empirical incidence of the offence, Dedieu argued that in reality there was no more incredulity, in the modern sense, in Cuenca than in Toledo; rather the archivist who compiled the catalogue for Cuenca created a category which did not exist for the inquisitors. See Caro Baroja, *Formas complejas*, 197-199; J.P. Dedieu, 'Classer des causes de foi: Quelques réflexions' in *L'Inquisizione Romana in Italia nell'età moderna: Archivi, problemi di metodo e nuove ricerche* (Rome: Ministero per i beni culturali e ambientali, 1991), 327. Even so, since my research confirms that expressions of unbelief in Cuenca were indeed frequent, it would be fruitful to investigate whether Conquense and Toledan inquisitors differed in the attention that they devoted to these offences and whether there was a disparity in the empirical incidence of expressions of religious unbelief according to region. Reference to trials in other tribunals would help to clarify this issue.

[15] Dedieu, *L'Administration*, 44-45.

[16] See Caro Baroja, *De la superstición*, 257-280, especially 258. In the context of early modern England, Michael Hunter has discussed the inclusive use of the word 'atheism' to sensationalize in a single, pervasive stereotype a broad range of phenomena that were believed to present a threat to religion. See Michael Hunter, 'The Problem of "Atheism" in Early Modern England', *Transactions of the Royal Historical Society,* Fifth Series, 35 (1985), 135-157.

[17] John Edwards, 'Religious Faith and Doubt in Late Medieval Spain: Soria circa 1450-1500', *Past and Present,* 120 (1988), 3-25, especially 13-16, 21 and 24. It is worth pointing out that Edwards's interpretation of the significance of propositions has been disputed by Sara Nalle, who believes that the sixteenth-century cases heard in Cuenca, rather than being defiant challenges to Catholic doctrine, were said in the context of justifying reckless living.

manifested among the common people in the sixteenth century.[18]   This revisionism represents a timely shift away from the sterile issue of atheism and the failure to recognize the manifold manifestations of religious unbelief.[19] Locating my research within the context of this current of revisionism, I should like to suggest that expressions of popular scepticism and idiosyncrasy are significant indicators of the quality of faith and belief of those who uttered them, and hence permit an assessment of the impact of the Tridentine indoctrination programme.

The attitudes and utterances which provoked trials for blasphemy and propositions reveal scepticism about, and idiosyncratic variations on, virtually every essential doctrine of the faith, and most especially those which the post-Tridentine Church had been so determined to inculcate in ordinary people. These included the greatest mysteries of the Church - the Eucharist, Parthenogenesis (Virgin Birth) and the Resurrection, as well as the fate of souls after death. The doctrine of the Real Presence in the consecrated host was assimilated with great difficulty by the mass of the population.[20] The defendant Diego de Valdés expressed a typical view when he asserted that the host was merely a lump of bread - if God was in heaven he could not be physically present in the host.[21] Other defendants ridiculed companions for believing in a

---

See Nalle, *God in La Mancha,* 60-61. In my view, the Conquense material bears out Edwards's interpretation.

[18] See Kamen, *Phoenix*, 89-90.

[19] Conversely, Maureen Flynn maintained in a recent article that 'few if any seem to have doubted, in a philosophical sense, that [God] existed'. She attributes the many denials of God 'muttered under the breath' by sixteenth-century Spaniards to the liberating effect of anger which allowed them 'to expand beyond their cultural boundaries and explore a world totally different from that which they normally experienced'. Maureen Flynn, 'Blasphemy and the Play of Anger in Sixteenth-Century Spain', *Past and Present*, 149 (1995), 29-56, especially 48-49 and 51. However, this surely begs the question: if these people were able to step outside their cultural boundaries in moments of anger, were they not also capable of doing so in moments of more considered reflection? One did not need to be angry in order to entertain philosophical doubts or sceptical views. Flynn's perspective is conditioned by her focus on blasphemy, which she correctly, in my view, interprets as 'credulous forms of belligerence and delinquency rather than ideological scepticism'. What she misses is that blasphemous thoughts and utterances could co-exist, in a given individual, with genuine scepticism. Many seventeenth-century Conquenses were both blasphemers and sceptics.   The interesting question which remains to be investigated is the precise relation between blasphemy, religious idiosyncrasy and scepticism.

[20] For this point, see Jaime Contreras, *El santo oficio de la inquisición de Galicia: poder, sociedad y cultura* (Madrid: Akal, 1982), 561.

[21] Leg 415, Exp 5829, Diego de Valdés (Belmonte, 1625). Similar views were found in other tribunals. Contreras refers to one defendant who denied the Real Presence because God was in heaven and was not so stupid as to put himself into the hands of a man like the priest! (Contreras, *Santo oficio,* 666).

host made of dough.[22]   Gabriel García Jiménez publicly stated that those heretics who did not believe in the Real Presence of God in the host might be right.[23] The view that God's mightiness could not be imprisoned inside a piece of bread was an expression of simple popular logic or what Henry Kamen has called 'the common heritage of popular reason'.[24] It owed nothing to the Lutheran notion of the sacrament as a sacred memory of the Last Supper; instead, more radically, it merely treated the host as a material object. It is interesting to note that the significance of the mass could also be distorted by idiosyncratic interpretations rather than being rejected outright. Juan Berdejo, for example, maintained that since Our Lord was in heaven, he did not descend to the consecrated host, but instead sent an angel on his behalf. God's power was present there in the same way as when a captain general brings an order from the king.[25] Thus, rather than denying the Christian mystery of the mass, this defendant adapted it according to his own logic.

The two elements relating to the Virgin Mary which provoked unorthodox utterances were Parthenogenesis (her virginity before, during and after the birth of Christ) and Immaculate Conception (her status as the first human being to lack the stain of original sin). Popular logic found it hard to accept that Christ was conceived without the intervention of a human male.[26] Julián Martínez Conejero assured fellow villagers, on the authority of what he had read in a book, that the Virgin had not been able to conceive without sexual union.[27] Francisco Engidaso García insisted that the Moors were right to dispute the Virgin birth, which he ridiculed, asking 'have you seen any woman who remained a virgin after giving birth?'[28] Whereas Mary's virginity provoked outright scepticism, her Immaculate Conception generated idiosyncratic notions.[29] Marcos García understood that the Virgin was conceived without

---

[22] See, for example, Leg 441, Exp 6190, Cristóbal de Mesa (Priego, 1633).

[23] Leg 444, Exp 6223, Gabriel García Jiménez (Alcogulaje, 1634).

[24] See Kamen, *Phoenix,* 90-91.

[25] Leg 381, Exp 5408, Juan Berdejo (Iniesta, 1613).

[26] Similarly, many Galician peasants found it easier to accept that Christ had been born and died to redeem our sins than that Mary could remain a virgin after giving birth. See Contreras, *Santo oficio,* 671.

[27] Leg 471, Exp 6438, Julián Martínez Conejero (Roda, 1647).

[28] Leg 596, Exp 7210, Francisco Engidaso García (Vara de Rey, 1737), fols. 44-51 and 60.

[29] The expression of deviant notions regarding the Immaculate Conception should be seen in the context of the growing controversy over the doctrine in the seventeenth century. In 1622, an interdiction issued by Pope Gregory XV forbade expression in public or in private of any opinion contrary to the Immaculate Conception. Great effort was expended in Spain to ensure respect for the doctrine, though it remained the object of fierce dispute and the cause of serious dissension among theologians. The public importance attributed to the doctrine, and the significance attached to the Marian cult in general, which, in Spain, assumed dimensions unknown elsewhere, may have provoked a reaction amongst ordinary people. See Henry

original sin, but deduced that for this reason she must have been the offspring, not of St Anne and St Joachim - even though they were her parents - but of God. He also held several other idiosyncratic interpretations of doctrine: that Christ and the Virgin had no relatives in the world, that Christ was not a descendant of Adam and Eve, that he partook of no earthly nature, that he had not died as God but only as a man and that he did not suffer in any way.[30] Clearly this defendant was not afraid to impose his own authority on normative doctrine.

The notion of resurrection and the existence of hell were also subjected to popular criticism and even derision. Marcos de Meca questioned how men could be resurrected in their bodies if they had been dead for more than four hundred years and eaten by fish.[31] Isabel María Vicente Sánchez y Martínez ridiculed the resurrection of the flesh on grounds of logic: how could dust and ashes be reconstituted into human form? How could those who were in hell be resurrected if they had already been judged, and those in heaven if they were already in glory?[32] The defendant Juan de Montoya Ponce de León who dismissed hell as a device used by preachers to terrify people into behaving as they wished was by no means uncommon.[33] Here, popular reason often found difficulty in reconciling the concept of 'God's justice' with condemnation. The defendant Ana María de Irupita, who refused to believe that God could do such a terrible thing as to condemn so many men, betrayed a not uncommon suspicion that divine justice was unfair or unreasonable and seems to have reflected an implicit but not fully articulated yearning for God's mercy to outweigh his justice.[34]

Rejection of traditional concepts of hell and the afterlife may indicate materialism rather than scepticism. The materialist espouses the view that matter is all there is, and excludes the existence of entities that are different

---

Kamen, *Spain in the Later Seventeenth Century 1665-1700* (London and New York: Longman, 1980), 292; Dedieu, *L'Administration,* 247-248; Bartolomé Bennassar, *The Spanish Character: Attitudes and Mentalities from the Sixteenth to the Nineteenth Century,* trans. Benjamin Keen (Berkeley: University of California Press, 1979), 76-77, 85 and 89.

[30] Leg 443, Exp 6209, Marcos García (San Clemente, 1633).

[31] Leg 420, Exp 5886, Marcos de Meca (San Clemente, 1626).

[32] Leg 599, Exp 7231, Isabel María Vicente Sánchez y Martínez (Albarracín, 1743), fols 4-5, 81, 85^v and 119.

[33] Leg 423, Exp 5934, Juan de Montoya Ponce de León (Belmonte, 1627). For further examples, see Leg 385, Exp 5480, Miguel del Moral (Buendia, 1614); Leg 385, Exp 5468, Miguel Ropero (Buendia, 1614); Leg 385, Exp 5469, Miguel Serrano (Buendia, 1614); Leg 390, Exp 5546, Francisco López Llorente (La Osa, 1616).

[34] Leg 552, Exp 6920, Ana María de Irupita (Valdeolivas, 1692).

from and superior to the matter of our ordinary experience.[35] One of the most common manifestations was the popular saying 'you won't see me do badly in this life nor suffer for it in the next' (no me verás en este mundo malpasar que en el otro no me verás malpenar), a phrase which enjoyed common currency in seventeenth-century Spain (although it appeared relatively infrequently among Conquense defendants).[36] Another common expression of the same sentiment was that 'there was nothing more to life than to be born and to die'.[37] Defendant Pedro de Torres voiced a prevalent opinion when he declared that there was no final judgement except death itself.[38] For these individuals, natural and human happenings were explicable at their own level without directly invoking the intervening agency of God; hence, matters of doctrine were an irrelevance and provoked disinterest or indifference rather than the hostility or aggression which often characterized the sceptic. Although some of these remarks were clearly uttered in anger or frustration and probably reveal a devil-may-care rhetoric rather than a genuine philosophical materialism, others seem to have been voiced in the context of serious and thoughtful debate on religious issues. Expressions of materialism were certainly far less frequent than expressions of scepticism (at least among inquisitorial cases) but their very existence does seem to demonstrate that an alternative philosophical understanding of life to the dominant norm was quite feasible, implying, contrary to Febvre, that some individuals were able to step outside the religious culture of their time.

Defendants in trials for propositions often showed considerable independence of thought, a flair for speculation, and great assurance and force in the exposition of their views. Some courted controversy by their passion for debate and argument for its own sake. The miller, Andrés de Sepúlveda, explained that it was not uncommon for students, ecclesiastics and professional men to meet at his house and enjoy intelligent conversation. On one occasion, a doctor present at the discussion said that the skill of arguing required that good students should defend what was not so and argue, for example, that his house was not his house but someone else's, or, since there is a God, defend the proposition that there was not. Another version related that Sepúlveda himself said that a good student would not espouse the same views as everybody else but, as an exercise, should endeavour to prove the opposite of what other people said and, as an

---

[35] M. Eliade (ed.), *The Encyclopedia of Religions*, 16 vols (New York: Macmillan, 1987), IX, 279.

[36] See, for example, Leg 412, Exp 5793, Jusep de Pastrana (Budia, 1624). The saying was frequent in other regions of Spain (Contreras, *Santo oficio*, 672).

[37] See, for example, Leg 427, Exp 6010, Bartolomé Cruz (Palomares, 1628); Leg 412, Exp 5794, Fernando Roldan, 1624.

[38] Leg 411, Exp 5767, Pedro de Torres (Sisante, 1624).

example, argue that there was no God. According to Sepúlveda, the accusation that he said he could prove that there was no God was a distortion of this innocent conversation, an account which was confirmed by the local sacristan. His taste for public speculation about doctrine provoked further trouble for him when he doubted aloud whether God could save a man who was predestined to go to hell. He attempted to legitimate his utterance by referring to a story he had heard from the sacristan, in which a religious, failing to reduce a sinner to the service of God, implored an image of Christ for help in saving the man's soul, only to receive the answer that he should take heart because, try as he might, he would not be able to save a man who was predestined to go to hell. Sepúlveda claimed that he had done nothing more than repeat this story recounted by the sacristan.[39]

The field-labourer Julián de Anguita not only told his fellow villagers that he did not believe in all the words of the Creed but also engaged a local priest in discussion about the reference in this prayer to Christ's sufferings at the hands of Pontius Pilate. Anguita wanted to know if Christ suffered of his own volition in order to redeem us rather than because Pilate and the Jews were more powerful than he. The priest assured him that God could have freed himself if he had wished but his death was necessary for the sake of our redemption. Anguita was apparently satisfied and acknowledged that the Jews did not have the power to kill Christ. He also argued with local priests about the fate of the souls of infidel Moors and Jews. Although the clerics reminded him of the Christian truth that all those who died unbaptized went to hell, he found difficulty in believing that God would condemn so many of the souls that he created every day, and was convinced that, except for those who took their own lives, there must be some hope of salvation. The mercy of God was so great that, as long as a man recognized God at his death and begged for pardon for his sins, then He would grant forgiveness, even to an infidel. As for tithes, he argued that payment was not mandatory since it did not figure among the Lord's Commandments, but had been introduced by the Church in the self-interest of clerics who did not have the right to impose it. The power of the Church to demand tithes and to decree Christ's law should be believed only if it could be demonstrated. Furthermore, there was no obligation to believe the law of Christ since this would be an infringement of free will.

Anguita was sufficiently bold to be prepared initially to defend his propositions before the inquisitors, but under the pressure of interrogation, he abandoned his personal readings and deferred to his interrogators. At first he insisted that since God was merciful and omnipotent, He could if He wished save any Moor or Jew who recognized the Lord as his God, regretted having

---

[39] Leg 538, Exp 6820, Andrés de Sepúlveda (El Picazo, 1671).

offended Him and asked His forgiveness. However, when pressed to answer clearly if he believed that the unbaptized could be saved, he said that he believed that Moors and Jews who were not baptized could not be saved. Similarly, he assured the inquisitors that despite his initial doubts, he believed in the Church's interpretation of the Creed, and that he knew full well that one could not believe what one wished with regard to the Christian religion, but that it was obligatory to believe in God and the teachings of the Church.[40]

The utterances of some defendants combined scepticism with imaginative idiosyncrasy in a way which defies any real attempt to separate them. After all, scepticism about an element of doctrine is not necessarily incompatible with belief in a wider sense. It is possible to deny the virginity of the Mother of God or the resurrection of Christ while still accepting the existence of these personages and their significance in every other sense to the Christian faith. Scepticism, then, by this definition, need not be total; as Thomas MacPherson emphasizes, in order to be able to describe someone as a sceptic it does not seem necessary to require that he should see no sense or truth in any part whatever of religious belief.[41] For this reason, the same individual may evince both lack of belief (scepticism) and distortion of belief (idiosyncrasy). Tailor Alonso Gómez, for example, maintained that he did not believe in God or heaven; then again, on other occasions, he asserted that God did exist but he was a Moor and Christ was simply another prophet, who had not been God before being Christ. On the other hand, there was no other God, nor king nor sacrament than Gómez himself. When apprehended and on his way to the tribunal, he told witnesses that there was no need to fear since God was passing by; when asked if he believed in God he said 'do not believe in God, believe in me.' The image of Christ was nothing more than a bit of wood which there was no need to revere, and the Holy Trinity did not exist. On the one hand, he rejected the host as a bit of bread; on the other, he maintained that the form of Christ was represented or imprinted there. Still, he refused to kneel for the holy sacrament since more than once he had seen the devil enter the host during mass. He was also known to have ridiculed the words of consecration on many occasions. When he was taken prisoner, he repeated the words and mimicked the actions of the priest; according to the prosecution, the purpose of this was to make people think he was deranged and thus escape punishment.

The idiosyncratic notions which he defended with most vehemence concerned the Virgin Mary. His own logic led him to conclude that since the Mother of God was not born a Christian, she must have been a Moor. When he was told

---

[40] Leg 522, Exp 6740, Julián de Anguita (Uña, 1662), fols 40, 43, 63-64^v, 66-67^v, 68^v-70, 72^v-73^v, 76^v, 81-88^v, 96^v-97.

[41] See Thomas McPherson, *Philosophy and Religious Belief* (London: Hutchinson, 1974), 115.

that the Virgin did not need to be a Christian since her conception was Immaculate and without sin, he replied that she like any other had to be brought up in her parents' faith. Asked how long he had believed erroneously that the Virgin was a Moor, he insisted that it was not an error, he had been told it by his parents who were good Christians, he had believed it all his life and he would defend what he believed. He explained that before Christ and St John baptized each other, there was no baptism; it followed that if the Virgin was born before baptism existed, she must have been a Moor. Another idiosyncratic belief which he sought to defend was that the Virgin had cursed those who had killed her son. After all, would not any father or mother curse those who treated their son unjustly? He was convinced that he had learned this idea from Christian doctrine, in particular the gospel of St John. Unable to refer the inquisitors to chapter and verse, he took refuge in his conviction that it was a matter of faith to believe that, if his son was killed, he would curse those who mistreated him. His idiosyncrasy derived from a sense of empathy with the Mother of God as parent and his trust in his own instinct rather than normative doctrine.

Gómez showed quite exceptional stubborness in defence of yet another idiosyncrasy: the Parthenogenesis which he attributed to the Virgin's mother St Anne. He was convinced that the Immaculate Conception of Mary was not the fruit of sexual union, but came about when an angel embraced St Anne, who remained a virgin after giving birth. St Joachim had no role in the conception of Our Lady because he was impotent. Gómez had believed this story ever since he learned his doctrine as a child from his parents and the Jesuits, and declared that he would believe it until the end of the world. The inquisitors told him that he was mistaken, that Mary was the natural child of St Joachim and St Anne, and that this had nothing to do with her Immaculate Conception, a prerogative granted by God in his omnipotence to his own mother. Not to be deterred, Gómez repeated that the Virgin was conceived without sexual union, that St Joachim was impotent and God alone was responsible for the conception and that St Anne remained a Virgin after giving birth. He was reminded that his remarks were contrary to the teachings of the Church and that he had made an error and strayed from the path of his salvation, convincing himself that it was true doctrine. He replied that he had thought about it hard ever since he was old enough to reason, and he knew that, since the sexual act was the source of original sin, there could have been no carnal intercourse in the conception of the Virgin or else it would not have been Immaculate. He was told that he did not know what he was talking about. The conception of the Virgin could still be Immaculate even though it involved sexual union. Gómez simply repeated his conviction to the contrary and, no doubt exasperated, his interrogators left the issue to one side and turned to other questions.

When interrogated again on this matter at a subsequent hearing, he was prepared to make concessions to the inquisitors but made it clear that he had not been convinced. He claimed that he had not previously been aware that the Church taught that Our Lady was the natural child of St Joachim as a result of carnal intercourse, but that he now believed the Church's teachings. When reminded that he had been informed of true doctrine in previous sessions, he answered simply that he was a good Christian. Asked why he had said that the Virgin was not conceived by sexual union, he answered that, since God had allowed Christ his son to be conceived by the Holy Spirit without the sexual act, he could also have allowed his mother to be conceived in the same fashion (a statement which seems to echo the inquisitor's remark in the earlier hearing about God granting the prerogative of Immaculate Conception to his mother). He confirmed that he now believed what the Church taught. Asked what it was that the Church taught, he would not say any more. Asked if he believed that Christ alone, and no other person, was conceived by the Holy Spirit, he said that if it had been proven, and if he was told that he must believe it, what else should he do but believe it? He had learned his doctrine from the Jesuits and had heard the sacristan of the church in Guadix tell him that the Virgin had been conceived without the sexual act when St Joachim embraced St Anne. But, if it was now proven that this was not true, then he believed it to be proven. Told to answer directly, either affirmatively or negatively, he said that if it was proven that St Anne was not a virgin when she gave birth and that Our Lady was conceived by sexual union, then it would be true and he would believe it, but that he did not know if it was proven or not. Asked in what manner it could be proved, he said how did he know, and that he had nothing else to say. He then added defiantly that if the Church had something to tell him which would help to remove his doubts he wanted to know, but that otherwise he had nothing else to say except that it was necessary to know what the Church's proof was. He was told that the Church's guide was the Holy Spirit, and that its head was the Pope and that what he decreed in matters of faith and doctrine was the infallible truth and must be believed by every faithful Christian; the Church needed no other proof and he had erred in asking for it. He said that he believed whatever was proven and whatever the Church said. In reality, his position had moved little since he had been arrested and had insisted that he would defend what he said 'now and for a hundred years'. In this respect, Gómez was relatively unusual since other defendants conformed more readily to the discourse of the inquisitors.

It is clear that the inquisitors were not sure what to make of Gómez. Despite the fact that his resistance on the question of the Immaculate Conception showed a clear ability to reason and sustain a logical argument, his answers seemed to the inquisitors quite demented and expert opinions were sought on his state of mind. One doctor concluded that, even though he exhibited reasoning powers, his utterances invariably became confused and ended in nonsense. When he was insulted, he never became angry but just laughed. Another noted that when told to perform a certain action, no sooner had he begun than he forgot what it was. A Franciscan and a Dominican friar who observed him also came to similar conclusions: in conversation he lacked the power of reason, became confused and misunderstood what was said to him. They were agreed that his ravings should not be taken seriously. However, quite a different picture was painted by the Dominican Fray Gaspar del Valle who was asked to visit the accused in prison shortly after he was arrested and to discuss religious questions with him. On the basis of an hour's conversation with the defendant, he concluded that there were no signs of madness since, on matters other than the faith, he spoke rationally and logically, with humility and respect. His errors regarding doctrine had probably been inherited since he always repeated and adamantly defended identical nonsense every time. There is every reason to trust this man's judgement, since the observation took place before the inquisitorial hearings, whereas those who concluded that he was deranged only came into contact with him after he had given his testimony. Remembering the prosecutor's opinion that the accused pretended to be mad when he was apprehended in the hope that he might be released, it is quite feasible that, once he realized the trouble he was in, he was able to feign madness in order to escape the consequences of his unorthodoxy. Indeed, if he did employ this strategy, it worked because his case was suspended, he was expelled from Cuenca and ordered not to return on pain of two hundred lashes.[42]

If defendants such as Gómez took pleasure in their ability to question and subvert Christian authority, others were caused considerable soul-searching and anxiety by doubts regarding the faith. These were defendants who, rather than mocking normative doctrine, or aggressively asserting their own interpretations, yearned to be convinced but found their convictions rooted in shifting sands. In 1609, Francisco de Marcilla, a twenty-three-year-old student of Latin, laid before the inquisitors some extraordinary doubts about the Catholic faith which had troubled him over a period of four years and which revealed that there was scarcely an area of Christian doctrine which had remained immune from his enquiring mind. After many hours of anxious deliberation, he had become convinced that Christ was not the true God. Was it not possible, after all, that the miracles which had been attributed to Jesus had not taken place? Or, alternatively, might they not have been performed by him even if he had not been God? Where matters were so considerably open to doubt, it seemed best to believe what could be demonstrated by natural law. Thus, it was surely

---

[42] Leg 523, Exp 6742, Alonso Gómez (Campo de Criptana, 1662).

sufficient to believe simply in the One True God and to follow the precept 'do unto others', without being obliged to believe as a matter of faith in all the other articles and precepts of the Church. Contemplation of the existence of so many religious sects had set him on this track of thought. Since all these people were clearly in error, was it not also possible that he too was misguided in the Catholic faith that he professed? Might not even the Pope and other ecclesiastics err in matters of faith? Indeed, this seemed quite likely since they were men like others and enjoyed free will. Reading the condemnations issued by the Council of Trent against certain heresies, he wondered - although he was not certain - whether the Council had been mistaken and its opponents had been right. It seemed debatable, for example, that one could never know that one had reached a state of grace. After all, if one did one's best in life, then one did one's duty by God, and hence God would grant one his grace; and it seemed to him that one should be able to know if one had done one's best.

The relationship between Man and God perplexed him considerably. To what extent could Man exercise his free will and to what extent was God the true instigator of all Man's deeds? After all, if it was conceded that Man could decide for himself in part - a necessary corollary of free will - should it not also be assumed that he could decide for himself *in toto*? If so, then things occurred without the need to posit the existence of a prime mover. But, conversely, if a prime mover was necessary for contingencies not influenced by Man, then surely he must also be necessary for Man's doings. In the end, he came to suspect that, if Man truly did enjoy free will to choose one course of action over another, then God did not know what Man intended to do at any moment.

As regards Man's salvation, his speculations led him to propose 'religious universalism'. He wondered whether each person might not be saved in the religion that he professed, considering that it would be rather harsh for all Moors to be condemned - or all Christians for that matter - supposing that there was only one true religion. At other times, he doubted whether there were such things as salvation and condemnation; perhaps there was no more to life than to be born and to die like irrational animals. This much, he felt, could be perceived by the use of natural reason. He even speculated on several occasions that if it was Nature that produced us, then possibly God did not exist at all.[43]

Marcilla's readiness to articulate a position which showed a remarkably cool detachment from the religious cosmovision of his day should surely lead us seriously to question Febvre's assurance that at this time the non-existence of God was inconceivable. It is highly significant that Marcilla's views were not propounded in moments of anger or frustration, but rather originated in dispassionate reflection. His incipient materialism, for example, was the product

---

[43] Leg 380, Exp 5393, Francisco de Marcilla (Villanueva de la Jara, 1609-1612).

not of a devil-may-care rhetoric but of sustained logic and reasoning. Even more significantly, his gnawing, philosophical doubts were directly related to his detailed knowledge of Christian doctrine; such an ambitious questioning of so many areas of authority could only emerge from thorough exposure to the precepts of the faith. It may come as no surprise, then, that the inquisitors' attempt to resolve his doubts by requiring him to attend further instruction in doctrine seems to have been to no avail; in fact, Marcilla appeared a second time before the tribunal in 1611, plagued by the same doubts. The inquisitors' leniency with him on the first occasion was repeated. Just as in 1609 he had been permitted to forswear his offence in secret, without formal sentence on condition that he receive instruction in doctrine, so in 1611 he was again absolved and entrusted to the care of a priest to instruct him in the faith. Once again this condition was to remain a secret in order to protect his good name. Clearly the extra instruction after his first appearance had not borne fruit. The more he knew, it seems, the more he was plagued by doubt.[44]

---

[44] The sort of religious doubt exhibited by Marcilla should, of course, be distinguished from the religious scepticism to which reference has been made above. Here I follow Geddes MacGregor and define doubt as 'vacillation, perplexity, irresolution'. See Geddes MacGregor, 'Doubt and Belief', in Eliade, *Encyclopedia*, IV, 425. The word doubt derives from the Latin *dubito*, related to *duo*, two; to doubt means, therefore, 'to be of two minds, to stand at the crossroads of the mind', a definition which epitomizes Marcilla's predicament. The crucial distinction between doubt and scepticism is that, whereas belief in any of the doctrines of religion is incompatible with scepticism about those doctrines, it is not incompatible with doubts about them. We can be both committed to a belief and at the same time sometimes doubt it. To be committed and yet to have doubts is not the same as not to be committed at all and it is this lack of commitment which characterizes the sceptic. Doubt, therefore, is not to be equated with unbelief, but rather with a vacillation between the two opposites, unbelief and belief. Thomas McPherson agrees that what we believe is balanced by what we doubt; reasons for doubting take their place together with reasons for believing. See McPherson, *Philosophy*, 18, 20, 21 and 115. See also Edwards, 'Religious Faith and Doubt'. Edwards takes the view that there is no necessary contradiction between faith and doubt; the faithful *and* doubting experience of late medieval Sorians seems not contradictory but comprehensible. See John Edwards, 'Reply to John Somerville', *Past and Present*, 128 (1990), 155-161, 160. For a discussion of different positions on the relation between faith and doubt, see, for example, M. Jaime Ferreira, *Doubt and the Religious Commitment: The Role of the Will in Newman's Thought* (Oxford: Clarendon Press, 1980), 2-5. It follows, then, that doubt is the complement of belief. This has important implications for the relation between doubt and faith. If, as MacGregor asserts, doubt and belief are as inseparable from each other as arteries and veins in the human body, then doubt, far from being antithetical or alien, is in fact an intrinsic part of faith. Indeed, insofar as faith rises beyond the doubt that is at the same time its necessary presupposition, all authentic religious faith is, in MacGregor's words, 'a descant on doubt' (MacGregor, 'Doubt and Belief', 424-425). Manifestations of religious doubt in the seventeenth century, an age of pervasive religious faith, might not, then, be quite the aberration they appear to be.

The leniency of the tribunal, though worthy of note (to what extent did the inquisitors hereby implicitly acknowledge the legitimacy of such doubts as an inherent part of religious faith?), is not entirely surprising. In the eyes of the inquisitors, Marcilla's doubts were not heretical; nor, for that matter, were the forms of religious scepticism and idiosyncrasy exhibited by the other defendants examined above. Although they were prosecuted by the Inquisition, all these defendants remained ordinary members of the Catholic faithful.[45] Indeed, it is important to recognize that they were typical products of post-Tridentine education and 'indoctrination'. Under interrogation, all proved knowledgeable about the basics of Christian doctrine. Marcilla's doubts originated in a very detailed understanding of the Church's teachings. Gómez knew that the Holy Trinity consisted of Father, the Son and the Holy Spirit, three separate persons and One True God. Sepúlveda was aware that heaven was the abode of God, the angels and the saints and the destination for saved souls. He understood from the Creed, the articles of faith and the catechism that hell was inhabited by devils and the souls of men who died in mortal sin, and that its sufferings were for all time. He knew too that millers would go to hell if they did not perform their job honestly. These defendants' idiosyncratic deviance derived from the free rein they had given to their imaginations. Anguita admitted that nobody had taught him his interpretation of the words in the Creed, but that he had simply thought of it himself; his idea that Moors and Jews could be saved without baptism had also been generated spontaneously in his imagination; and his notion that free will was 'the will that everyone had to do what they wished' was an idea that 'just popped out of his head'. Similarly, Gómez said that his idea that Christ asked his mother who his father had been just popped into his head. The fact that these unorthodox statements did not originate in ignorance

---

[45] These forms of religious deviance should be clearly differentiated from formal heresy. First, whereas heresy was a self-conscious break from the Church, the aberrations and idiosycrasies of these defendants were often unconscious; frequently they did not realize that they had distorted normative doctrines. There was no intention to break with the Church as an institution. Indeed, the very willingness to introduce deviant elements into the faith suggests a fundamental acceptance of that faith. Second, many of these defendants did not so much dispute Christian authority as attempt to supersede it, or arrogate it to themselves. Often they suffered from an excess of, rather than a lack of, religious zeal. Their principal error was that by engaging in their own interpretation of religious phenomena, they attributed greater significance to their personal experiences and intuitions than to official doctrine. Finally, this form of religious deviance was characteristic of large numbers of the Old Christian population, whereas the number of heretics was very small. If the prosecuting counsel described the utterances of offenders in the language of heresy (for example, by comparing them to Arians, Hussites or Lutherans), this was little more than 'a juridical artifice', since technically heresy was the only offence that the Holy Office could punish, cf. Jean-Pierre Dedieu, 'The Inquisition and Popular Culture in New Castile' in Haliczer (ed.), *Inquisition and Society*, 129-145, especially 131.

of doctrine, but, on the contrary, derived from considerably more than rudimentary knowledge has considerable implications in assessing the impact of the Tridentine programme.

Although it is impossible to assess what proportion of the population in general experienced and gave expression to these phenomena, it is clear from the considerable attention devoted to them by the Inquisition that they were not the preserve of a minority and were less marginal than has been supposed. As the figures in the Appendix show, investigations of cases of blasphemy and propositions (not all of which necessarily led to trials) were the principal occupation of the tribunal in the seventeenth century and first half of the eighteenth century. These offences generated more inquisitorial activity than any other in the periods 1610-1650, 1670-1680 and 1740-1750, and constituted the second most important area of activity after Judaizers in the periods 1650-1670 and 1710-1720, and offences committed by clerics in the periods 1680-1710 and 1730-1740. Only in 1720-1730 did they drop into third place. To the evidence of relative weight may be added relative share. These offences constituted nearly 50% of all the business of the Conquense tribunal in the 1610s, as much as 40% in the 1620s and about 30% in the 1630s and 1730s-1740s. They accounted for more than 25% in the 1640s, 1670s and 1700s, and between 15% and 20% in the 1680s and 1690s. The fall-off in their share in the 1650s-1660s (down to approximately 10%) and 1710s-1720s (around the 10-15% mark) coincided with intense activity against *conversos* which left little time for lesser offences. If the period 1610-1750 is taken as a whole, these offences constituted on average about a quarter of the activity of the Conquense tribunal (ahead of Judaizers at about 23% and clerics at about 21%) and thus accounted for more business than any other offence. If the category were extended to include all offences of the word, then the figure would be even higher, since it would take in the fornicators and many of the clerics, whose offences were usually verbal and included blasphemy and propositions.[46] Furthermore, Cuenca was not atypical of the Peninsula. Propositions accounted for about 24% of the total activity of the Zaragoza tribunal in the period 1615-1700 (with superstitions a close second at 22%) and 22% of the entire total of

---

[46] Apart from during the 1610s (and to a lesser extent in the 1620s and 30s), activity against propositions regarding fornication (that sexual relations between two unmarried consenting adults was not a sin) and estates (that the estate of marriage was superior to that of celibacy) never formed a substantial part of business in the seventeenth and eighteenth centuries (the peak of activity was in the 1560s-1580s). Persecution of clerics was the third (and sometimes the second) most important category from the 1610s to the 1670s. In the 1680s, 1690s, 1700s and 1730s, it became easily the most important. In the 1740s, it was the second most important but was not considerably below first position. The drop in the 1710s and 1720s (like that of propositions) was due to the anti-*converso* flurry.

business conducted by the Spanish Inquisition as a whole (including Sicily, Sardinia and America but excluding Cuenca and Madrid) in the same period, again ahead of any another offence (Judaism was the second with about 18%).[47] If the period is extended to the century and a half between between 1540 and 1700, propositions still led with about 27% of all activity in the Spanish Inquisition as a whole (followed by Muslim practices at about 24%, and Judaizers a distant third at about 10%). The data bank provided by Contreras and Henningsen show that propositions formed a considerable proportion of the total business of all tribunals, especially in Castile where they were the principal activity in every tribunal in this period except Cordoba and Murcia.[48]

Although it can be demonstrated that these offences were a principal occupation of the tribunal, it is much more difficult to assess how typical they were of the Old Christian population at large. One approach is to determine how representative inquisitorial defendants were of the general population. Most historians agree that inquisitorial sources offer a complete cross-section of Spanish society.[49] Certainly Conquense defendants were representative of the

---

[47] Toledo, on the other hand, followed a different pattern. Propositions were the second most important offence in the period 1615-1700 (about 19% of activity) after Judaizers (about 44% of activity); the gap was considerable. See J.-P. Dedieu, 'Los cuatro tiempos de la inquisición' in Bartolomé Bennassar, *Inquisición española: poder político y control social* (Barcelona: Editorial crítica, 1981), 15-39, 31. Elsewhere, Dedieu suggests - if I have interpreted him correctly - a share of about 18% for propositions in the period 1621-1700 (in second place after Judaism at 46.5%) and about 21.5% for propositions in the period 1701-1820 (suntil in second place after Judaism at about 29.5%). These figures represent a considerable decrease by comparison with 1561-1620 when propositions accounted for about 45% of business, a long way ahead of the second most important, Muslim practices, on about 13%. Even so, over the longer period 1540-1700, propositions generated by far the greatest number of cases. See Dedieu, *L'Administration*, 240.

[48] Jaime Contreras and Gustav Henningsen, 'Forty-Four Thousand Cases of the Spanish Inquisition (1540-1700): Analysis of a Historical Data Bank' in Henningsen and Tedeschi (eds), *The Inquisition,* 100-129, especially 114.

[49] On the cross-section of Spanish society, see Dedieu, 'The Archives of the Holy Office of Toledo as a Source for Historical Anthropology' in Henningsen and Tedeschi (eds), *The Inquisition,* 158-189, especially 161. Sánchez Ortega observed that the victims of an inquisitorial trial represented more closely the average Spaniard than did those of lay tribunals. See María Helena Sánchez Ortega, *La mujer y la sexualidad en el antiguo régimen: La perspectiva inquisitorial* (Madrid: Akal, 1992), 20. Nalle showed that Conquense defendants were representative of the general population. More than two-thirds of the Conquenses interrogated by the tribunal between 1570 and 1610 about their knowledge of doctrine were artisans, farmers, field hands or shepherds, while only small fractions were noble or practised a profession. There was a small but not pronounced urban bias: half of the defendants came from towns of 500 households or larger at a time when one-third of the diocese's inhabitants lived in towns of that size. It is true, however, that women were greatly under-represented. See Sara T. Nalle, 'Literacy and Culture in Early Modern Castile', *Past*

population in most respects, including social class, occupation, and age range.[50]
It would certainly be wrong to assume that these defendants, simply because
they were victims of the Inquisition, were somehow exceptional. As Ginzburg
noted for Menocchio, their distinctiveness had very definite limits.[51] Of course,
the fact that they were representative does not by itself prove how typical their
particular offences were but it is clear, at least, that these defendants were not
especially unusual in any sense.

It might be thought that these defendants were exceptional insofar as some of
them claimed to have derived their ideas from books, but in reality the access of
the *pueblo llano* to printed matter should not be underestimated. Modern
research has shown that literacy levels among the mass of the population in
Golden Age Spain were high, book ownership was relatively common, and
there was considerable popular consumption of devotional literature. Using the
Conquense inquisitorial records, Nalle has demonstrated that levels of literacy
during the sixteenth and seventeenth centuries were much higher than scholars
previously estimated. Rates, for males at least, compared favourably to
northern European ones, and showed no great divergence between rural and
urban defendants. By the seventeenth century, over half the male inhabitants of
the cities of Madrid, Avila, Toledo and Cuenca were literate and the ability to
read was not unusual in villages.[52] Not only were literacy rates high but book-

---

and Present, 125 (1989), 65-95, especially 73 and 49; see also Nalle, *God in La Mancha*, 118-
121.

[50] Among the defendants in trials for blasphemy and propositions examined for this survey,
the largest group, as would be expected, was made up of farmers and agricultural workers
(about 30%), who constituted the largest social group in Conquense society. Among the
others, a great variety of professional activities were represented, including millers, bakers,
tailors, cobblers and bootmakers, locksmiths, blacksmiths, innkeepers, woolcarders and
woolcombers, soldiers, healers, doctors, lawyers, students, servants, builders, scribes, town
officials, vagabonds and one or two living off private means. The age range varied from
twenty to seventy years old, with a fairly even distribution among those in their twenties,
thirties, forties and fifties (about 16-18% in each group), and far fewer over the age of sixty
(less than 10%; the remaining percentage is accounted for by those whose age is unknown).
This distribution of professions and age groups suggests that the defendants were
representative of the population in general. Only distribution regarding gender reveals a
disproportionate bias in favour of men (90%), confirming a distortion already noted by Dedieu
and Nalle.

[51] Ginzburg, *The Cheese and the Worms*, xx-xxi.

[52] Whereas in 1540-1600, 41% of urban males and 34% of rural males were literate, in
1600-1660, the corresponding figures were 66% and 50% respectively. The figures for male
defendants brought before the tribunal of Toledo were even higher. See Sara T. Nalle,
'Popular Religion in Cuenca on the Eve of the Catholic Reformation' in Stephen Haliczer
(ed.), *Inquisition and Society in Early Modern Europe* (London and Sydney: Croom Helm,
1987), 67-87, 84 n.3; Nalle, 'Literacy and Culture', 66-69; Nalle, *God in La Mancha*, xvi;
Kamen, *Phoenix*, 347-348.

ownership was by no means rare. One person out of every eight interviewed by the Conquense Inquisition in the period between 1570 and 1610 owned printed matter, and over half of these were farmers, artisans and field hands.[53] It is clear, then, that significant sections of the rural population did have access to books.

Nalle has also shown that one of the most important uses of popular literacy was to facilitate private religious devotion. The best-selling authors of the Golden Age were, after all, religious writers such as Fray Luis de Granada and Antonio de Guevara. Furthermore, inventories of bookshops in the sixteenth century reveal that a substantial percentage of stock was given over to cheaply priced devotional works, an indication that there was a mass market for this form of literature. This is borne out by the fact that as many as 67% of Conquense defendants interviewed between 1570 and 1610 owned books which could be defined as 'ecclesiastical' or 'devotional'.[54] This keen interest in religious matters and thirst for religious printed material provides an important backdrop to the personal interpretation of doctrine.

At the same time, the expression of religious idiosyncrasy did not rely exclusively or even primarily on printed material, and independent thought was possible without access to the printed word. The sermons and preaching to which the *pueblo llano* were exposed, and the everyday gossip in houses and village squares, were the primary source of information for inhabitants of principally an oral culture.[55] Paradoxically, the mass Christianization programme imposed by the post-Tridentine Church in the second half of the sixteenth century unwittingly contributed to religious scepticism and idiosyncrasy. Although the Church's efforts were designed to impose doctrinal uniformity, in fact more systematic acquisition of a minimum theological knowledge furnished a greater pool of material with which to weave personal interpretations.[56] We know that there was a substantial improvement in the ability of Spaniards in New Castile to memorize what the Church now defined as a requisite minimum: the basic Catholic catechism, the fundamental prayers of the Church (Pater Noster, Ave María, Credo and Salve Regina) and the

---

[53] Nalle, 'Literacy and Culture', 77.

[54] See Nalle, 'Literacy and Culture', 80-85 and 91-92. On 'best-sellers', see K. Whinnom, 'The Problem of the "Best-Seller" in Spanish Golden-Age Literature', *Bulletin of Hispanic Studies,* 57 (1980), 189-198.

[55] For the oral transmission of religious culture, see, for example, Augustin Redondo, 'La Religion populaire espagnole au XVI siècle: un terrain d'affrontement?' in Coloquio Hispano-Francés, *Culturas populares: Diferencias, divergencias, conflictos* (Madrid: Casa Velázquez, 1986), 334.

[56] Here I differ from Nalle who suggests that access to religious material universally promoted a common belief system. See Nalle, *God in La Mancha*, xvi.

Lord's Commandments. Data collected by Dedieu reveals a major
transformation in the ability of male defendants in Toledo (women were not
represented in his sample) to satisfy these basic requirements of the Church. In
brief, the number of defendants who were able to recite the basic prayers
correctly nearly doubled (rising from 40% to 75%) between the 1550s and the
1570s, and success rates increased further in the seventeenth century.[57] Nalle
found a similar improvement in knowledge of the basic prayers among
Conquense defendants in the same period; the number of those who knew the
prayers by heart doubled between the period 1544-1567 and 1568-1579 (rising
from one third to two thirds), and even these high levels were surpassed in the
period 1610-1661. As for agriculturalists, whereas in the period 1564-1580,
60% of farmers and 30% of fieldworkers could recite their prayers correctly, in
the period 1581-1600, the corresponding figures for correct recitation of
catechism were 88% and 60% respectively.[58] Both Dedieu and Nalle
recognized that, since inquisitorial prisoners were not among those who had
best learned Church doctrine, it is probable that the success rate was even
higher for the population as a whole. Dedieu went so far as to assert that a true
process of Christianization of the mass of the population took place in the
Archbishopric of Toledo during the second half of the sixteenth century, while
Nalle felt that for the first time in the history of the Church, the majority of lay
men and women in the region of Cuenca became practising Catholics.

It is all the more significant, then, that expressions of popular scepticism and
idiosyncrasy, far from being eliminated, continued in the seventeenth century.
The content of the utterances of seventeenth-century defendants has only to be
compared with that of sixteenth-century defendants, such as Conquense
Bartolomé Sánchez, to appreciate the essential continuity and the failure of the
Church offensive to make inroads in this area.[59] The most notable difference
between Sánchez and his seventeenth-century counterparts lay not so much in

---

[57] See Dedieu, 'Christianization in New Castile', 2-6, 15-18 and 22; and Dedieu,
L'Administration, 51-52.

[58] See Nalle, *God in La Mancha*, 118-23, 127, 131-32 and 210; and Nalle, 'Popular
Religion in Cuenca', 86, n.36.

[59] Bartolomé Sánchez, tried by the Conquense tribunal in 1553-1554, formulated his own
ideas about doctrine which he proudly maintained sprang from his imagination inspired by
divine grace. For him, the Eucharist was 'no more than flour and water mixed together', of
which Christ formed no part, the cross was just a post, the Pope was a villain and papal
indulgences did nothing to get souls out of purgatory. He would only confess his sins to God,
refused to baptize his children, and declared that the Christian faith was the worst of the three
religions of the book. He dismissed images of the Virgin and saints as idols and worshipped
only the Trinity of God Father, Son and Mother! He even claimed to be the Messiah Elijah,
come to enact the justice of God for those whom the Inquisition had killed without cause. See
Nalle, 'Popular Religion in Cuenca', 71-72, 74-76, 82.

the content of utterances as in the attitude towards the tribunal. The manner in which Sánchez gleefully instructed the inquisitor in his own personal theology was unknown in the seventeenth century. Even the headstrong Alonso Gómez confined himself to evasiveness and a stubborn refusal to disavow his ideas. Where Sánchez confronted the inquisitor head on, Gómez measured carefully what he said. Defiant pride in swimming in the margins of faith, so characteristic of Sánchez or Menocchio, was absent among seventeenth-century defendants. Insofar as these offenders understood and chose to avoid the dangers of being labelled a heretic, the Inquisition had succeeded in making its definition of heterodoxy understood. However, to make this definition respected, and, what is more, respected beyond the doors of the tribunal, was another matter entirely. These defendants bowed to inquisitorial authority when in its presence, but many expressed open contempt for the tribunal when its reach seemed distant. A not inconsiderable number were reported to have said that they did not care if they were denounced to the Holy Office since they did not fear it and were sure they would be released without punishment if they claimed they had been drunk. Clearly the tribunal's objective, conceived in the second half of the sixteenth century, that everyone should begin to censor himself for obscenities that he had uttered and for thoughts that passed through his mind had not been achieved.[60] Neither fear of the Inquisition nor Tridentine indoctrination was enough to repress expressions of scepticism or idiosyncrasy.

To some extent, the attitude of the Inquisition towards these offences contributed. Its efforts to instil higher standards of morality among Christians were concentrated on suppressing the widespread beliefs that sexual relations outside marriage were not a sin and that the married state was superior to celibacy. Although the sharp decline in prosecutions for these offences in the seventeenth century might be interpreted as a sign of the success of the Church's campaign, it is more probable that the tribunal succeeded only in making people realize that extra-marital sex was considered sinful and hence refrain from publicly defending it. It is much harder to show that the population actually interiorized the clerical definition (especially regarding sex with

---

[60] Regarding the inquisitorial goal of self-censorship to be exercised by Old Christians, see Contreras and Henningsen, 'Forty-Four Thousand Cases', 123. The authors attribute the marked reduction in the number of cases heard by the Inquisition after 1614 (e.g. from 15,000 cases for minor offences in 1560-1614 to 9000 in 1614-1700) principally to institutional ageing but also, in part, to the success of the post-Tridentine campaign against Old Christians, although they recognize that the latter is difficult to document. The cases of expression of religious scepticism and idiosyncrasy suggest that, in this area at least, the campaign had limited success.

prostitutes) or that they modified their behaviour.[61] A similar campaign against
blasphemies and propositions in the later sixteenth century seems to have had
little influence on people's actual behaviour; indeed, the cases considered here
indicate that defendants were either unaware that their ideas were unorthodox
or that, where they were aware, they were not afraid to boast of them openly.
Furthermore, despite being condemned as sinful, propositions were rarely
punished severely enough to modify deeply ingrained behaviour. Although
banishment from one's place of residence was indeed a severe punishment, it
was only imposed on the most serious or unrepentant offenders; even recidivists
like Sepúlveda received relatively light sentences. Alonso Gómez, who may
have feigned insanity, was simply expelled from Cuenca, which was not in any
case his native town or place of residence. Although four years' banishment
was imposed on Anguita, the sentence was later commuted to two years after
he appealed on the grounds of his age, which he was able to exaggerate with
impunity. Most offenders were simply reprehended, or absolved on account of
their gross ignorance, rustic background or feeble mental capacity. Since their
offences did not constitute formal heresy, none of these defendants was ever
obliged to abjure *de vehementi* (the abjuration reserved for the gravest
offences).

But the persistence of religious scepticism and idiosyncrasy cannot be
attributed simply to the failings of the Inquisition as an institution. There were
deeper factors at work. The transformation of popular faith in the second half
of the sixteenth century had its limits, as Dedieu points out, since it was founded
upon mechanical repetition of formulae which must have remained obscure.
Emphasis on mere repetition - designed to simplify doctrine so that it was within
the capabilities of the humblest peasant to master - both postponed genuine
understanding and precluded learning through discussion and debate.[62] In their
houses and the public square, in gossip and conversation, the *pueblo llano*
engaged in the dialogue in doctrine denied to them by official channels. Thus,
by insisting on greater dissemination of simplified doctrine, the post-Tridentine
Church furnished the material for idiosyncratic readings while at the same time
failing to secure deference to the normative version. Indeed, the very attempt to

---

[61] See Nalle, *God in La Mancha*, 64-69; and Dedieu, 'The Inquisition and Popular
Culture', 139. Contreras points out that the diminishing severity of the tribunal with regard
to fornicators in the seventeenth century should not be taken to indicate that the attempted
reform of sexual customs produced the desired result in Galicia. See Contreras, *Santo oficio*,
564-565.

[62] The aim of the rote learning was to give preachers and confessors a foundation on which
to build by commenting upon doctrine and rendering it explicit, for example, through sermons
and confessions. The point was to oblige people to recognize that the clergy alone held the
key to the sacred. See Dedieu, *L'Administration*, 51-52.

exert greater efforts to set limits to the diversity of religious culture may have provoked a more fervent search for individualism in doctrine.[63] It is interesting that it was precisely those notions which the Church tried hardest to impose that were most contested by the population. If the aim of the Counter-Reformation was to 'turn collective Christians into individual ones', then it may come as no surprise that religious idiosyncrasy flourished.[64] Spanish religious life had always been characterized by a search for personal spirituality which created a tension between authority and interiority.[65] It is possible that the Counter-Reformation offensive simply made this conflict more acute.

The persistence of expressions of religious unbelief demonstrate that the objective of the Catholic Reformation - 'the gradual enforcing over an entire society of a clerical definition of what was permissible or not' - was not achieved by the Church's indoctrination programme.[66] Indeed, far from eroding unbelief or creating greater religious uniformity, increased familiarization with doctrine may have simply encouraged idiosyncratic variations on themes devised by Christian authority. Dissemination of normative doctrine did not enslave recipients to the ideological constructs of the dominant and people were not coerced into abandoning the construction of their own meanings.[67] As Ginzburg has observed, 'culture offers to the individual a horizon of latent possibilities - a flexible and invisible cage in which he can exercise his own conditional liberty'.[68] Seventeenth-century Conquense defendants exercised their imagination across this horizon in ways that were not marginal but central to their religious experience.

---

[63] For the limits to diversity of religious culture, see Anne J. Cruz and Mary Elizabeth Perry (eds), *Culture and Control in Counter-Reformation Spain*, Hispanic Issues, 7 (Minneapolis: University of Minnesota Press), ix.

[64] See J. Bossy, 'The Counter-Reformation and the People of Catholic Europe', *Past and Present*, 62 (1970).

[65] Nalle, *God in La Mancha*, 208.

[66] For this definition of the aims of the Counter-Reformation, see Chartier, 'Culture as Appropriation', 232.

[67] See Rostas and Droogers (eds), *The Popular Use of Popular Religion in Latin America*, 5 and 10.

[68] Ginzburg, *The Cheese and the Worms*, xx-xxi.

Appendix

Activity of the Conquense tribunal, expressed as percentages for each offence according to decade; the figures represent cases investigated by the tribunal, not all of which led to trials. The source for the figures for cases is Dimas Pérez Ramírez, *Catálogo del archivo de la Inquisición de Cuenca* (Madrid: Fundación Universitaria Española, 1982).

decade	P	J	M	L	A	B	F	S	H	C	V
1610	47	9	4	<1	<1	3	9	5	4	9	8
1620	41	17	<1	0	<1	<1	5	8	4	15	7
1630	31	15	<1	<1	1	<1	6	9	5	17	14
1640	28	10	<1	<1	1	1	2	14	9	15	19
1650	9	64	<1	<1	0	1	<1	5	5	5	9
1660	12	58	0	0	0	1	<1	5	4	9	10
1670	28	20	0	0	0	8	2	15	3	16	8
1680	17	12	0	0	0	4	1	13	3	41	9
1690	19	19	0	0	0	1	0	15	1	39	6
1700	26	11	1	1	0	6	0	9	5	34	8
1710	15	30	5	5	0	11	0	10	11	12	6
1720	11	51	<1	<1	<1	2	<1	7	1	21	5
1730	29	3	0	0	0	8	2	11	5	36	6
1740	32	2	0	0	0	4	2	22	1	28	9

Key

P   Propositions/Blasphemy/Incredulidad (*pueblo llano* only)
J   Judaizers
M   Mohammedanism, i.e. Muslim practices
L   Lutheranism/ Calvinism
A   *Alumbrados*, Iluminados, visionarios
B   Bigamy
F   Fornication, Estates
S   Superstition, Sorcery, Witchcraft, Astrology
H   Acts against the Holy Office
C   Offences committed by clerics (priests, friars, nuns and other religious), including solicitation, blasphemy, propositions, errors in sermons and superstition
V   Various, miscellaneous

The system of classification is based on that of Henningsen and Contreras, who distinguished ten main groups, reflecting the inquisitors' own categories.[69] The only alterations I have made have been to separate fornication/estates from the category of propositions in order to focus more clearly on the latter, and to widen the category of 'solicitation' to 'clerics' and thus take in other offences committed by both secular and religious clerics including blasphemy and propositions. In this way, it is easier to analyse the relative weight of those propositions and blasphemies committed by the *pueblo llano*.

Figures have been rounded up or down to avoid fractions of percentages which suggest a misleading level of accuracy. It is important to remember that the figures can only provide a rough picture and can never be definitively accurate since the total of inquisitorial business is an unknown quantity. Figures of less than one percent have been recorded as <1.

---

[69] See Contreras and Henningsen, 'Forty-Four Thousand Cases'.

Bibliography

Bennassar, Bartolomé, *The Spanish Character: Attitudes and Mentalities from the Sixteenth to the Nineteenth Century*, trans. Benjamin Keen (Berkeley: University of California Press, 1979)

Berman, David, 'The Repressive Denials of Atheism in Britain in the Seventeenth and Eighteenth Centuries', *Proceedings of the Royal Irish Academy*, 82C (1982), 211-245

Blázquez Miguel, Juan, *Madrid: Judíos, herejes y brujas. El Tribunal de Corte (1650-1820)* (Toledo: Arcano, 1990)

Bossy, J., 'The Counter-Reformation and the People of Catholic Europe', *Past and Present*, 62 (1970).

Caro Baroja, Julio, *Las formas complejas de la vida religiosa: Religión, sociedad y carácter en la España de los siglos XVI y XVII* (Madrid: Akal, 1978)

----------, *De la superstición al ateísmo: Meditaciones antropológicas* (Madrid: Taurus, 1974)

Chartier, Roger, 'Culture as Appropriation: Popular Cultural Uses in Early Modern France' in Steven L. Kaplan (ed.), *Understanding Popular Culture: Europe from the Middle Ages to the Nineteenth Century* (New York: Mouton Publishers, 1984), 229-253

Christian, William A., Jr., *Local Religion in Sixteenth-Century Spain* (Princeton: Princeton University Press, 1981)

Contreras, Jaime, *El santo oficio de la inquisición de Galicia: Poder, sociedad y cultura* (Madrid: Akal, 1982)

-----------, and Gustav Henningsen, 'Forty-Four Thousand Cases of the Spanish Inquisition (1540-1700): Analysis of a Historical Data Bank' in Gustav Henningsen and John Tedeschi (eds), *The Inquisition in Early Modern Europe: Studies on Sources and Methods* (Illinois: Northern Illinois University Press, 1986), 100-129

Cruz, Anne J. and Mary Elizabeth Perry (eds), *Culture and Control in Counter-Reformation Spain*, Hispanic Issues, 7 (Minneapolis: University of Minnesota Press)

Davis, Natalie Zemon, *Society and Culture in Early Modern France* (London, Duckworth, 1975)

Dedieu, Jean-Pierre, *L'Administration de la Foi: L'Inquisition de Tolède (16-18 siècle)*, Bibliothèque de la Casa de Velázquez, vol. 7 (Madrid: Casa de Velázquez, 1989)

----------, 'Classer des causes de foi: Quelques réflexions' in *L'Inquisizione Romana in Italia nell'età moderna: Archivi, problemi di metodo e nuove ricerche* (Rome: Ministero per i beni culturali e ambientali, 1991)

----------, 'Los cuatro tiempos de la Inquisición' in Bartolomé. Bennassar, *Inquisición española: poder político y control social* (Barcelona: Editorial Crítica, 1981), 15-39

----------, 'Christianization in New Castile. Catechism, Communion, Mass, and Confirmation in the Toledo Archbishopric, 1540-1650' in Anne J. Cruz and Mary Elizabeth Perry (eds), *Culture and Control in Counter-Reformation Spain,* Hispanic Issues, 7 (Minneapolis: University of Minneapolis Press, 1992), 1-24

----------, 'The Inquisition and Popular Culture in New Castile' in Stephen Haliczer (ed.), *Inquisition and Society in Early Modern Europe* (London and Sydney: Croom Helm, 1987), 129-145

----------, 'The Archives of the Holy Office of Toledo as a Source for Historical Anthropology' in Gustav Henningsen and John Tedeschi (eds), *The Inquisition in Early Modern Europe: Studies on Sources and Methods* (Illinois: Northern Illinois University Press, 1986), 158-189

Edwards, John, 'The Priest, the Layman and the Historian: Religion in Early Modern Europe', *European History Quarterly,* 17 (1987), 87-93

----------, 'Religious Faith and Doubt in Late Medieval Spain: Soria circa 1450-1500', *Past and Present,* 120 (1988), 3-25

----------, 'Reply to John Somerville', *Past and Present,* 128 (1990), 155-161

Eliade, M. (ed.), *The Encyclopedia of Religions,* 16 vols (New York: Macmillan, 1987)

Febvre, Lucien, *The Problem of Unbelief in the Sixteenth Century: The Religion of Rabelais,* trans. Beatrice Gottlieb (Cambridge, Mass.: Harvard, 1982)

Ferreira, M. Jaime, *Doubt and the Religious Commitment: The Role of the Will in Newman's Thought* (Oxford: Clarendon Press, 1980), 2-5

Flynn, Maureen, 'Blasphemy and the Play of Anger in Sixteenth-Century Spain', *Past and Present,* 149 (1995), 29-56

Ginzburg, Carlo, *The Cheese and the Worms: The Cosmos of a Sixteenth-Century Miller,* trans. John and Anne Tedeschi (London: Routledge, 1980)

----------, 'The Dovecote has Opened its Eyes: Popular Conspiracy in Seventeenth-Century Italy'. in Gustav Henningsen and John Tedeschi (eds), *The Inquisition in Early Modern Europe: Studies on Sources and Methods* (Illinois: Northern Illinois University Press, 1986), 191-195

Greyerz, Kaspar von (ed.), *Religion and Society in Early Modern Europe 1500-1800* (London: German Historical Institute, 1984)

Hunter, Michael, 'The Problem of "Atheism" in Early Modern England', *Transactions of the Royal Historical Society,* Fifth Series, 35 (1985), 135-157

Kamen, Henry, *Spain in the Later Seventeenth Century 1665-1700* (London and New York: Longman, 1980)

----------, *The Phoenix and the Flame: Catalonia and the Counter-Reformation* (New Haven and London: Yale University Press, 1993)

McPherson, Thomas, *Philosophy and Religious Belief* (London: Hutchinson, 1974)

Monter, William, *Frontiers of Heresy: The Spanish Inquisition from the Basque Lands to Sicily* (Cambridge: Cambridge University Press, 1990)

Muchembled, Robert, *Popular Culture and Elite Culture in France 1400-1750* (London: Louisana State University Press, 1985)

Nalle, Sara T., *God in La Mancha: Religious Reform and the People of Cuenca 1500-1650* (Baltimore and London: John Hopkins University Press, 1992)

----------, 'Literacy and Culture in Early Modern Castile', *Past and Present,* 125 (1989), 65-95

----------, 'Popular Religion in Cuenca on the Eve of the Catholic Reformation' in Stephen Haliczer (ed.), *Inquisition and Society in Early Modern Europe* (London and Sydney: Croom Helm, 1987), 67-87

Pérez Ramírez, Dimas, *Catálogo del archivo de la Inquisición de Cuenca* (Madrid: Fundación Universitaria Española, 1982)

Redondo, Augustin, 'La Religion populaire espagnole au XVI siècle: Un terrain d'affrontement?' in Coloquio Hispano-Francés, *Culturas populares: Diferencias, divergencias, conflictos* (Madrid: Casa Velázquez, 1986)

Rostas, Susanna and André Droogers (eds), *The Popular Use of Popular Religion in Latin America* (Amsterdam: Popular Uses, 1993)

Scribner, Bob, 'Is a History of Popular Culture Possible?', *History of European Ideas,* 10:2 (1989), 175-191

Sánchez Ortega, María Helena, *La mujer y la sexualidad en el antiguo régimen. La perspectiva inquisitorial* (Madrid: Akal, 1992)

Whinnom, K., 'The Problem of the "Best-Seller" in Spanish Golden-Age Literature', *Bulletin of Hispanic Studies,* 57 (1980), 189-198

Part III

Cross-Cultural Awareness

7

The Religious Background of the Sephardic Ballad

Hilary Pomeroy

Whilst the purpose of my paper is to discuss the treatment of religion, or to be more precise the 'tres leyes', in the *romancero sefardí*, I must point out that the survival of the Sephardic ballad owes much to those very forces of *fervor y fanatismo*.

However complex and varied the reasons for the expulsion of the Jews from Spain, the wording of the expulsion edict is couched in terms of religious fanaticism.[1] It is translated into English by Edwards as follows:

> a great danger to Christians has clearly emerged, this having followed, and still continuing, from the activity, conversation [and] communication which [these Christians] have maintained with Jews. [These Jews] demonstrate that they always work, by whatever ways and means they can, to subvert and remove faithful Christians from our holy Catholic faith, to separate them from it, and attract and pervert [them] to their wicked belief and opinion.[2]

The Catholic Monarchs are thus compelled 'to throw the said Jews out of our kingdoms'. The edict continues:

---

[1] The original passages of the 1492 Castilian expulsion edict quoted are as follows: 'Consta e pareçe el gran dueño que a los christianos se a seguido e sigue de la participaçión, conbersaçion, comunicaçion que han tenido e tienen con los judios, los quales se prueban que procuran siempre por quantas bias e maneras pueden subvertir e subtraer de nuestra santa fee catolica a los fieles christianos e los apartar della e atraer e perbertir a su dañada crençia [sic] e opinion, ynstruyendolos en las çeremonias e observançias de su ley[...]. E asi mismo damos liçençia e facultad a los dichos judios e judias que pueden sacar fuera de todos los dichos nuestros reinos e señorios sus bienes e haziendas por mar e por tierra con tanto que no saquen oro ni plata ni moneda amonedada ni las otras cosas vedadas por las leyes de nuestros reynos'. See Luis Suárez Fernández, *Documentos acerca de la expulsión de los judíos* (Valladolid: CSIC, 1964), 392, 394.

[2] John Edwards (ed.), *The Jews in Western Europe 1400-1600*, Manchester Medieval Sources (Manchester: Manchester University Press, 1995), 49-50.

> Also we give licence and faculty to the said Jews and Jewesses to take their
> goods and property out of all our said kingdoms and lordships, by sea and by
> land, provided that they do not take out gold and silver or minted coins, or the
> other things forbidden [for export] by the laws of our kingdom.

Luis Suárez Fernández has emphasised this financial hardship imposed upon the
community by the terms of the edict:

> Naturalmente las dificultades para la venta de casa y heredades fueron muy
> grandes porque, con un excedente brusco en la oferta y un plazo fijo y sin
> prórroga, los cristianos presionaban a los judíos haciendo buenos negocios y
> pagando cantidades ridículas por bienes cuantiosos (50-51).

The graphic eyewitness account written by the chronicler Andrés Bernáldez
describes the hardships of the journey into exile and reiterates that the only
alternative for the Jews was conversion:

> Salieron de las tierras de sus nacimientos chicos y grandes, viejos y niños, a pie
> y caballeros en asnos y otras bestias y en carretas, y continuaron sus viajes
> cada uno a los puertos que habían de ir; e iban por los caminos y campos por
> donde iban, con muchos trabajos y fortunas, unos cayendo, otros levantando,
> otros muriendo, otros naciendo, otros enfermando, que no había cristiano que
> no hubiese dolor de ellos, y siempre por do iban los convidaban al baptismo, y
> algunos con la cuita se convertían y quedaban, pero muy pocos, y los rabíes los
> iban esforzando y hacían cantar a las mujeres y mancebos y tañer panderos y
> adufos para alegrar la gente, y así salieron de Castilla (Suárez Fernández, 57).

This description is significant in that it tells us that the Jewish exiles, divested of
many of their financial assets, took with them invisible assets. These were the
culture and language of Spain. Whilst it is possible that they sang psalms or
other liturgical songs, it is not impossible that we have here a first reference to
the Jews taking their heritage of Spanish ballads into exile, particularly as this is
a song tradition associated with women.

Over the decades, Spanish became a means of identifying Sephardic Jews,
distinguishing them from other groups such as the Romaniot Jews already living
in Turkey and Greece. The Spanish ballads became the most popular
manifestation of Sephardic culture. In Israel, to this day, elderly Sephardic
women meet together to sing *romansas*. In so doing, unlike the Jews of the late
fifteenth and sixteenth centuries, they are not evoking some sentimental
attachment to Spain, but rather recalling the countries of their youth, Greece,
Turkey or Bulgaria. Over the centuries, the Sephardic ballad has become the

symbol, not of the Spain from which the Jews were exiled, but of Spain's replacement, the countries of the Sephardic diaspora.

Among the reasons for the survival of the Spanish language and culture amongst the Sephardim, we must include the religious and political structure of the Ottoman Empire and of North Africa. In the Ottoman Empire, the millet system granted ethnic minorities 'religious and cultural freedom, as well as considerable administative, fiscal, and legal autonomy under their own ecclesiastical and lay leaders'.[3] The Jewish refugees from Spain were thus allowed to form their own separate communities and permitted to speak Spanish. These Sephardic Jews continued to sing Spanish ballads long after they had fallen out of favour in Spain. It is thanks to the descendants of those expelled Jews that many Spanish ballads have survived into the twentieth century to be collected and transcribed.

The Spanish, subsequently the Sephardic, ballad proved to be an ideal form of entertainment in a religious milieu. The ballad is sung unaccompanied. It was therfore an especially appropriate form of entertainment on the Sabbath and Holy Days, when it is forbidden to play a musical instrument. Furthermore, every Sabbath morning, the Jewish community would listen to an extract of the Pentateuch sung in Synagogue. On many occasions, the contents of those Sabbath portions resembled the thematic categories into which Spanish ballads have been divided.[4] These categories include ballads about prisoners and captives, faithful love, unhappy love, the adulteress, rape and abduction, incest; themes often present in the Pentateuch. This familiarity with sung narrative, both in the Synagogue and at home, reinforced the popularity and survival of the Sephardic ballad.

As Samuel G. Armistead has pointed out: 'The Sephardic ballad corpus, in its two quite different branches - in the eastern Mediterranean communities and in North Africa - is surely one of the most conservative, if not the most conservative, of all the Hispanic subtraditions. It has indeed preserved a great number of medieval ballad types that are known nowhere else in oral tradition today' (Armistead, 3). The background, then, of the major body of the Sephardic corpus is that of medieval Christian Spain with its frontier wars between Christian and Moor. Guarinos, the Spanish admiral, is captured during such fighting:

---

[3] Avigdor Levy, *The Sephardim in the Ottoman Empire* (Princetown, New Jersey: Darwin Press, 1992), 42.

[4] Samuel G. Armistead, *El romancero judeo-español en el archivo Menéndez Pidal: Catálogo-índice de romances y canciones,* 3 vols (Madrid: Cátedra-Seminario Menéndez Pidal, 1978).

> cuando moros y cristianos   salían a guerreare
>
> (*El cautiverio de Guarinos*, 1.2),

as is don Bueso's sister:

> guerrean los moros   por campos de oliva
>
> (*Don Bueso y su hermana*, 1.2).[5]

Two possible fates awaited captives such as Guarinos and don Bueso's sister: conversion or slavery. According to Bel Bravo: 'en el reino musulmán de Granada no había tolerancia para el cristianismo y sí, en cambio, grandes facilidades para abrazar la fe musulmana'.[6] The Moorish king offers Guarinos vineyards, wealth and his sister to be Guarino's wife, as rewards for converting to Islam:

> Olvida la ley de Cristo,   la de morito tomare (1.10).

The Moorish woman in *Melchior y Laurencia* falls in love with Melchior. She urges him to convert and marry her:

> que te volvas a mi ley,   de Mahoma tu profeta (1.24).[7]

Similarly, the Moorish woman in *Leonisio de Salamanca* demands of her Christian captive: 'Reñega de D--s, reñega (1.20)' (Bénichou, 274).

In *El alcaide de Alhama*, conversion is to Christianity. The ballad is related from the point of view of the Moorish commander who laments his losses:

> [...] yo perdí mi honra y fama,
> perdí hijos y mujer,   las glorias que bien amaba (1.6-7).

Worst of all, his beloved daughter, 'la flor de Granada', has been carried off by the Spanish forces. The commander's attempts to pay his daughter's ransom have failed and he is left to mourn the physical and spiritual loss:

> La respuesta que me dieron,   que se volvió cristiana (1.10).

---

[5] Unless otherwise stated, quotations are taken from the Halia Isaac Cohen manuscript collection of ballads from Tangier which I am transcribing and editing for my doctoral thesis.

[6] María Antonia Bel Bravo (ed.), *Diáspora sefardí*, Colección Sefarad (Madrid: Mapfre, 1992), 20.

[7] Paul Bénichou, *Romancero judeo-español de Marruecos*, La lupa y el escalpelo (Madrid: Castalia, 1968), 272.

Conversion is not the fate that awaits don Bueso's sister. During the Middle Ages, as the historian Charles Verlinden has stated: 'Christianity confronted Islam, and the adherents of the two religions reduced each other to slavery'.[8] Usually, such slaves were given domestic tasks. Don Bueso's sister is made to carry bread to the ovens and to do the royal washing:

> Mandadla, señora, con el pan al horno[...]
> Mandadla, señora, a lavar al río (l.10, 14).

In *Las hermanas reina y cautiva,* the Moorish queen asks for a Christian slave:

> La reina cherifa mora, la que mora en Almería,
> dice que tiene deseo de una cristiana cautiva (l.1-2).

Conde Flores's wife is therefore abducted and made to become 'una esclaba en la cosina'. The captured Christian of *El cautivo del renegado* endures a harsh regime as a slave, forced to wear chains and a bit. In this moving ballad, the Christian and the Moor's wife fall in love. This selfless woman encourages the Christian to leave her and escape

> Siempre ella me decía; -Cristiano, vete a tu tierra [...]
> Vale más tu libertad, que amor en tierra ajena (l.14, 17).

A curious feature of the Sephardic ballad is the absence of Jews as individuals (other than in the few biblical ballads which mainly date from pre-expulsion times). The very rare ballad, *La expulsión de los judíos de Portugal*, exists exclusively in the Sephardic tradition. Historical fact has here become confused. The King (presumably of Portugal, for his country is not specified) has married his daughter to the king of Castile. Christians, Moors and Jews set out to greet their new queen:

> y saliéronme a encontrar tres leyes a maravilla (l.7).

Each of these 'leyes' is described with reference to its most salient characteristics:

> los cristianos con sus cruses, los moros a la turquilla,
> los judíos con sus leyes (l.8-9).

---

[8] Charles Verlinden, 'Slavery, Slave Trade' in Joseph R. Strayer (ed.), *Dictionary of the Middle Ages*, 13 vols (New York: Charles Scribener's Sons, 1988), XI, 334-340, 338.

The Christians carry their crosses, the Moors dress in their exotic fashion, and the Jews carry their scrolls of the law. In a unique reference to the expulsion of the Jews from Spain, the new queen declares that she will rid the country of Jews:

> En la siudad de mi padre,   no hubo judío ni judía.
> Y ahora, si D--s me ayuda,   lo mismo haré en las mías (l.10-11).

Halia Isaac Cohen's text ends here, but that in Menéndez Pidal's 1929 *Catálogo del romancero judío-español*, goes on to describe the Jews' departure from Portugal:

> Ya sacan á los judíos,   los sacan de la judería,
> de ellos se iban por mar,   de ellos por tierra iban.[9]

Surviving versions of the ballad deteriorate at this point, concluding with the queen falling dead or her headdress falling off.

There are two other Sephardic ballads where the three religions are grouped together. In *La buena hija*, now known only in the Moroccan tradition, the girl ask her father, the Cid, why he is upset:

> si te han hecho mal los moros,   les mandaré yo a matare,
> si os han hecho mal cristianos   les mandaré a cautivare,
> y os han hecho mal judíos   les mandaré a desterrare (l.5-7).

The reply in Halia's version is:

> no me ha hecho mal ninguno,   nadie a mí me ha hecho male (l.8).

Bénichou's text, however, reveals Jewish sympathies:

> —Ni me han hecho mal los moros,   ni los mandes a matare;
> ni me han hecho mal quistianos,   ni los mandes a cativare;
> ni me han hecho mal judíos,   gente es que mal no hazen (Bénichou, 180, l.7-9).

The Halia Isaac Cohen text of *Moriana y Galván* is equally discreet:

> Si te han hecho mal los moros,   les mandaré yo a matare,
> si te han hecho mal cristianos,   les mandaré yo a cautivare,
> si te han hecho mal judíos,   les mandaré a desterrare.

---

[9] Ramón Menéndez Pidal, 'Catálogo del romancero judío-español', *Cultura española* (Madrid: Imprenta ibérica, 1929), IV, 1045-1077; V, 161-199; see IV, 1064.

—No me ha hecho ma[l] ninguno,   nadie a mí me a hecho male (l.16-19).

The response in Larrea (78-81) is more detailed and, once again, expresses sympathy with the Jewish community:

—Ni me han hecho mal los moros,
ni los mandes tú matare;
ni me han hecho mal cristiano,
ni los mande a cautivare;
ni me han hecho mal judíos,
gente son que mal no hacen.

(Larrea, 81)

If we compare this with the sixteenth-century Spanish text, it will be seen that 'judíos' are not mentioned in the early text:

si os enojaron mis moros   luego los hare matare
o si las vuestras donzellas   hare las bien castigare
y si pesar los Christianos   yo los yre a conquistare [...]
No me enojaron los moros   ni los mandeys vos matare
ni menos las mis donzellas   por mi reciban pesare
ni tampoco los Christianos   cumple de los conquistase (l.15-17; 20-22).[10]

Not only do Sephardic ballads have few references to Jews, but references to Christianity are actually retained. As Armistead and Silverman have pointed out, the heroes and heroines are Christian.[11] The cultural background is Christian:

El Romancero hispánico, a pesar de los que hayan elegido cultivarlo, tenía su origen en la poesía heroica medieval de los castellanos militantemente cristianos[...]. Los protagonistas patricios de los romances sefardíes [...] están concebidos como miembros de aquella nobleza cristiana que había logrado la supremacia política y cultural a finales del medioevo (Armistead and Silverman, 145-146).

---

[10] Antonio Rodríguez-Moñino and Daniel Devoto (eds), *Flor de enamorados* (Barcelona, 1562) (Valencia: Castalia, 1954).

[11] Samuel Armistead & Joseph H. Silverman, *En torno al romancero sefardí: Hispanismo y balcanismo de la tradición judeo-española* (Madrid: Seminario Menéndez Pidal, 1982), 127-148.

In addition, their adventures and misfortunes take place in a setting that is unmistakably Christian. There are numerous references to the Church, as the following examples show:

> A las puertas del perdón,   a misa entrara
>
> > (*Aliarda enamorada en misa*, 1.2)

> ya le entierran en la iglesia,   la noche le sonaría
>
> > (*La muerte del duque de Gandía*, 1.18)

> la infanta como lo supo,   tiróse de su altar[...]
> a él le entierran en la iglesia,   y a ella en el campo real
>
> > (*El conde Niño*, 1.16, 18)

There are also references to the clergy.   These have an occasional ironic undertone.   Of Virgilio's wife it is said:

> Hija era del obispo,   sobrina del Señor rey (1.4).

An irreverent note is also sounded in various versions of *La bella en misa*.   So beautiful is the woman entering the church that the priest forgets his words:

> Ella entrando a la misa,
> la misa s'arrelumbró,
> el papás qu'está meldando,
> de meldar ya se quedó.
> -Melda, melda, el papasico,
> que por tí no vengo yo (1.29-34).

The beauty goes on to say that if her lover will not marry her:

> Tomaré al Papa de Roma (1.41).[12]

The confessor features in several ballads, such as *El pájaro verde:*

> que llamen a confesor,   como de buena cristiana (1.35).

He is summoned in *Raquel lastimosa*, a ballad sung at Sephardic weddings, despite its theme of adultery:

---

[12] Moshe Attías, *Romancero sefardí: Romanzas y cantes populares en judeo-español*, 2nd edn (Jerusalem: *Ben Zvi Institute*, 1961), 14.

No la mates de repente,   llámala al confesador.-
Con un criado de casa   por el confesor mandó
Acabó de confesarla,   allí muerta la dejó (l.16-18).

Events take place on saints' days, notably on the 'mañanita de San Juan'. Guarinos, for example, is captured on this day:

Mañanita era, mañana,   mañanita de San Juane,
cuando moros y cristianos   salían a guerreare.
(El cautiverio de Guarinos, l.1-2)

The unfortunate count Niño chooses this day to sing his magic song:

Levantóse el conde Niño,   mañanita de Sanjuane.
(El conde Niño, l.1)

Another inauspicious day is Easter Monday. It is on Easter Monday that Don Bueso's sister is abducted by the Moors:

Lunes era, lunes,   de Pascua florida.
Guerrean los moros,   por campos de oliva (l.1-2).

All these allusions to the Christian background of Spain, to churches, mass, priests, nuns, friars, Popes, saints' days, wars between Christian and Moor, exist at background level. There does exist, at the same time and possibly within the same text, a deliberate removal of certain Christian elements. This process is referred to by Bénichou as 'dechristianisation' (286-290). Here, Christian elements are deliberately removed when they might appear to compromise the personal beliefs of the singer. In *Leonisio de Salamanca*, the opening line has been deliberately changed from:

En el nombre de Jesús   y su madre soberana,
(Bénichou, 275)

to:

En el nombre dilo tú   y su madre soberana.
(Bénichou, 274)

In most versions of *La vuelta del marido*, the wife states that she will become a nun, as will her daughters:

> Si a los catorse no viene,   monja yo me quedaré (1.15).

whilst in others, this reference is removed:

> Si a los catorce él no vino,   yo nunca me vo casar (1.6).[13]

   The pennant in Menéndez Pidal's synthetic version of *Vos labraré un pendón* is described thus:

> de un cabo pondré la luna   y del otro pondré el sol,
> del otro santa María,   del otro san Salvador.

(Menéndez Pidal, 190)

The saints are removed in Moroccan versions:

> A un lado pondré la luna   y al otro el ojo del sol,
> De las estrellas menudas,   os las pondré yo alrededor (1.12-13)

   The Sephardic ballad contains very few features that are specifically Jewish. I have already mentioned the deliberate and sympathetic inclusion of Jews as a group in *Moriana y Galván* and *La buena hija*. Hebrew words are occasionally used to denote religious institutions. There is very occasional use of the 'euphemistic third person' to distance misfortune from the speaker. The abductor, in *El raptor pordiosero*, explains that he is blind, using the third person to distance his affliction from both the singer and the audience:

> —No le topeš culpa,   qu'él allá es siego— (1.12).[14]

The unfortunate captive, in *Las hermanas reina y cautiva*, reluctantly accepts the keys to the 'despensa':

> Ya las tomara, señora,   por la gran desdicha suya.
> Que ayer condesa y marquesa   hoy esclaba en la cosina (1.16-17).

   So, to what extent has fervour and fanaticism kept the *romancero sefardí* alive? The religious fanaticism that caused the expulsion to take place transported the custodians of the Spanish ballad to countries where those exiles were able, in their isolation, to maintain this tradition. Their survival was further encouraged by the fact that the form of the ballad fitted in with the religious practice of the Jews. What greater irony than that the Spanish ballad,

---

[13] Cf. my unedited version, recorded in Belgium in 1994.

[14] Cf. my unedited version, recorded in Istambul in 1993.

with its Christian protagonists and Christian background, has been preserved most faithfully by the Sephardic Jews, living in Moslem countries?

Bibliography

Armistead, Samuel G., *El romancero judeo-español en el archivo Menéndez Pidal: Catálogo-índice de romances y canciones,* 3 vols (Madrid: Cátedra-Seminario Menéndez Pidal, 1978)

---------- & Joseph H. Silverman, *En torno al romancero sefardí: Hispanismo y balcanismo de la tradición judeo-española* (Madrid: Seminario Menéndez Pidal, 1982)

---------- with the collaboration of Oro Anahory Librowicz, *Romances judeo-españoles de Tanger: Recogidos por Zarita Nahón* (Madrid: Cátedra-Seminario Menéndez Pidal, 1977)

Attías, Moshe, *Romancero sefardí: romanzas y cantes populares en judeo-español,* 2nd edn (Jerusalem: *Ben Zvi Institute,* 1961)

Bel Bravo, María Antonia (ed.), *Diáspora sefardí,* Colección Sefarad (Madrid: Mapfre, 1992)

Bénichou, Paul, *Romancero judeo-español de Marruecos,* La lupa y el escalpelo (Madrid: Castalia, 1968)

Edwards, John (ed.), *The Jews in Western Europe 1400-1600,* Manchester Medieval Sources (Manchester: Manchester University Press, 1995)

Larrea Palacín, Arcadio, *Romances de Tetuán,* 2 vols (Madrid: Instituto de estudios africanos, 1952)

Levy, Avigdor, *The Sephardim in the Ottoman Empire* (Princetown, New Jersey: Darwin Press, 1992)

Menéndez Pidal, Ramón, 'Catálogo del romancero judío-español', *Cultura española* (Madrid: Imprenta ibérica, 1929), IV, 1045-1077; V, 161-199

Pisonero, Isidoro & Hilary Pomeroy (eds), *Donaire,* 6 (London: Embajada de España, 1996)

Antonio Rodríguez-Moñino and Daniel Devoto (eds), *Flor de enamorados* (Barcelona, 1562) (Valencia: Castalia, 1954)

Suárez Fernández, Luis, *Documentos acerca de la expulsión de los judíos* (Valladolid: CSIC, 1964)

Verlinden, Charles, 'Slavery, Slave Trade' in Joseph R. Strayer (ed.), *Dictionary of the Middle Ages,* 13 vols (New York: Charles Scribener's Sons, 1988), XI, 334-340

8

A Comparison of the Devotional Systems in the *Viaje de Turquía*

Encarnación Sánchez García
translated by Michael Truman

Dialogues are a highly developed genre in Spanish Golden Age literature. First appearing at the beginning of the sixteenth century, they reached their zenith between 1530 and 1590, and were still in vogue for much of the seventeenth century.[1]

A not insignificant number of great authors, ranging from the Valdés brothers (in the first half of the sixteenth century), to Fray Luis de León (in the second half of that century) and Cervantes (in the early seventeenth century) took the dialogue and nurtured it with love, often obtaining extraordinary results. Humanism, acknowledging its debt to Antiquity, again offered the dialogue as one of the simplest, yet highest forms of literary expression. In Italy, in particular, the way in which this revisiting of the classical past turned humanist dialogue, and then the *cinquecentesco,* into a genre which Castiglione described as 'alla foggia de molti antichi' is very well known.[2]

---

[1] For a general view, see Jacqueline Ferreras, *Les Dialogues espagnols du XVI siècle ou l'expression littéraire d'une nouvelle conscience* (Paris: Didier, 1985). The author has collected up to 83 works in Spanish. Jesús Gómez, *El diálogo en el Renacimiento español* (Madrid: Cátedra, 1988) also includes in the *corpus* dialogues in Latin, and adds works in Spanish, reaching a total of 173. Prior to this, Luis Andrés Murillo, 'Diálogo y dialéctica en el siglo XVI español', *Revista de la Facultad de Letras*, 4 (1959), 56-66, claimed that: 'Entre 1525 y el fin de la centuria apareció toda una literatura de diálogos filosóficos, religiosos, morales, satíricos, científicos, técnicos, históricos, artísticos y de pasatiempo. El número de diálogos escritos durante esa época se acercó a un millar' (57), but this seems to be an arbitrary figure. The oldest dialogue in Spanish is the *Tratado de la inmortalidad del ánima*, by Rodrigo Fernández de Santaella, published in Seville by L. Polono and J. Cromberger in 1503. This was followed (in chronological order) by a series of dialogues in Latin (those of Luis Vives, *inter alia*) up to 1526, when Diego de Sagredo's famous *Medidas del Romano* was published by the press owned by Ramón de Petras, which was extremely active at that time in Toledo.

[2] Carlo Cordié (ed.), *Il Cortegiano* (Turin: Mondadori, 1991), 15. For the dialogue genre in humanist and Renaissance Italy, cf. Francesco Tateo, 'La tradizione classica e le forme del dialogo

In Spain, 1553 can be taken as the date marking the mature assimilation of the classical past, since this was the year in which Plato's *Convivium* was published in Salamanca.[3] There are, moreover, two other noteworthy dates: in 1561, León de Castro used the *Convivium* in his *Clase de mayores* at the University of Salamanca;[4] in 1565, in Alcalá, regulations on the teaching of Greek were put into effect and, in the orders under which the academic authorities prescribed texts as compulsory reading to university chairs, Lucian's *Deorum dialogi* appears in the *Cátedra de menores*. This author's works were also required reading in the *Cátedra de medianos*.[5]

Alongside the direct assimilation of these models, the classical past makes its influence felt in modern times through Erasmus, who occupied centre stage from the second decade of the sixteenth century onwards. Quite apart from this, the idea of revisiting the Greco-Roman past spread, like delicately worked filigree, to the Iberian Peninsula through the influence of Italy's output of literature in the dialogue genre. This reached its apogee with Boscán's translation of Castiglione's *Il Cortegiano*. It was Boscán who was the precursor of the Italian style, which has had some effect upon the development of the models for dialogues which were adopted in Spain.[6]

---

umanistico' in his *Tradizione e realtà nell'Umanesimo italiano* (Bari: Dedalo Libri, 1967), 223-249.

[3] The title in Greek (which is not quoted for typographical reasons) is followed by: *Platonis Convivium, seu de amore, Dialogus moralis, Salmanticae, Excudeabat Andreas a Portonanis, primus ab Academia condita Graecarum literarum Typographus. Anno M.D.LIII.*

[4] Cf. José López Rueda, *Helenistas españoles del siglo XVI* (Madrid: CSIC, 1973), 160; and Francisco Rico, *El pequeño mundo del hombre* (Madrid: Alianza, 1986), especially 126 ff. and 170-189.

[5] The orders governing the teaching of Greek in Alcalá, put into effect by Juan de Obando, are to be found in the *Libro de Reformas de la Universidad de Alcalá* (Archivo Histórico Nacional de Alcalá de Henares, Book 525-F, fols 43ᵛ and 44ʳ), cf. José López Rueda, 257 ff.

[6] Cf. Margherita Morreale, *Castiglione y Boscán: El ideal cortesano en el Renacimiento español* (Madrid: Real Academia Española, 1959). Boscán's translation of *Il Cortegiano* appeared in 1534 and, by the end of the century, it had run to sixteen legal editions: cf. José Simón Díaz, *Bibliografía de la literatura hispánica* (Madrid: CSIC, 1950-1984), VII, no. 5.111-5125 and 6.582. Lore Terracini, *Lingua come problema nella letteratura spagnola del Cinquecento* (Turin: Stampatori, 1979) mentions the 'affinità d'impostazione e d'idee' between *Il Cortegiano* and Valdés's *Diálogo de la lengua* (in which Valdés claimed that he had not read Boscán's Spanish translation) and points out that they were united by 'l'ideale della lingua, che possiamo continuare e chiamar cortigiana', 18. The significance, and the influence of *Il Cortegiano* were largely attributable to Boscán's widely distributed translation, but this translation, in a way that is paralleled in the excample that Lore Terracini gave with regard to Juan de Valdés, would probably have widened horizons, and created favourable conditions for such developments, rather than acting as a blueprint. Cf. Jesús Gómez, *El diálogo en el Renacimiento español*, who observes that 'sólo dos diálogos españoles del s. XVI imitan la forma literaria del *Cortesano*: *El Scolastico* de Cristóbal de Villalón y, muy secundariamente, *El Cortesano* de Luis Milán' (12).

These varied influences should not simply be understood in terms of rhetoric, but also with reference to the direct *imitatio* of content, with the transposition of large amounts of material. In this respect, it should not be forgotten that critics have scarcely touched upon the question of genre, and have solved the problem of the - almost invariably - multiple instances of *imitatio* by offering hasty judgements on the lack of originality or plagiarism in the text.

It is into this latter category that the *Viaje de Turquía* falls.[7] Written in about 1557, it is an anonymous dialogue in which three old friends from the University of Alcalá meet again many years later at the gates of a town in Old Castile. Their names - Juan de Voto a Dios, Mátalas Callando and Pedro de Urdemalas - form part of Spain's folklore heritage. Pedro, who has travelled far from Spain, and has returned as a pilgrim, tells his friends about the circumstances surrounding his period of captivity in Turkey. His story begins with his capture near the island of Ponza, and describes his journey from there to Constantinople, the time he spent in Turkey, (during which he practised as a physician), his escape three years later, his return journey across the Aegean, then through Italy from Messina to Genoa, and ends with his arrival in Castile. He concludes his account by declaring to his friends his intention to settle in Spain in order to continue his work as a doctor once he has returned from his pilgrimage to Santiago de Compostela, after fulfilling a promise made to St James during his captivity.

This long narrative occupies two thirds of the book, and accounts for the first day of the dialogue; the second day is divided into two parts, in which the Turks' life and customs are described, together with the origins of the latter, ending with a lesson on the history of the Byzantine Empire from Constantine the Great to Manuel Palaeologus. Both the second day and the prologue are, in fact, an expansion, a *rimaneggiamento* or corrupted version of treatises on the Turkish question which had been published in Italy in the previous decade.

---

[7] There are five manuscripts of the *Viaje de Turquía*. The one known as M-1, preserved in the Biblioteca Nacional in Madrid under catalogue number 3871 is, as Marcel Bataillon maintained, 'la base de toute édition future'. Cf. Marcel Bataillon, 'Les manuscrits du *Viaje de Turquía*' in Alexandru Rosetti (ed.), *Actele celui de al XII lea Congres International de Linguistica si Filologie Romanica* (Bucharest: Akademiei Republici Socialiste Rômânia, 1971), II, 37-41. The latest edition, by Fernando García Salinero (Madrid: Cátedra, 1980; repr. 1986) is a transcription of M-1, but omits the *Turcarum Origo* (the last part of the second day of the dialogue), as did previous publishers. On this question, cf. Franco Meregalli, 'Partes inéditas y partes perdidas del *Viaje de Turquía*' in the *Boletín de la Real Academia Española* (1974), 193-201, which claims that the *Turcarum Origo* is an integral part of the text of the *Viaje*. Cf. Florencio Revilla and Ana Vian, 'Para la lectura completa del *Viaje de Turquía*: edición de la *Tabla de materias* y de la *Turcarum Origo*', *Criticón*, 45 (1989), 5-70. All the quotations in this chapter relate to the García Salinero edition, hereinafter referred to as *Viaje*.

(These were primarily the works of Giovanantonio Menavino and Bartolomé Georgievits, the latter translated into Italian by Domenichi.)

It should be added that the *Viaje de Turquía* was not published until 1905, when Serrano y Sanz included it in a volume of the *Nueva Biblioteca de Autores Españoles* devoted to autobiographies and memoirs. He assumed that Pedro's account was true, and suggested that Cristóbal de Villalón might have been the author. Thirty years later Marcel Bataillon proved that it was, in fact, a literary fabrication, insisting that the *rimaneggiamento* was plagiarized, and attributed it to Andrés Laguna, a humanist and papal physician. Subsequently, a group of scholars (I shall mention only two, both of them Italian - Anna Corsi Prosperi and Cesare Acutis) has declared itself in favour of the hypothesis that Laguna was the author; those who remain unconvinced include the Americans Dubler and Markrich, the brothers Luis and Juan Gil and, in the eighties, Fernando García Salinero.

The last decade or so has seen the emergence of a third group. Its members include both those who are against attributing the authorship to Laguna (Franco Meregalli, Caterina Ruta), and those who are in favour of doing so (Jacqueline Ferreras), but they have come together to try to shift the focus away from the question of clarifying the authorship issue above all else, and towards the exploration of other aspects of the text.

Prominent in this group is Augustin Redondo who, in a study published in the *Homenaje a Eugenio Asensio,* compares the traditional devotional systems advocated in the Franciscan Fray Antonio de Aranda's *Verdadera información de la Tierra Santa*, which is quoted in the *Viaje de Turquía*, with the new system proposed in the latter.[8] Thus, although Aranda's text 'se presenta como un libro que exalta la devoción más tradicional, apoyándose en exterioridades (peregrinaciones, indulgencias, reliquias, milagros)' (Redondo, 398), the position adopted by the author of the *Viaje de Turquía* emerges as a very different one, and is identical to that of groups in Spain which, in earlier years, had accepted the teachings of Erasmus. From Redondo's analysis it is clear that the reception accorded to Erasmus in Spain triggered a compound reaction which, based initially on the reading of the texts themselves and early translations, then engendered original texts which helped to ensure the propagation of the *philosophia Christi*. The reaction to the main thrust of its arguments from the most conservative elements in the Catholic Church subsequently provoked a further batch of texts from the Spanish Erasmian movement, including, specifically, the masterpiece which is the subject of this

---

[8] Augustin Redondo, 'Devoción tradicional y devoción erasmista en la España de Carlos V. De la *Verdadera información de la Tierra Santa* de Fray Antonio de Aranda al *Viaje de Turquía*' in Luisa López Griguera and Augustín Redondo (eds), *Homenaje a Eugenio Asensio* (Madrid: Gredos, 1988), 391-416.

study - the *Viaje de Turquía*. Redondo cites the translation by Cristóbal de Virués of some of the *colloquia* of Erasmus (1529), especially the one entitled *Peregrinación*. In this dialogue, the Benedictine, Virués, adds some of his own comments to Erasmus's text, *De visendo loca sacra* (1526). Redondo points out, with philological obsessiveness, the personal comments which have been added, *inter alia:* 'Virués pone en tela de juicio, con fino espíritu crítico y acertada visión histórica, el valor de la peregrinación a Jerusalén, de las reliquias traídas de la Tierra Santa, o presentadas como tales, y el de las indulgencias unidas al universo de las romerías' in which 'no está lejos de pensar como Alfonso de Valdés'; 'parece como si a Erasmo (que embiste contra el comercio de las reliquias en el coloquio *Peregrinación*) y a los dos humanistas castellanos citados, fray Antonio de Aranda les estuviera contestando cuando insiste sobre la reverencia que se ha de guardar con las reliquias, aun con las falsas' (Redondo, 403-404).

It is precisely in an area such as this (the rejection of false relics), which is so fraught with difficulties and dangers yet, at the same time, so essential for Catholic reform, that Virués makes an observation of his own which would be an appropriate prologue for this study. Commenting on the exaggerated acts of religious devotion of the pilgrims passing along the Way of the Cross, he declares:

> Quando pasamos por aquella sancta vía o calle besamos aquella piedra [sobre la cual dicen que se reclinó la Virgen al ver caer a su Hijo con la cruz a cuestas], por lo qual los moros o turcos no sólo nos tienen por locos pero aún por ydólatras, creyendo que adoramos las piedras. Y de despecho, muchas vezes la hallamos untada e no de bálsamo: e como digo desta piedra, assí acaesce en todas las que besamos que están en el campo o en la ciudad sin estar cubiertas, conviene saber sin edificio cerrado.[9]

The question of relics and of the sense behind pilgrimages to the Holy Land is seen here in relation to the problem of the evangelization of the Muslim world. The latter is another world which is physically close (especially in the Holy Land); this world's expressions of disapproval need to be assuaged in order to avoid provoking controversy and summary judgements on Catholic insanity and idolatry. This consideration of the judgement of the other world is already hinted at in the comment of the Benedictine, Virués. As I have demonstrated elsewhere, the concept of this other (Muslim) world comes to life in the

---

[9] *Colloquios familiares* (no number, no place, published in 1529), fol. XXXVI[r], quoted from the copy in the University of Valencia; cited by A. Redondo, 404.

development of the literary and formal structure of the *Viaje de Turquía*.[10] What I wish to stress at this juncture is the way in which the pure Erasmian roots of the 'inward' Christianity professed by the main character in the *Viaje*, Pedro de Urdemalas, appear to be present in the basis for 'the exploration and presentation of this "other" world (i.e. Turkey and all that is between it and Spain)', this being one of the main contributions of the *Viaje* (Sánchez García, 460). As I also hope to prove, the attitude of the anonymous author of 'the masterpiece of literature which is both serious and entertaining, and for which Spain is indebted to her Erasmian humanists' is in line with that of Virués: an awareness that Christians' acts of devotion in the Holy Places were witnessed by followers of another monotheistic religion, and that this in itself was having an influence on Catholic consciousness.[11] However, this 'auténtico humanista reformador' (Redondo, 405), the author of the *Viaje,* went a step further than Virués by including in a dynamic and highly complex system his criticism of the religious devotion of the *viri oscuri* (represented in this text by Juan de Voto a Dios). What Virués saw as the need to protect the Way of the Cross from the spite of the infidel, and to safeguard the dignity, decorum and decency of the ground on which Christ lived, suffered and died is simply the starting point for the author of the *Viaje*.

II

It is not necessary to search hard in the text of the *Viaje* to encounter the theme which interests us: alms, relics and hospitals are the three opening *motifs* in the dialogue, and are tightly intertwined from the very beginning of the conversation between the two friends Juan de Voto a Dios and Mátalas Callando, even before Pedro de Urdemalas appears, dressed in his outlandish apparel. These three *motifs*, in turn, encompass a fourth one, which is really a 'macrotheme', that of pilgrimages. The foul-mouthed Mátalas Callando attacks the cleric Voto a Dios thus:

> Veinte y más años ha que nos conosçemos y andamos por el mundo juntos y en todos ellos, por más que lo he advertido, me acuerdo haberos visto dar tres vezes limosna; sino al uno: ¿por qué no sirves un amo?; al otro: gran necesidad tenía Santiago de ti; al otro: en el ospital te darán de cenar; y a bueltas desto, mil consejos airadamente porque piensen que con buen zelo se les dize (*Viaje*, 100).

---

[10] E. Sánchez García, '*Viaje de Turquía*: Consideraciones acerca del género' in *Revista de Literatura*, 56, 112 (Madrid: CSIC, 1994), 453-460.

[11] Marcel Bataillon, *Erasmo y España*, trans. Antonio Alatorre (Mexico-Buenos Aires: Fondo de Cultura Económica, 1950), II, 280.

Not content with branding his fellow traveller as an uncharitable hypocrite, he immediately turns in the same speech to the subject of relics (which, like the previous one on alms, is inextricably linked to that of pilgrimages):

> Mas dexado esto aparte, en todo el año podíamos salir a tiempo más a vuestro propósito: ¿no miráis quánto bordón y calabaza? ¿cómo campean las plumas de los chapeos? Para mí tengo que se podría hazer un buen cabezal de las plumas del gallo de señor Sancto Domingo. Bien haya gallo que tanto fructo de sí da. Si como es gallo fuera oveja, yo fiador que los paños vaxaran de su preçio. ¿Pensáis que si el clérigo que tiene cargo de rrepartirlas hubiera querido tratar en ellas, que no pudiera haber embiado muchas sacas a Flandes? (*Viaje,* 101)

Here, the initial connection between the abundance of pilgrims and false relics (produced to satisfy the demand) is soon laced with the irreverent Mátalas Callando's sarcasm. He becomes more self-confident and, referring to the 'pobres aplagados' for whom his companion Voto a Dios is preparing a sort of prison, maintains that they are hypochondriacs who will never want to go home, since they 'tenían sanas las llagas' but 'enfermas las bolsas' (*Viaje,* 102) and, when Voto a Dios refutes his argument with 'opinión es de algunos de nuestros theólogos que son obligados a restituçión de todo lo que demandan más de para el substentamiento de aquel día, so pena de malos christianos' (*Viaje,* 102), Mátalas Callando then launches his main attack: [12]

> Mejor me ayude Dios, que yo los tengo por christianos quanto más por buenos. Ni preçepto de todos los de la ley guardan [...] Ellos, primeramente no son naturales de ningún pueblo, y jamás los vi confesar, ni oír misa, antes sus bozes ordinarias son a la puerta de la iglesia en la misa mayor y en las menores de persona a persona, que aun de la devoción que quitan tienen bien que restituir... (*Viaje,* 102-103). [13]

In Mátalas Callando's mind, being a Christian seems, in principle, to be linked to the notion of belonging to a national community: those who belong to a town or village, or to a group, are Christians. Good Christians obey the precepts of the law, and here Mátalas Callando mentions the most important ones - attendance at confession and mass. Finally, Mátalas Callando considers sin (which implies the duty to return stolen goods), which forms part of the behaviour of these

---

[12] 'El intento del ospital de Granada que hago es por meter todos éstos y que no salgan de allí y que se les den sus raziones. Para éstos son propios los ospitales y no los habían de dexar salir dellos sino como casa por cárzel [...]' (*Viaje,* 102).

[13] 'Yo los tengo' (instead of 'Yo los tenga'): negatives without particles are a very common stylistic feature of the *Viaje*; here, moreover, an indicative has been slipped in instead of the subjunctive, which should have been used here. This is also common in the text.

beggars (something which is more subtle and impalpable than the excess of alms to which Voto a Dios has just referred): the poor, noisy and restless, detract from the devotion of the faithful, and will later be called to account for it.[14] In this context, it is clear that Mátalas Callando's understanding of religious devotion is fundamentally the same as the definition given by Covarrubias fifty years later:

> Comúnmente se entiende por devoto el que frecuenta los Sacramentos, asiste a las horas Canónicas, monasterios, ermitas, altares, reza las devociones y oraciones del Oficio Divino.[15]

Covarrubias's definition, although it refers to the Catholic system, is applicable in the *Viaje* to the other two systems. The adverb *comúnmente*, with which the definition in the *Tesoro* begins is, for our theme, a revealing one, since it identifies what follows as 'común opinión, recibida por todos' (Covarrubias, 345), in other words as a norm, which, in this case, Mátalas Callando represents. Mátalas Callando believes, then, that those pilgrims and beggars who are more concerned with displaying relics or seeking alms (or even stealing) than with following the precepts of the Holy Mother Church do not show true devotion. Voto a Dios, however, takes the opposite view, which is not so subtle, and equates devotion with the concept of pilgrimage:

> Gran devoçión tienen todas estas naçiones estrangeras; bien en cargo les es Santiago (*Viaje*, 104).

The two friends adopt clearly differentiated positions, although these are not the only differences of opinion: when, indeed, Urdemalas appears, dressed as a 'fraire estrangero' (*Viaje*, 106), but before he is recognized by his two friends, he makes several brief utterances on penitence in Greek: *Metanoia* (penitence), o *Theos choresi* (May God forgive you) and *Ef logite pateres* (Fathers, your blessing). These are both greetings and invitations to repent. There is more to come: as soon as his identity is revealed, Pedro tells the others that this is a temporary state: 'Aunque me veis en el ábito de fraire peregrino, no es ésta mi profesión' (*Viaje*, 109), but while he is in this state he will respect all the obligations that it imposes: '¿Mudar hávitos yo? Hasta que los dexe colgados de aquella capilla de Santiago en Compostella, no me los verá hombre despegar

---

[14] This concern that nothing should divert attention from worship is, to some extent, an opinion shared by one Martín Azpilcueta, *Commento en romance...* [Coimbra: 1545]; cf. M. Bataillon, II, 178-181.

[15] Sebastián de Covarrubias, *Tesoro de la lengua castellana o española*, Martín de Riquer (ed.), reprint (Barcelona: Altafulla, 1987), 465-466.

de mis carnes' (*Viaje*, 110). Urdemalas resists their entreaties to abandon the cloth, and embrace expediency and common practice: 'por cumplir con el vulgo' (*Viaje*, 111), something which he rejects out of hand: 'Digan, que de Dios dixeron; quien no le paresciere bien, no se case conmigo' (*Viaje*, 111), although he does find a way to spend two days in Juan's house:

> Esperemos a que sea de noche para no ser visto, y estonces entraremos en vuestra casa, y holgarme he dos días y no más, y éstos estaré secreto sin que hombre sepa que estoy aquí, porque ansí es mi voto. Después de hecha mi romería y dexado el ábito, haced de mí zera y pabilo (*Viaje*, 111).

The new Christian dimension which Pedro brings to his old friends' Castilian view of the world is, in essence, that he puts his Christian belief into practice, challenging what others might think as well as commonly held opinions, and holds himself accountable only to his own conscience.[16] If such internal rigour exists, pilgrimages can form part of the devotional system of a Christian. The pilgrimage to Santiago de Compostela is good if it is a way to seek penitence and purification. Pedro's thoughtful piety shows in his conversations with the other two, causing Mátalas Callando to exclaim:

> Dos horas y más ha que estamos parlando y no se os ha soltado una palabra de las que solíais, sino todo sentencias llenas de philosofía y religión y themor de Dios (*Viaje*, 123).

and in the crescendo which the last three syntagms form there is evidence of his recognition of the novelty and the superiority and the holiness of Pedro's message. This message is essentially the *philosophia Christi*, which the *Enchiridion* did more to popularize than any other book.[17] In this and other texts, Erasmus insists that the philosophy of Christ is to be lived, rather than debated, and Pedro, in his turn, exemplifies this zeal.

For Pedro, everything in the realm of the sacred is now fired with this new spirit, so he freely voices his opinions on the need to return money embezzled from sums given as alms for the building of hospitals, as well as on the need to do away with false relics, suggesting: 'esas dar con ellas en el río' (*Viaje*,124). He also refers to harmful literature, such as Aranda's book: 'tan grande modorro era ese como los otros que hablan lo que no saben, y tantas mentiras

---

[16] Mátalas Callando acknowledges the superiority of Pedro's point of view: 'Gran ventaja nos tienen los que han visto el mundo a los que nunca salimos de Castilla' (*Viaje*, 116). Pedro identifies and elaborates on the reason: 'Yo estoy al cabo que vos nunca estubistes en Hierusalem ni en Roma, ni aun salistes d'España, porque *loquela tua te manifestum fecit*, ni aun de Castilla [...]' (*Viaje*, 123).

[17] cf. M. Bataillon, *Erasmo y España*, I, 87.

diçe en su libro' (*Viaje*, 125); but Pedro not only deals with those themes, which had been the first to emerge in the great debate in which the whole of Europe had passionately engaged at the dawn of the Renaissance; his new epistemology also offers views on burial (*Viaje*, 158), confession (*Viaje*, 165-166), preaching (*Viaje*, 166-168) and the mass.   On the latter, for instance, when Juan comments that some priests who have been to Italy and France 'han traído la costumbre...de decir la misa rezada a voces, y todo se lo reprehenden porque dizen que no se usa', Pedro expresses the following view:

> ¿Qué se me da a mí de los usos, si lo que hago es bien hecho? En verdad que lo de dezir alto la misa que es una muy buena cosa; porque el precepto no manda ver misa, sino oírla, y es muy bien aunque haya mucha gente todos participen igualmente (*Viaje*, 168).

Religious ceremony is not rejected, but its value is expressed in relative terms; faced with his friend's perplexity, Pedro does not climb down, but ends up by passing judgement on the case with philological obsessiveness, focusing on the letter of the precept which, in the last analysis, involves breathing the new spirit into the ceremonies: participating means actively giving life to the sacrifice.

Finally, Pedro also welcomes the *Modus orandi* of Erasmus, and explains the importance he attached to silent prayer when he was surrounded by enemies during his escape: [18]

> Ninguna quenta tenía con los *pater nostres* que rezaba, sino con solo estar atento a lo que deçía. ¿Luego pensáis que para con Dios es menester rezar sobre taja? Con el coraçón abierto y las entrañas, daba un arcabuzazo en el çielo que me paresçía que penetraba hasta donde Dios estaba; que deçía en dos palabras: Tú, Señor, que guiaste los tres reyes [...] y libraste a Santa Susana del falso testimonio, y a Sant Pedro de las prisiones y a los tres muchachos del horno [...] ten por bien llevarme en este viaje en salvamento *ad laudem et gloriam omnipotentis nominis tui;* y con esto, algún *pater noster* (*Viaje*, 265).

This, then, is a living prayer in which the soul is raised to God, although the conversational and humorous tone which characterises the whole dialogue gives substance to things which are as abstract as the soul (in the references to the *coraçón abierto* and the *entrañas*), or prayer (in the reference to the *arcabuzazo*), which the prudish might consider blasphemous.

Our hero, Urdemalas, judges humanist Christianity to be appropriate for the Catholic world, since if the west has created and acknowledges the superiority of humanism, it cannot fail to adopt its most precious fruit, the *philosophia*

---

[18] M. Bataillon, II, 169-173.

Christi which, by blending classical literature and Christianity, raises classical philosophy to God, making it divine. It is in this context that the astonished Mátalas Callando's judgement that the hero's new eloquence, expressed in 'sentencias llenas de philosofía, y religión y themor de Dios', can now be fully understood.

The classical origins of this Christianity make a hero of Pedro, sustaining him during his captivity. This is exemplified in an incident during the period spent in Turkey, in which Pedro, who by then was a famous doctor enjoying considerable esteem in the court of the Grand Turk, and who had some freedom and material comforts, resists pressure from his master to become a Muslim. His master, attempting to break him by making him work hard and humiliating him, sends him to work with the slaves as a stonemason's labourer. On seeing him in such circumstances, a Turkish agent asks him:

> Di, christiano, aquella philosophía de Aristótil y Platón, y la mediçina de Galeno, y elocuençia de Çiçerón y Demósthenes, ¿qué te han aprobechado?

And Pedro replies:

> Hame aprobechado para saber sufrir semejantes días como éste (*Viaje*, 188).

We are now in a position to classify the two other devotional systems analysed by Pedro de Urdemalas. They occupy distinctive, well-defined positions in Pedro's epistemology: although the sublime form of Christianity in the *philosophia Christi* is well suited to the west of the Renaissance period, the apostolic Christianity which he professes is well suited to the orthodox east. Urdemalas makes it clear that the reason for the continuing schism in the east lies not in the importance attached to dogma, but in the lack of scholarship amongst the Greeks:

> Yo, hablando muchas vezes con el patriarca y algunos obispos, les deçía que por falta de letrados estaban diferentes su Iglesia y la nuestra romana (*Viaje*, 284).

And he summarizes the main reasons behind the dispute:

> En el baptiçar diçen que somos herejes, porque es grande soberbia que diga un hombre: *Ego te baptizo*, sino *Dulos Theu se baptizi: el sierbo de Dios te baptiza*. [...] En la misa no hay pan para senzeño [...] porque [dicen que] el pan sin levadura es como cuerpo sin ánima, y habiéndose de convertir en Christo aquéllo, no puede si no tiene ánima. Son todos una jente quasi tan sin razón como los turcos (*Viaje*, 284-285).

A Byzantine conflict? This is probably how Urdemalas sees it, given that he makes no attempt to refute the points raised by the Greek Orthodox Church against the Catholics. In his system, dogma seems to be a subject for reflection which is part and parcel of reason itself, yet there is no scope for discussing the question with the Greeks, who are almost as irrational as the Turks.

Nevertheless, Orthodox Christianity is a coherent system which Urdemalas respects, criticizing some things and praising others. Pedro points to the evangelical poverty of Orthodox priests, and their concomitant abstinence; he testifies to this because, during his flight, he hid amongst the Monte Sancto friars and knows 'muy bien que hazen la mayor abstinençia del mundo siguiendo siempre ellos y los clérigos griegos la orden evangélica' (*Viaje*, 273); strict observance is admired by Urdemalas, who tells his friends that '[todos los griegos] tienen quatro Quaresmas' (*Viaje*, 282), and he ponders:

> No digo yo fraire, ni en Quaresma, sino un plebeyo en viernes, que esté malo, que se purgue, no comerá dos tragos de caldo de abe, ni un huebo, si pensase por ello morir o no morir, y aun irse al infierno; en eso no se hable, que entre un millón que curé de griegos jamás lo pude acabar, sino unas pasas o un poco de aquel pan cocto de Italia (*Viaje*, 283).

This meticulous observance, which is sometimes carried to extremes which drive our hero to despair, covers all things religious (prayer, the celebration of the sacrifice of the mass, respect for places of worship, the keeping of the commandments) and turns, in some instances, through over-zealousness, into superstitious tension, which Pedro condemns. On one occasion he claims that the Greeks were 'tan escrupulosos' that they did not dare warm themselves around a fire made from wood left in a hermitage, 'diçiendo ser sacrilegio' (*Viaje*, 295), but they accused him of showing a lack of 'themor [...] de Dios en hurtar lo ajeno' (*Viaje*, 296), because he had made use of that same wood. Pedro's judiciousness is not affected by this clash of cultures: after commenting that the Greeks are cowards, slanderers, drunkards and ignoramuses, he points to their mercy and compassion. He respects the Greek Orthodox monk's devotion to his calling and considers that observance of this very rule is so commendable that it is adequate as a plea for salvation:

> Ellos al paresçer tienen vida con que se pueden bien salvar, y no piden a nadie nada ni son importunos (*Viaje*, 289).

Pedro accepts the Orthodox system, which is so formalistic, so concerned with literalism and, therefore, so far removed from the *philosophia Christi*, as a form of Christianity which is appropriate for the illiterate east, since 'ni en Atenas ni en toda Greçia hay escuela ni rastro de haber habido letras entre los griegos, sino la jente más bárbara que pienso haber habido en el mundo' (*Viaje*, 317). The Christian doctrine of the east is ideally suited to such a group of human beings 'según son de idiotas' (*Viaje*, 299), since it represents a structured set of norms with its own internal harmony. Although 'el más prudente de todos es como el menos de tierra de Sagayo' (*Viaje*, 317), the method of Orthodox devotion is, in itself, good because it is part of the structure of the society in which it flourishes, even though it is contrary to the ideal form of Christian worship which Urdemalas himself practises and preaches. Although 'las orationes particulares, como no sean misa ni horas de la Iglesia, son a la apostólica, muy breves' (*Viaje*, 275), Urdemalas finds that they are counterbalanced by the daily worship which he observed in a monastery, in which 'los ofiçios eran tan largos como maitines de la Noche Buena y çiertamente, sin mentir, duraron quatro horas' since they pray from 'el Salterio, del primer psalmo hasta el postrero' (*Viaje*, 276) every day 'dos vezes, una a bísperas, otra a maitines' (*Viaje*, 276). This contrast between long and short acts of worship plays its part in the occasion; it rhythmizes time and makes it sacred. The exemplary value which Orthodoxy places upon praying aloud is also dependent on the place which it occupies in Pedro's discourse; it is, indeed, the starting point for Urdemalas's description of Greek Christianity, thus stressing the extremely important role which it plays within the devotional system of the east, in terms of a discipline which provides cohesiveness in a world organized in furtherance of fanatical resistance, a concept so apparent in that 'tan grande miseria [en que] están los pobres christianos' (*Viaje*, 282) who are under Turkish rule.

The *lupus in fabula* - the Turk - also has a place in Urdemalas's discourse. The standard by which everything is judged is still *humanitas*. When Pedro tells his friends about his apotheosis as a doctor to the Court in Constantinople, and the honours he received from his master, Zinán, Voto a Dios exclaims:

> Estoy tan afiçionado a tan humano prínçipe, que os tengo embidia el haber sido su esclabo, y no dexaría de consultar letrados para ver si es líçito rogar a Dios por él (*Viaje*, 232).

And Urdemalas, rather more cautiously, replies:

> Después de muerto tengo yo el escrúpulo, que en vida ya yo rogaba mill vezes al día que le alumbrase para salir de su error (*Viaje*, 232).

In this statement the hero, while not discounting the possibility to which Juan alludes, refers forcefully to the official Catholic doctrine on salvation.

Apart from that, the moral virtues of the Turks are very wide-ranging, according to Pedro's discourse: humility (*Viaje*, 196), patience (*Viaje*, 202), magnificence (*Viaje*, 231) and humanity are virtues possessed by Zinán, a high dignitary and Pedro's master at the Court of Constantinople, whose gentility shines through the accounts in the *Viaje*. Tolerance (*Viaje*, 253; 487), stoicism (*Viaje*, 261-262), kindness and soldiership (*Viaje*, 253; 455-457) are characteristics which the people as a whole share. They also have, of course, some quite significant defects, such as cruelty (*Viaje*, 240), fickleness (*Viaje*, 213) and obstinacy (*Viaje*, 230).

On a more general level, when Urdemalas analyses the question of the Muslim religion, he takes as his starting point, as is his wont, the relationship between this faith and reason. Everything is clear from the outset, since Pedro begins by stating that 'para atraer Mahoma a su vana secta a los simples que le siguieron, ordenó su Alcorán tomando de la ley de Moysén y de la nuestra sancta, de cada una lo que conosçió ser más apacible y agradable a la gente' (*Viaje*, 386).

Thus, Islam's original sin of synthesizing only the milder, more agreeable laws of the Old and New Testaments is explained, because it is a message intended for the *simples*. Our hero stresses this underlying irrationality when he maintains that 'no cabe demandarles razón de cosa que hagan, porque lo tienen de defender por armas y no disputar' (*Viaje*, 389). Having established this, Pedro is in no fear of being misinterpreted and can, therefore, recognize Islam's merits. These include the value of ceremonies such as circumcision (*Viaje*, 87-388), confession (understood as the cleansing of the body before the prayer of the faithful [Viaje, 388]), and, above all, the deeply-felt metrical prayer which the faithful recite:

> Çinco [vezes al día], con la mayor devoçión y curiosidad; que si ansí lo hiziésemos nosotros, nos querría mucho Dios (*Viaje*, 389).

This *devoçión*, the touchstone of the Muslim system of worship, fosters cohesiveness, since it is emphasised that 'oran estas çinco vezes, que no queda ánima viba de turco ni turca, pobre ni rico, desde el emperador hasta los moços de cozina, que no lo haga' (*Viaje*, 389).

Pedro stresses the exemplary nature of a devotional tradition interpreted as the discipline of prayer, when he warns his friends, who are surprised at the frequency and intensity of these prayers:

> Mirad qué higa tan grande para nosotros, que no somos christianos sino en el nombre (*Viaje*, 390).

In conclusion, as the hero of the story of his own captivity, the main character in the *Viaje*, a novel in embryonic form narrated by the author himself to his friends, heralds an idea of moral and religious reform, which can be identified with the *philosophia Christi* championed by Erasmus. This Christian hero left Spain as a callow student and returned as a doctor. Practising spiritual prayer, he has a strong appreciation of the classical tradition. Amongst the Muslims, he has borne witness to his Christian faith; amongst the followers of the Orthodox Church, he has been a model of prudence and reason. On the road to Santiago, he preaches in favour of conversion to that model which he himself represents. The Christian ideal he proposes is complex. Although on the one hand he upholds, with all the strength he can summon, a rational, anti-scholastic model of Christianity, which draws upon patristic tradition, does not reject the Greco-Roman classics and still embraces that 'deseo de convergencia, en su variedad, hacia la unión espiritual' which Erasmus had never tired of expounding in his many writings from *Querela pacis* onwards, he cannot, nevertheless, disguise a certain disillusionment with the notion of fostering hopes for worldwide religious unity.[19] This utopic vision implied the conversion of the other monotheistic religions to Christianity, a dream which had also been shared by Erasmus, and which Urdemalas considers outdated. In the *Viaje*, this is the hope nurtured by Voto a Dios, the theologian in the group and, in all senses, the most conservative. Each time Voto a Dios tentatively suggests the idea which Erasmus expounds in *Consultatio de bello Turcis inferendo* - that the Turks are half way towards being Christians: 'Una merced os pido, y es que, pues no os va nada en ello, que no me digáis otra cosa sino la verdad; porque no puedo creer que, siendo tan bárbaros, tengan algunas cosas que parezcan llebar camino' (*Viaje*, 395), Urdemalas pours cold water on his timid enthusiasm: '¿No sabéis que el diablo les ayudó a hazer esta seta? [...] Pues cada vez que quiere pecar es menester que lo haga a bueltas de algo bueno' (*Viaje*, 395). The hero's standpoint is that each creed should be respected, yet, at the same time, the distances between them should be rigorously maintained. If, in the final pages, Juan de Voto a Dios abandons his role as a corrupt and dissolute cleric and is converted to the model of Christian humanism which Pedro preaches, becoming a true *devoto*, this - I must emphasize - only takes place at the end because of Urdemalas's persistent efforts to convince him and bear witness to Christ. It should not be forgotten that Voto a Dios is a theologian, and not an *idiota*, a *simple* or a *bárbaro*. Pedro does not countenance simplistic enthusiasms when he observes similarities in the systems of religious devotion. He is well aware that the followers of Orthodoxy and Islam have their own set

---

[19] M. Bataillon, 'Erasmo, ¿europeo?', *Revista de Occidente*, Año VI, 2ª época, nº 58 (1968), 1-19, especially 12.

of norms, but he does not go so far as to advocate the future unification of the three religions mentioned in the book, as envisaged by Erasmus. Urdemalas has no qualms about recognizing that the Greeks and Turks can teach Christians in the Roman Church a great deal about divine worship and works of mercy. His cultural knowledge and experience is distilled into an historical and ethnographical rationale which provides reasoned responses to this range of systems. His human and cultural maturity allows him to recognize an intrinsic dignity in each of the three systems. The variants of the concept of devotion are, therefore, responses to ways of functioning which differ in each system; at the same time, each of these systems is in harmony with the *nomos* associated with the country which is under scrutiny. The discovery of traces of a mythical universal *Cristianitas* in the similarities in the three systems is something that Urdemalas, at this late stage in the century, and with his experience, would find difficult to accept.

Bibliography

Bataillon, Marcel, 'Les Manuscrits du *Viaje de Turquía*' in Alexandru Rosetti (ed.), *Actele celui de al XII lea Congres International de Linguistica si Filologie Romanica* (Bucharest: Akademiei Republici Socialiste România, 1971), II, 37-41

----------, *Erasmo y España*, trans. Antonio Alatorre (Mexico-Buenos Aires: Fondo de Cultura Económica, 1950)

----------, 'Erasmo, ¿europeo?', *Revista de Occidente*, Año VI, 2ª época, 58 (1968), 1-19

Covarrubias, Sebastián de, *Tesoro de la lengua castellana o española*, Martín de Riquer (ed.) (Barcelona: Altafulla, 1987)

Ferreras, Jacqueline, *Les Dialogues espagnols du XVI siècle ou l'expression littéraire d'une nouvelle conscience* (Paris: Didier, 1985)

García Salinero, Fernando (ed.), *Viaje de Turquía* (Madrid: Cátedra, 1986)

Gómez, Jesús, *El diálogo en el Renacimiento español* (Madrid: Cátedra, 1988)

López Rueda, José, *Helenistas españoles del siglo XVI* (Madrid: CSIC, 1973)

Meregalli, Franco, 'Partes inéditas y partes perdidas del *Viaje de Turquía*', *Boletín de la Real Academia Española* (1974), 193-201

Morreale, Margherita, *Castiglione y Boscán: El ideal cortesano en el Renacimiento español* (Madrid: Real Academia Española, 1959)

Murillo, Luis Andrés, 'Diálogo y dialéctica en el siglo XVI español', *Revista de la Facultad de Letras*, 4 (1959), 56-66

Redondo, Augustin, 'Devoción tradicional y devoción erasmista en la España de Carlos V: De la *Verdadera información de la Tierra Santa* de Fray Antonio de Aranda al *Viaje de Turquía* in Luisa López Griguera and Augustín Redondo (eds), *Homenaje a Eugenio Asensio* (Madrid: Gredos, 1988), 391-416

Revilla, Florencio and Ana Vian, 'Para la lectura completa del *Viaje de Turquía*: edición de la *Tabla de materias* y de la *Turcarum Origo*', *Criticón*, 45 (1989), 5-70

Rico, Francisco, *El pequeño mundo del hombre* (Madrid: Alianza, 1986)

Sánchez García, E., '*Viaje de Turquía*: Consideraciones acerca del género', *Revista de Literatura*, LVI (1994), 453-460

Tateo, Francesco, 'La Tradizione classica e le forme del dialogo umanistico' in Francesco Tateo (ed.), *Tradizione e realtà nell' Umanesimo italiano* (Bari: Dedalo Libri, 1967), 223-249

Terracini, Lore, *Lingua come problema nella letteratura spagnola del Cinquecento* (Turin: Stampatori, 1979)

9

Fervor sin fanatismo: Pedro de Valencia's Treatise on the *Moriscos*

John A. Jones

The treatment of the *moriscos* in Spain in the sixteenth and seventeenth centuries culminating in their expulsion in 1609 has been a controversial issue which has indeed been characterized by *fervor* and *fanatismo*. These elements were certainly evident in contemporary attitudes to the controversy, and they have also been displayed by many of the historians who have written on the matter since the sixteenth century. Fernández Guerra, referring to the change in attitudes to the Moors after their relatively good treatment immediately following the fall of Granada in 1492, states that:

> El fanatismo religioso, al cual nada importa que se derrame a torrentes la sangre humana ni que se falte a uno de los principios fundamentales de la sociedad, comenzó a incitar a los Reyes, poco después de la conquista y por boca de algunos prelados, para que mandasen que se bautizaran todos los moros rendidos, y los que no quisiesen hacerlo fuesen arrojados a Berbería.[1]

In reviewing the historiography of the *morisco* problem, Miguel Angel de Bunes Ibarra also asserts that:

> La minoría ha sido estudiada desde los prismas más conservadores, dominados por el fanatismo religioso y la xenofobia hasta los liberales, pasando por el marxismo y los economistas (Bunes Ibarra, 10).

Different attitudes have therefore been brought to bear on the issue, and the element of *fervor* has assuredly characterized both participants in and commentators on the controversy. At best, the quality of *fervor* may be seen as positive and creative; at worst, it produced the fanatical approach that eventually led to the polemical call for expulsion, an act which, according to

---

[1] Quoted in Miguel Angel de Bunes Ibarra, *Los Moriscos en el pensamiento histórico: Historiografía de un grupo marginado* (Madrid: Cátedra, 1983), 67.

Bunes, as soon as it was carried out 'empieza a pesar como una gran losa sobre la conciencia de los españoles' (Bunes Ibarra, 22). This conscience, however, was alive before the expulsion too. There were those who approached the question certainly with *fervor* but without *fanatismo*; there were individuals who held strong religious views but who advocated measures which were balanced and moderate. My aim in this paper is to draw attention to one such view, namely, that of the important humanist, Pedro de Valencia.[2]

Valencia was a figure of some stature who commanded considerable respect. Evidence of this was his appointment as *cronista* of Philip III in 1607. In this capacity, he produced several weighty papers on a variety of topics. However, some time before his appointment as *cronista* he was asked by the King's confessor, Fr Diego de Mardones, to present his views on the *morisco* question, a request which Valencia duly complied with, producing his treatise *Acerca de los moriscos de España* which he submitted on 25 January 1606.[3] This paper, written three years before the expulsion took place, offers a key illustration of *fervor* without *fanatismo*, and testifies to the presence of enlightened, balanced voices which, if heeded, might have averted the controversial events that took place.

Pedro de Valencia sent his treatise to Mardones with an accompanying letter which sets the tone of his exposition of ideas on the subject. Valencia acknowledges the existence of a serious problem, underlines the strength of feeling aroused, and stresses the importance of finding a rational solution. He makes points which echo arguments of the anti-*morisco* lobby but then goes on to suggest solutions to the problem which reveal a more rational and open approach. In his letter, Valencia thus assures Mardones that his paper is a response to the very real fear aroused by the *morisco* threat so that he has written it:

> en consideracion de el justo temor, y recato que S.M. y el Reyno deben tener de la infidelidad, y de el poder de los Moriscos, que viven en España (fols 1^r-1^v).

He has written extensively out of the 'deseo' and 'agonía' he feels to contribute to a solution of what he describes as a 'tan grave y acelerado mal' and a 'temor tan espantoso' (fols 1^v-2^r). Valencia's approach is one which seeks to win over

---

[2] On Pedro de Valencia, see Luis Gómez Canseco, *El humanismo después de 1600: Pedro de Valencia* (Seville: Universidad de Sevilla, 1993).

[3] The text consulted is a copy in Biblioteca Nacional MS 8888, 161 fols. References to it follow quotations within brackets. Minimal alterations have been carried out to the text except for giving the full words in the case of normal abbreviations, e.g., porq. > porque, and the addition of missing letters indicated by square brackets. Otherwise, the spelling, punctuation and use of capitals of the MS have been preserved.

the addressee's sympathy by attributing to him suitably worthy strength of feeling but then channelling that feeling towards calm, rational consideration of possible acceptable solutions. In other words, he acknowledges the existence of *fervor* which he attempts to preserve from *fanatismo*. He thus refers to Mardones's 'amor y deseo ardentissimo, [...] de la gloria de Dios [...]' (fol. 2^r), and then emphasizes his own objective stance:

> que digo en este papel mi sentimiento, sin aficion, ni odio, ni otra passion culpable, que con ninguna se debe contaminar, ni profanar el consejo que como dicen los sabios es cosa sagrada (fols 2^v-3^r).

Valencia thus points to the existence and value of strong religious fervour but also suggests how wise counsel may be jeopardized by blind, passionate feelings, a point which is highlighted by the contrasting terms he employs: on the one hand, *passion*, *culpable*, *contaminar*, *profanar*, and, on the other, *consejo*, *sabios* and *cosa sagrada*.

Valencia begins his treatise by reference to the state's duty to protect itself. He thus seems to be siding with those who advocate strong action against the supposed threat of the *moriscos*. But Valencia places this threat in the context of Spain's position as an imperial nation. The vocabulary he employs is somewhat double-edged, since it emphasizes both the strength and weakness of empire, thus pointing to some of the negative effects of expansion by force and conquest and implying that different measures might be advisable. For example:

> Al que muchos temen, y muchos ha rendido, y sugetado, muchos tambien lo asechan, y aborrecen, y de suio esta seguridad que promete la presumcion de fuerzas, y armas propias, ofende, i irrita a Dios. Cuya condicion, y uso antiguo y propio, es humillar, y rendir los grandes, y levantados, y engrandecer y levantar a los humildes, y pequeños (fol. 4^r).

Placed in the context of the *morisco* situation, the terms employed by Valencia become significant. On the one hand, there is a whole series of negative terms: *temen*, *rendido*, *sugetado*, *asechan*, *aborrecen*, *presumcion*, *fuerzas*, *ofende*, *irrita*, all associated with the use of violence, force and conquest; on the other, the reminder of God's ways, with echoes of the Bible in 'humillar y rendir a los grandes y engrandecer y levantar a los humildes y pequeños'. In support of the more lenient policies he favours, Valencia provides examples from history which illustrate the successful results of applying them. In fact, throughout the treatise, Valencia buttresses his arguments with historical, biblical and classical references. This, in fact, is typical of his writings generally, and is the fruit of the humanistic formation and methods which underpin his life and works.

If imperial power is no guarantee of security, Valencia continues, neither is adherence to the true religion of itself sufficient to achieve it. Rather, he highlights the importance of prudent action based on sound moral and political principles:

> Ni aun la profesión de la Religion Verdadera, y la confianza de el Divino favor, y amparo prometido a los Reynos, y Republicas, que proceden a la voluntad, y ley de Dios, se ha de usurpar para seguridad descuidada, ni para dexar de hacer en cada cosa, y negocio, lo combeniente en regla de prudencia moral, y politica para que suceda bien (fols 4^v-5^r).

He thus urges the need for special care in protecting the nation against the threats that assail it. But his arguments are again two-sided, for he sees Spain confronted by threats on all sides like an island battered by stormy seas, and this as a result of its position as a leading Catholic state:

> Porque la profesion unica de Potentado Catholico, y el *esfuerzo*, y *valentia* con que *ha hollado* a otras Naciones de Europa, y aventuradoseles con *arrogancia*, y *jactancia*, y las *riquezas de Oro y Plata*, y *señorio* de la Navegacion, y comercio de el Mundo, la hacen *odiosa*, y *embidiada*, y *asechada* de todos los Principes y Potentados de la tierra cercanos, y lexanos *fieles, y infieles* (fol. 5^v).

The relationship and associations between the words we have italicized imply a strong condemnation of the state while at the same time stressing the importance of proper defence of the nation, particularly against the Moorish threat which Valencia identifies as one of the greatest since, he argues, the Koran advocates the use of force to overcome non-believers and extract acceptance of the Islamic religion. He thus describes the Moors as 'inflamados con odio belicoso' (fol. 9^r). But Valencia also underlines the views current amongst Moors abroad of the situation in Spain, making criticisms subtly since the implied attitudes and actions are, at least in part, true. Externally the *moriscos* are thought of as:

> Oprimidos y tiranizados en servidumbre, con deshonra, y desprecio, ultrajados y forzados con violencia a dexar la ley de Mahoma [...] Presos, y privados de las haciendas, [...] azotados y quemados [...] (fols 10^v-11^r).

Valencia stresses that such views deserve a fitting response from Catholics. He suggests a course of action which requires a markedly different approach to the one perceived to be in existence by Moors abroad:

Nos conocemos obligados por precepto Divino a [a]marlos de Corazon, guardarles fee, y palabra, y desearles y procurarles todo bien, no castigarles sino legitimamente, y con conocimiento de causa, no matarlos ni herirlos, sino en Guerra Justa, porque aunque ellos nos sean y se hayan con nosotros, como Paganos, nosotros debemos havernos con ellos, como Cristianos, y no embidiarles esta ventaja, que les ha de estar mal en este Mundo, y en el otro (fols 14ᵛ-15ʳ).

In fact, Valencia tempers the implied criticism by pointing to the Moors as one of the most guilty parties in the matter of religious persecution and fanaticism. However, the significance of the above words would not be lost on those on the Christian side who were advocating repressive measures.

Another major argument Valencia develops is that of the desirable degree of integration of the *moriscos* in Spanish society. Initially, he again indicates faults and weaknesses on the part of the *moriscos*: their unreliability with regard to their adherence to Christianity; their efforts to keep apart from Christians and maintain their customs and practices. But he then turns the argument around and ends up affirming how Christians ought to ensure that the *moriscos* are not a group apart. Valencia emphasizes the Spanishness of the *moriscos* physically. They constitute an integral part of the Peninsula, 'pues ha casi novecientos años que nacen y se crian en ella [...]' (fol. 22ᵛ). Failure to acknowledge this will result in the dangerous situation of creating second-class citizens, something which is already well in the process of developing:

Porque ellos, de la forma, que aora estan no se tienen por Ciudadanos, no participando de la honra, y oficios publicos, y siendo tenidos en reputacion tan inferior, notados con infamia y apartados en las Iglesias, y Cofradias y en otras congregaciones y lugares (fols 22ᵛ-23ʳ).

This is all the more dangerous and undesirable given the sympathy the *moriscos* enjoy among the Turks, and their effect on the demographic balance of the Peninsula since they are the fastest growing group. Valencia also warns how, through a variety of reasons, they possess the potential to constitute a genuine military threat to the rest of Spain. In this way, and in adducing explanations for the fecundity of the *moriscos,* Valencia seems to be fuelling the arguments for aggressive or repressive action against them. However, he again uses these same points in order to promote the opposite approach, rejecting fanatical passion and vengeance in favour of action guided by reason and sound principles:

El haver representado la grandeza de la enemistad de las fuerzas, y de la comodidad para ofender, con que los Moriscos estan armados contra el Reyno, podia tener dos inconvenientes, o causarnos cobardia y desmayo, y desesperacion del remedio con la consideracion de la gravedad de la enfermedad, o incitar a ira, y enojo apasionado, y desmoderado para hacer castigo injusto, y de hecho tomar venganza de esta Gente, y procurar acabarla aunque fuese por via no justa. Ambos eran de temer, y otros si este discurso se escriviera para en publico, y para el Vulgo que suele moverse con liviandad a temor o indignacion. Seria culpado el que disolveret manus virorum bellantium, como le oponian al Profeta Jeremias [Jerem. 38], o quisiese irritar el Pueblo a injusta venganza: pero esta consultacion se propone a la Magestad del Rey nuestro Señor, y a las personas de su mas interior Consejo, de cuia fortaleza y entereza de animo generoso debemos estar ciertos no se perturbara con temor, antes con la presencia de el peligro, y con el celo de la Gloria de Dios, y de el publico bien, y de la reputacion propia, y de el Reyno, se inflamara y incitara, y mostrara mayor su valor, y brio en la maxima necesidad [...] (fols 37^v-38^v).

Valencia thus makes a good psychological point, drawing a distinction between the masses, prone to emotionalism and fanaticism, and those in positions of responsibility who are able to exercise calm control and objective judgement. Following this line of argument, he directs his comments to the supreme authority, the King himself, whom he describes as 'un Rey tan pio, y benigno, y verdaderamente Cristiano, y Catolico [...]'(fol. 39^r), which is sufficient to satisfy and assure him that 'por ningun riesgo, ni provecho, ni comodidad temporal hara cosa con que sepa, que se ofende la Divina Magestad del Rey supremo, que es el unico temor de los Reyes Cristianos, y de todos los animos generosos' (fol. 39^r). Valencia goes on to emphasize the need to base all action on sound Christian principles that do not go against the demands of justice and right Christian practice.

Having established this basis for any action that might be taken, Valencia then sets out the available options as he sees them. These are eight:

Muerte(1), excision,(2) captividad,(3) expulsion,(4) translacion,(5) dispersion,(6) conversion,(7) permixtion, sugecion o aseguracion (8) (fol. 54^r).

These options are dealt with by Valencia not in strict order nor separately. Rather, the discussion in some instances crosses over from one to the other in cases where the options are closely linked either by the nature of the measures involved or the risks entailed or the likely results. Thus, *muerte* and *excision* are dealt with as one, *translacion* and *dispersion* also overlap, and so forth. The underlying approach, however, in all cases is an acknowledgement of the existence of a problem, reference to the possible use of force in some way to solve it but preference for measures which are conciliatory and humane. Valencia thus continues the strategy of appearing to go along with some of the anti-*morisco* arguments only to deflate or counteract them at a later point with a very different course of action.

With regard to the use of force and the killing of *moriscos*, Valencia raises interesting points. He relates the use of force to cowardly and tyrannical rulers and considers it as essentially unjust and unchristian. Whatever provocation some *moriscos* may have offered, it does not justify the use of violence against them as a group. And even if grounds for a just war against them could be established, wholesale slaughtering of *moriscos* could not be countenanced. He thus rejects a policy of ethnic cleansing which perhaps appealed to some parties at the time. Instead, he advocates compassion and moderation:

> Aunque huviera causas de Justa Guerra y toda la Nacion mereciese castigo de muerte, se deben compadecer los Reyes, y las Republicas, y no enfurecerse para tan grande crueldad, como seria matar Pueblos enteros (fols 66ᵛ-67ʳ).

The Church seeks 'edificacion' and not 'destruccion' (fol. 59ᵛ). This is what characterizes her attitude towards its weaker members. Interestingly enough, Valencia underlines that when it is necessary to deal with any infringements by *moriscos* of directives prohibiting them from continuing their practices and customs, they should be dealt with by ordinary, civil judges and not by the Inquisition whose methods are counter-productive:

> El santo oficio [...] que es mui estricto, Juicio, para gente tan flaca, y vemos que se enojan, y endurecen, mas con el, y no se edifiquen [...] (fols 62ᵛ-63ʳ).

Furthermore, he warns against using religion as a cloak for what are essentially political issues. Religion should not be employed as a justification for the killing of *moriscos*:

> Y quando una cosa se hace por conveniencia Política y por comodidades, o intentos humanos quererla cubrir con nombre de piedad, celo, y religion es astucia, que ofende mucho a la Divina simplicidad y bondad (fol. 63ʳ).

He still recognizes threats and dangers to the state, particularly those posed by the Turks, in the face of which the country needs to be in a state of preparedness in order to ward off possible attack, but any war that it engages in must be a just one. So as to curtail any risk of the *moriscos* acting as spies or plotting in any way against the state, Valencia suggests they should be given settled, sedentary occupations, and they should not be allowed to live in mountainous areas but in flat, open lands. Thus, he goes some way towards accepting that the *moriscos* pose a threat. But he is quite explicit on grounds of natural justice and feasibility in his rejection of the use of force and expulsion:

> El acabar los Moriscos con muerte, o con expulsion ya mostré que ni es justo, ni hacedero, ni en manera alguna conveniente (fol. 126ᵛ).

Whatever security measures may be taken, he encourages and advocates a process of genuine integration through just and fair treatment based on basic principles of Christian life. For example, he urges the employing of *morisco* children in Christian families, thus embarking on a process of education which might ultimately have an effect on the parents:

> Los hijos si llegan a ser honrados, doctos, y pios, procuraran que sus Padres y Parientes olviden el Mahometismo y rehuyan el parecer Moros (fol. 154ʳ).

After rejecting the use of violence and the forcible moving of *moriscos* to other areas, Valencia begins to indicate some of the alternatives he most favours. In the process, he provides an interesting statement aimed at retaining the support of his reader which provides an indication of his underlying technique and the likely impact of his paper. Referring to the principal solution, he states:

> El principal de ellos, y que si se obtuviese, montaría por todos, es la verdadera conversión a la fee, pero no trato primero de el, porque no me parece que procedere con claridad, siguiendo en el decir la orden, que me parece conveniente a la execucion, y ante todas cosas quiero pedir por merced, y por el amor de Dios, y de el publico bien, que no se juzgue de lo que voy diciendo hasta que acabe de decirlo todo (fols 85ᵛ-86ʳ).

His paper may be seen to put forward a series of arguments and points which build up a case. It is the impact of these overall that matters. There is an interrelationship between the parts, a development of a line of argument which can only be properly appreciated in the context of the paper as a whole. In this way, Valencia displays his reliance on, and faith in, the power of words when used skilfully. This, as we have seen, is evident too in his presentation of arguments in language intended to engage the sympathies of those whose attitudes and methods he is about to attack and reject.

Valencia also warns against a futile search for quick solutions. The *morisco* problem can only be solved by hard work and a willingness to confront the issues involved:

Pensar que un mal tan grande, y peligroso, se haya de remediar ligeramente sin trabajo, ni cuidado, ni perdida, ni riesgo, es contra toda prudencia, y experiencia (fol. 92ᵛ).

As Valencia develops his arguments, two main strands emerge as the basis of the solution he favours to the *morisco* problem. These are real integration into Spanish society and proper conversion. The first of these is evident when he discusses the proposal to disperse the *moriscos* throughout the Peninsula, a discussion which raises many interesting points, including the probable losses in economic terms which will ensue. For our purposes, however, what is worthy of note is his advice on how dispersion should be carried out, moving the *moriscos* in small groups so that they do not form ghettos or small communities. He also acknowledges the cost in human terms of carrying out such a policy of dispersion:

que en fin es destierro, y descomodidad grande para los que han de ser esparcidos, y han de perder mucho de sus haciendas [...] (fols 92ᵛ-93ʳ).

He, therefore, asserts that such a measure must be justified very carefully, and he also warns against exploiting such a situation in order to loot and take over the property of the *moriscos*.

Hand in hand with this sympathetic approach to the *moriscos* and their plight, Valencia has equally understanding views concerning the thorny matter of conversion. Forcible conversion and compulsion to carry out Christian practices are futile for:

El que no es Cristiano, ni gusta de oir Missa, por que aborrece la fee, no aprovecha, ni le vale nada para con Dios, ni para con los Hombres llevarle forzado, lo que hace al caso es persuadirle el animo, para que ame el culto Divino y lo busque por su conveniencia y devocion (fols 90ᵛ-91ʳ).

The implication is that for conversion to be effective it has to be carried out in an understanding way which is sensitive to the views and outlook of the *moriscos*. It is only in this way that a genuine spiritual, internal commitment may be achieved. The current situation is one in which *moriscos* have been baptized, forced to practise Christianity but have no genuine internal understanding of or adherence to the Christian faith. Thus:

Lo que aora se hace para la enseñanza de los Moriscos que es compelerlos a oir Misa, y sermones, y aprender la Doctrina, aunque se hiciera con todo cuidado, son diligencias, que presuponen fee, y persuasion interior, y pia afeccion a la religion Cristiana (fols 104ᵛ-105ʳ).

But the *moriscos* do not have this internal disposition, and so all the other measures are ineffective. Spain, which has evangelized peoples throughout the world, is thus failing to effect a proper conversion of people on its own territory, people who, though baptized, have undergone a genuine process of conversion:

> Mui de extrañar es que sea España la que rodea el Mar y la Tierra, y llega hasta los fines de el Oriente, y de el Occidente, a Chile, a la China, y al Japon, por convertir Infieles que no seria mui culpable si no los fuese a buscar, y que no cuide, ni haga diligencia para la conversion, o confirmacion en la fee de estos que tiene dentro de casa, que estan bautizados, y le corre obligacion de enseñarlos y confirmarlos, y que le va tanto en hacerlo para lo espiritual, y temporal (fols 103ᵛ-104ʳ).

Valencia also specifically attacks the low level of preaching that pertains, censuring preachers for indulging in displays of wit and eloquence rather than spreading the word of God. There is therefore a need for good teachers and preachers who will set the example that is required. In this context, he calls for an expression of good intent through prayer and other Christian practices which might attract the *moriscos* by good example:

> seria bien acordado que S.M. pidiese Jubileo a su Santidad para sus Reynos con obligacion de Ayunos, Limosnas, y Oraciones, y aun con obligacion, que tuviesen todos de hacer estas diligencias, y procurar ganarlo, para encomendar a Dios este negocio, que no pareceria, ni estaria mal, que los Moriscos vieran que nos afligiamos, y ayunabamos por su salvacion, mas les edificaria esto, que llamarlos de Perros Moros. Y si pareciere que no conviene tan publica diligencia, a lo menos se encargue en cada lugar y Iglesia, y Monasterio por medio de sus superiores esta solicitud (fols 109ᵛ-110ʳ).

The different attitude illustrated in the negative reference to 'Perros Moros' is strongly rejected by Valencia as a way of ensuring compliance by the *moriscos* with Christian practices. He again goes part of the way towards meeting the advocates of a hard-line approach by acknowledging that, if proper conversion is to take place, pressure must be brought to bear on the *moriscos* to abandon their ceremonies, dress and other practices, but importantly he stresses again that this should be done in a humane way and not through the harsh ways of the Inquisition:

> sera mui importante para la conversion, que los Moriscos sean compelidos con pena a dexar de usar las ceremonias trajes y costumbres de Moros, con tal que esta compulsion haya de ser mansa, no rigorosa: pero ordinaria, y sin

intermision, no hecha por el Tribunal de el Santo Oficio de la Inquisicion, porque con el proceder tan exacto se obstinan, y se conjuran, para no declarar unos contra otros, y los castigos graves, muertes, Galeras, Azotes y confiscaciones de bienes, no los reciven como correciones, sino como venganzas de enemigos, y se empeoran mas y mas (fols 110^r-111^r).

Valencia thus points to the counter-productive results of a system and an approach based partly on externals, and which is adversarial. Instead, he calls for 'amor' and 'charidad' to be the guiding principles in the process of conversion (fol. 123^v).

Importantly, too, Valencia goes on to highlight probably one of the most important aspects of the problem - the perception of the other. Social, economic, religious and other factors have created a gulf between the *moriscos* and the rest of Spain in which each side sees the other as different. This is the crux of the problem, and the solution Valencia advocates is *permixtion*, a concept which he derives from the model of the Roman Empire and from the writings of Seneca. By it, Valencia means 'total mezcla, que no se pueda discernir, ni distinguir qual es de aquesta o aquella Nacion' (fol. 122^v). He thus seeks to eliminate the notion of otherness as a factor in this whole issue.

Valencia's comments in this respect exhibit several aspects of interest relating to the context of empire, the tensions of regionalism and even perhaps the matter of religious divisions brought about by the Reformers. In the context of this paper, they raise the whole process of *convivencia, reconquista* and the *mudéjares* who could have been assimilated but who were kept apart, thus perpetuating a notion of otherness which accounted for, or at least aggravated, the problem. When forcibly converted, the *moriscos* constituted a marginal group of people who were, at least nominally, Christians and who were physically no different from the rest of the population. Yet, they saw other Spaniards as different to themselves, and the Spaniards for their part also saw the *moriscos* as the other. And this despite the fact that the Moorish element had been a feature of Spain for centuries, and the *moriscos* were in many cases the product of generation after generation of Moors born and bred in Spain, and hence indistinguishable from other Spaniards. Valencia, therefore, advocates not that *moriscos* should have equality of rights and opportunities with other Spaniards but rather that the division between the two groups should disappear:

Conviene pues, no que los Moriscos sean iguales en los oficios y honra de el Reyno con los Cristianos viejos, sino que los Moriscos se acaben, y que solamente queden y haya en el Reyno Cristianos Viejos: que sea toda la Republica de un nombre en su Gente, y de un animo sin division [...] (fol. 126^v).

He goes on to show the futility of creating divisions in society since they merely lead to conflict and dissension, and criticizes those who pride themselves on the title of *cristianos viejos* and zealously deny this to others. This type of difference and division only creates antagonisms. In fact, Valencia extends the argument to other types of barriers, borders and divisions between the various regions of Spain, which he sees as cracks or fissures that might lead to schisms threatening the unity of the state. The only valid divisions he accepts are those between good and bad people, between vice and virtue wherever these may be found. Examples from history corroborate the fact that all prudent rulers have been guided by this principle. Valencia therefore champions a brotherhood of peoples which cuts across national boundaries in a unity which is akin to the irenicism encouraged by many of his contemporaries in the context of religious divisions.

Valencia concludes his treatise with some general observations of interest to the nature and content of the document he has written. He admits he has deliberately omitted material he could have included, he claims to have no expert knowledge in the matters he has written about, and he offers his thoughts for others to use as they think fit, taking from his treatise whatever they find helpful. He restates the measures that should be taken:

> En la materia de este tratado, dicho he mi parecer con resolucion; elijiendo para cura total la dispersion en primero lugar, y despues de ella (en orden, no en dignidad) la conversion, y finalmente para sanidad perfecta, la permixtion (fol. 157ᵛ).

After thus clearly affirming his views, he concludes with a plea which highlights some of the qualities which should guide the relevant persons in how they deal with this matter:

> Dios por su bondad abra los ojos de este Reyno, y le de a los Superiores y Consejeros de el Espiritu de Prudencia y consejo para que conozcan y elixan, y aliento y fortaleza para que hagan luego con tiempo lo mas conveniente al servicio de el Rey, nuestro Señor, a el publico bien de el Reyno, y a la edificacion, y aumento de la Iglesia catolica para Gloria de Dios [...] (fol. 160ʳ).

Valencia thus ends the treatise as he begins. His approach is not a forceful, confrontational one but one which respects and recognizes the authority of those entrusted with the resolution of the *morisco* problem, appears in part to accept the validity and attitudes of the critics of the *moriscos*, but tactfully and subtly opts for other lines of approach to the problem. The way the treatise is written, therefore, is important since it offers an illustration of the relationship between writer, reader and text.

The use of language in the *morisco* controversy is an interesting one. This applies to the controversy as it took place, to the writings which followed the expulsion and to later seventeenth-, eighteenth- and nineteenth-century historiography of the dispute. Some of the worst aspects of the controversy were reflected in what was said and written about the expulsion soon after its occurrence. Márquez Villanueva reminds us of this when referring to the apologists of the expulsion and the works they produced which were based on the lowest standards of honesty and justice, and used language to cover over a fundamentally unjustified act of aggression against a marginal group.[4] These early works were the product of uneasy consciences, and were aimed at soothing and allaying a collective sense of guilt which the nation experienced. An early example of this, Márquez Villanueva emphasizes, was a report produced by one of the architects of the expulsion, Juan de Ribera, Bishop of Valencia, whose 'lenguaje se vierte en moldes eufemísticos para eludir el nombre escueto de los horrores que allí propone. No gusta, por ejemplo, de evocar las crudas realidades de un masivo exilio a tierras musulmanas. "Berbería" es allí una palabra desagradable, que se evita a todo trance pronunciar, aun a riesgo de que no quede nada de claro a dónde se desterrarán los *moriscos*' (Márquez Villanueva, 215). But it is in describing Ribera's sermon delivered on 27 September 1609, five days after the edict of expulsion was promulgated, that Márquez Villanueva highlights how language, oral and written, was going to be manipulated to justify the expulsion and present it in a positive and acceptable light. In his revisionist study, Márquez Villanueva does not mince his words in referring to Ribera's sermon:

> Mediocre como pieza de oratoria sacra, no debe ser juzgada en cuanto tal, porque en realidad persigue otro orden de finalidades. Su estilo digno y asequible, su hábil manipulación de emociones y sentimientos, el desarrollo simplificado al alcance de todos, el tono en apariencia moderado, hacen, en cambio, de la pieza una obra clásica en cuanto a técnicas de propaganda en un sentido moderno (Márquez Villanueva, 268).

Thus, an apparently innocent, spiritual sermon was in reality a clever piece of political propaganda through skilful manipulation of language. This use or abuse of words continued to characterize writing about the expulsion. The language used was cowardly and misleading, and it was echoed and re-echoed in letters, minutes, memoranda and apologetical statements. According to Márquez Villanueva, it is the use of language at its basest level and hardly worthy of the great classical age of which it forms a part. It is a language born

---

[4] Francisco Márquez Villanueva, *El problema morisco (desde otras laderas)* (Madrid: Libertarias, 1991).

of troubled consciences and which leads to a 'desrealización expresiva'
(Márquez Villanueva, 29). Márquez Villanueva sees this phenomenon as one
which hides complicity on a national scale with the shameful act of expulsion,
and one which deserves to be exposed for what it is:

> El lenguaje no es una realidad inerte ni exenta de responsabilidades morales. El
> fenómeno lingüístico que rodea a la expulsión continúa forzando, a siglos de
> distancia, una complicidad en la misma a que es ya hora de poner fin. No existe
> en España una conciencia popular o colectiva de la expulsión, como sí la hay
> (con todos sus defectos) acerca de la Inquisición. Toca ahora al lenguaje
> deshacer el daño que él mismo causaría y ello es responsabilidad de cuantos nos
> dedicamos a estos estudios (Márquez Villanueva, 292).

The linguistic context highlighted by Márquez Villanueva provides us with
the background against which Pedro de Valencia's work must be seen.
Valencia's paper constituted one of the few contemporary expressions of
opinions concerning the *moriscos* based on rational, balanced arguments. His
paper, along with a few others, testifies to the existence of a dispassionate,
tolerant current of thought in Spanish society of the time which to a small extent
redeems the negative features outlined by Márquez Villanueva. What is also
interesting about Valencia's treatise is that, in its own way, it displays the use
and manipulation of language to achieve its own aim. In this respect, we must
underline that the paper is the product of a humanist whose life was dedicated
to words and their uses. Furthermore, by the time Valencia wrote this study he
had acquired long experience in the skilled practice of the interpretation of
words and the expression of ideas. His long-standing association with his friend
and mentor, Benito Arias Montano, had involved Valencia in continuing tasks
of copying, editing, translating, explaining and defending the works produced by
Montano.[5] Defending the works of Montano when they were under attack and
censure after Montano's death in particular involved Valencia in issues of
interpretation and expression and in the writing of long papers in which he had
to employ all his humanistic skills and resources in order to put his case
forward. But Valencia also produced other papers in which his literary skills are
clearly evident. His treatise on the Granada discoveries of 1588 and 1595, and
his *Discurso acerca de las bruxas* are perhaps two of the best examples.[6]

---

[5] See J. A. Jones, 'Las advertencias de Pedro de Valencia y Juan Ramírez acerca de la
Biblia Regia', *Bulletin Hispanique*, 84 (1982), 328-346, and 'The Censor Censored: the Case
of Benito Arias Montano', *Romance Studies*, 25 (1995), 19-29.

[6] These may be found in Biblioteca Nacional MS 2316, 30 fols and Escorial MS I. III. 31,
fols 130^r-176^v respectively. The latter was published by M. Serrano y Sanz, *Revista de
Extremadura*, 2 (1900), 289-301; 337-347. MS 2316 is being edited by Ms Grace Magnier

Valencia's treatise on the *moriscos* therefore should be seen against this background. As we have seen, it is written in a tone and manner which does not take up or rise to the provocative aspects of the problem. Valencia keeps his addressees in mind, to some extent goes along with their general line of thinking only to subtly lead them towards the solutions that he favours. He criticizes as much by what he says as by what he leaves unsaid. The point of his argument is often made by implication rather than in an explicit manner. The paper, therefore, is itself a piece of skilled manipulation of language but based on powerful moral principles. It reflects the power of words and the impact of skilful structuring and ordering of ideas. Valencia is able to achieve a balance in his writing which tempers the criticisms he delivers. This feature, which is characteristic of his writing generally, perhaps explains why, despite his long association with Arias Montano and despite the controversies he was involved in, Valencia himself always steered clear of censure.

Whatever merits Valencia's paper possesses, he was not, as we know, successful in persuading the authorities to follow the rational line he advocated. The infamous expulsion took place. It is only in recent years that this event has been reassessed in a more balanced, accurate and revisionist way. In this context, the importance of figures such as Valencia has to be highlighted. Although not successful in dissuading the authorities from proceeding with the expulsion of the *moriscos*, Valencia's treatise stands as a testimony to moderation and tolerance, to religious fervour free from fanatical prejudice, in a Spain in which rational argument was often displaced by 'ciegas pasiones populares'.[7] To this extent, Valencia's treatise represents an important contribution not only to a specific issue but also to a wider debate about Spanish historiography. It is a document of absorbing interest in the context of a period in which words and their meaning were matters of intense debate and at times even of life or death. It is, therefore, a document which fully merits the attention and diffusion it is now receiving.[8]

---

and will appear in Exeter Hispanic Texts. Ms Magnier has also written an excellent MA thesis, 'The Assimilation of the Moriscos Reflected in Golden Age Drama and in Selected Contemporary Writings' (unpublished Master's thesis: University College Dublin, 1992) which contains valuable comments on Pedro de Valencia's treatise on the *moriscos*. I am grateful to Ms Magnier for a copy of this thesis and of Valencia's treatise.

[7] Márquez Vilanueva, 116, refers to these words used by D. Eduardo Saavedra in a speech to the Real Academia on the expulsion of the *moriscos*. See *Memorias de la Real Academia Española*, VI (1899), 191.

[8] Valencia's treatise will be published in the near future as part of the research project directed at the University of León, Spain, by Professor Gaspar Morocho Gayo, who is overseeing the publication of the complete works of Pedro de Valencia.

John A. Jones

Bibliography

Bunes Ibarra, Miguel Angel de, *Los moriscos en el pensamiento histórico. Historiografía de un grupo marginado* (Madrid: Cátedra, 1983)
Gómez Canseco, Luís, *El humanismo después de 1600: Pedro de Valencia* (Seville: Universidad de Sevilla, 1993)
Jones, J. A., 'Las advertencias de Pedro de Valencia y Juan Ramírez acerca de la *Biblia Regia*', *Bulletin Hispanique*, 84 (1982), 328-346
--------, 'The Censor Censored: the Case of Benito Arias Montano', *Romance Studies*, 25 (1995), 19-29
Magnier, Grace, 'The Assimilation of the Moriscos Reflected in Golden Age Drama and in Selected Contemporary Writings' (unpublished Master's thesis: University College Dublin, 1992)
Márquez Villanueva, Francisco, *El problema morisco (desde otras laderas)* (Madrid: Libertarias, 1991)
Memorias de la Real Academia Española, VI (1889)
Para el illustríssimo cardenal arçobispo de Toledo, Don Bernardo de Rojas y Sandoval, mi señor sobre el pergamino y láminas de Granada in Biblioteca Nacional MS 2316, 30 fols
Valencia, Pedro de, *Acerca de los moriscos de España*, in Biblioteca Nacional MS 8888, 161 fols
--------, *Discurso acerca de las bruxas*, in Escorial MS I. III. 31, fols 130^r-176^v and in M. Serrano y Sanz (ed.), *Revista de Extremadura*, 2 (1900), 289-301; 337-347

Index